KINDRED
SPIRITS

Knickerbocker Writers and American Artists, 1807-1855

John Neilson
THE DEVIL'S PULPIT
(*The Talisman* for 1828)

The University of
North Carolina Press
Chapel Hill

KINDRED
SPIRITS

Knickerbocker Writers
and
American Artists, 1807-1855

JAMES T. CALLOW

To My Family

PREFACE

The general topic of this book, the relationship between the visual and the literary arts, is not new. Nor will the reader be surprised to find that, in the United States during the first half of the nineteenth century, this relationship was especially close. When already similar professions flourish together in time and place, their outlooks, goals, materials, and methods are expected to resemble each other. Moreover, scholarship has proved the validity of these expectations, modern books and articles having shown, for example, that Hawthorne applied painters' techniques to his fiction, that Emerson shared the functionalist theories of the sculptor Horatio Greenough, and that John Neal, an eccentric Yankee novelist, was one of America's earliest art critics.

Even some of the Knickerbockers, at present a less popular group than the New Englanders, have not been passed by in the sporadic search for links between literature and the fine arts. Of course, signs that this search would be rewarding have long been well known. Washington Irving informed his readers as early as 1819 that he considered his craft akin to the painter's when he called himself "Geoffrey Crayon" and one of his works *The Sketch-Book*. And in 1849 the friendship between a Knickerbocker poet and a Hudson River artist was celebrated in Asher Durand's "Kindred Spirits," a frequently reproduced picture of William Cullen Bryant and the painter Thomas Cole in the midst of a spectacular mountain landscape. Encouraged perhaps by these clues, scholars in the last twenty years have turned up other evidence of writer-artist relationships in the Knickerbocker period. Their work is of course the basis for all further study of this topic.

But these scholars have limited themselves to the major Knicker-bockers (Irving, Bryant, and Cooper) and to a very few of their lesser contemporaries (only Gulian Verplanck, James Kirke Paulding, and John Howard Payne come to mind), while the art-connections of two or three dozen other Knickerbockers have never been revealed. The consequences of this neglect vary considerably. In the case of Fitz-Greene Halleck, who had relatively little to do with the art-world, they are slight. But in the case of Nathaniel Parker Willis they are serious. A rival of the best Knickerbockers in talent and contemporary reputation, Willis enjoyed many friendships with painters and sculp-tors, held interesting ideas about architecture and landscape gardening, and was possibly the only journalist of his day to make informal essays out of art reviews. He therefore deserves attention, as do John Inman, Theodore Fay, George Pope Morris, Alfred Billings Street, Cornelius Mathews, Prosper M. Wetmore, and other neglected Goth-amites who in various ways belong to the history of American art.

Moreover, the thousands of manuscripts from the Knickerbocker period have never been used as much as they deserve to be. The greatest problem has been to locate these unpublished materials, espe-cially those of artists; for there is no finding list of artists' papers comparable even to *American Literary Manuscripts* (1960), itself an incomplete tool. Yet these unprinted documents, lying in sweet re-pose in attics and libraries, hold important clues to the cultural history of nineteenth-century America; and it is in them that the day-to-day meetings of artists and writers are to be discovered.

This book is an attempt to build upon but greatly supplement previous studies. First of all, its frame of reference is large; for it discusses several dozen Knickerbockers—as a group and as individuals —and relates them to the scores of American artists who were their contemporaries from approximately 1807 to 1855. Second, it relies chiefly on manuscript sources—including the very useful minutes of The Sketch Club—to reconstruct the complex patterns of artist-writer friendships in New York City. Third, it surveys the abundant art-material in literary periodicals issued from 1825 to 1855, a subject covered only tangentially in Frank Luther Mott's standard history of American magazines. Fourth, although it does not ignore the already well-known place of landscape painting in the works of the Knickerbockers, it also examines the place of other arts—namely, architecture, city planning, and genre painting—in these same works.

On the other hand, this study has certain boundaries. It does not say as much about the period from 1807 to 1824 as about the period from 1825 to 1855, when the literary and visual arts were more mature. Nor does it cover Melville, Poe, or Whitman, who lived and worked in New York but deserve more extensive treatment than could presently be afforded them. Furthermore, with some exceptions this book does not discuss the relations between the Knickerbockers and foreign artists or elaborate upon the use of artists as characters in fiction written by Knickerbockers. Finally, although the approach is interdisciplinary, it draws heavily only upon the literary and visual arts—without denying, however, that these two arts flourished as parts of a world of religion, philosophy, politics, education, science, music, and folklore.

In the first two chapters the focus is on the lives of the Knickerbockers. In the next five it is on their writings. The first chapter considers New York City as the literary and art capital of the United States and concentrates on the opportunities it provided for a mingling of artists and writers in co-operative ventures such as clubs, academies, and lotteries. The second chapter, narrowing the focus of the first, explores the details of friendships between the Knickerbockers and American artists, thus supplying a motive for the literary support of the fine arts which is the dominant theme in the rest of the book. The third chapter is devoted to the publicity afforded artists by the literary magazines of New York City. Here and in appendixes it has been necessary to index practically all the art-material in *The Knickerbocker, The New-York Mirror, The Literary World,* and a few other journals to uncover the rich treasures awaiting historians. The fourth chapter tells how the Knickerbockers educated the public to an enhanced appreciation of native landscape painting; and the fifth chapter, after analyzing the techniques shared by these painters and writers, examines the landscape gift books on which they worked together. The sixth chapter is devoted to "genre," a term which, if taken to mean the depiction of people in everyday life, is applicable to literature and painting alike. The Knickerbockers, it will be shown, not only praised the genre artist for portraying such materials but also supplied him with subjects. The seventh chapter considers the place of architecture, city planning, and landscape gardening in Knickerbocker literature.

Underlying all the chapters is the thesis that the Knickerbocker writer, attaining popularity earlier and controlling a larger public than the American artists, was able to help these artists in more ways than the artists could help him, but that the artists never gave up trying to repay these favors. The result was a healthy atmosphere of reciprocity in which American literature and art generally thrived.

ACKNOWLEDGMENTS

My interest in the Knickerbockers stems from the inspired teaching of Dr. G. Harrison Orians, Professor of English at the University of Toledo. Although ideas which I absorbed in his classes many years ago are impossible to isolate here, this book is undoubtedly full of them.

At the very beginning of my research I sought out Dr. Edgar P. Richardson, at that time Director of the Detroit Institute of Arts, and he helped me to see the possibilities of my project.

My inquiries to individuals, societies, libraries, and institutions elicited useful materials and suggestions. It is a pleasure to recall my correspondence with Dr. Ralph M. Aderman, Professor of English, The University of Wisconsin—Milwaukee; The American Antiquarian Society; Mr. John C. Bagley, of Fray, Bagley, and Chadderdon, Counselors at Law, Catskill, New York; Dr. James F. Beard, Jr., Professor of English, Clark University; Boston Public Library; Mr. Herbert O. Brigham, Librarian, Newport Historical Society; Dr. William Cullen Bryant II, College of General Studies, Columbia University; Charleston County Free Library; Charleston Library Society; Dr. Curtis Carroll Davis, Baltimore, Maryland; Miss Margaret Dennis, Reference Librarian, Lehigh University Library; The Free Library of Philadelphia; The Frick Art Reference Library; Mrs. Elisabeth H. Gazin, Chief of Reference and Circulation, Smithsonian Institution Library; Dr. William H. Gerdts, of the University of Maryland; Mr. Conrad G. Goddard, Cummington, Massachusetts; Miss Elizabeth L. Godwin, Roslyn, Long Island; Mr. Frederick M. Godwin, Katonah, New York; Dr. Harold E. Hall, the Nebraska Wesleyan University;

Mr. James J. Heslin, Director, The New-York Historical Society; The Historical Society of Pennsylvania; The Houghton Library, Harvard University; The Henry E. Huntington Library and Art Gallery; Mr. Samuel S. McConoughey, Head, Social Sciences Department, Toledo Public Library; Maryland Historical Society; The Morristown Library; The Museum of the City of New York; New York University Library; The Newberry Library; The Newburgh Free Library; Mr. Gouverneur Paulding, of *The Reporter*; Mr. Vernon C. Porter, Director, The National Academy of Design; The Rhode Island Historical Society; Dr. Stephen T. Riley, Librarian, the Massachusetts Historical Society; Sleepy Hollow Restorations, Incorporated; Smithtown (New York) Public Library; South Carolina Historical Society Library; South Carolina State Library Board; The State Historical Society of Wisconsin; Mr. George A. Stauter, of the Minneapolis-Honeywell Company; University Microfilms; The University of Chicago Library; The University of North Carolina Library; The Library, University of Pennsylvania; The University of Virginia Library; Mrs. Mary Cole Van Loan, Catskill, New York; Wadsworth Atheneum; Mr. Lewis Hammond Webster, Librarian, The Century Association; The Western Reserve Historical Society; University Libraries, Western Reserve University; Mrs. Grinnell Willis, Greenwich, Connecticut; Mrs. Martha F. Wiggin, Town Clerk, Bedford, New Hampshire.

My most faithful correspondents were Mr. Theodore Bolton, former Librarian of The Century Association; Mr. William P. Campbell, Assistant Chief Curator of The National Gallery of Art; Dr. Kenneth J. LaBudde, Director of Libraries, The University of Missouri at Kansas City; and Dr. Jules D. Prown, Curator Designate, Garvan and Related Collections of American Art, Yale University Art Gallery.

In the quest for manuscripts and rare publications I visited The William L. Clements Library; The General Library of the University of Michigan; The Toledo Public Library; The Toledo Museum of Art; The Cleveland Public Library; The Library of Congress; Yale University Library; The Suffolk Museum, Stony Brook, Long Island; The Pierpont Morgan Library; The New-York Historical Society; The Columbia University Libraries; The Century Association; The

New York Society Library; The New York Public Library; The Albany Institute of History and Art; The New York State Library. In every instance I was given expert and kindly aid.

Mr. Robert W. Hill, Keeper of Manuscripts, The New York Public Library, has shown an unfailing interest in my project.

I also appreciate the kindness of the hospitable Mrs. Philinda Rand Anglemyer and her family, who made available their collection of materials relating to the painter John Rand. Mrs. Anglemyer has continued to answer my many questions.

The University of Detroit Library extended me, among other things, an efficient interlibrary loan service, adequate microfilm-reading facilities, and an enlightened circulation policy. In the Detroit Public Library and its separate Burton Historical Collection I have found the bulk of the published material used in this book. The library of The Detroit Institute of Arts, with its collection of Thomas Cole Papers, also proved well worth visiting; and The Archives of American Art, a grandly conceived project to microfilm the manuscripts of all American artists, has been helpful from the very beginning of my research. To each of these libraries I extend my deepest appreciation.

Professors Clyde P. Craine, Jr., Eugene F. Grewe, Fred Hayes, John Mahoney, Frank Paulsen, Robert J. Reilly, Edwin H. Rutkowski, Aloysius G. Weimer, and many more of my colleagues at the University of Detroit have helped me in various ways, as have certain former members of the faculty—Professor C. Carroll Hollis, Mr. Howard Sullivan, Professor Ralph R. Kibildis, and Professor Herbert H. Petit. I am especially grateful to the Rev. Robert J. Kearns, S. J., Director of Libraries, for friendly assistance and unflagging encouragement. The colleague to whom I am most indebted is Professor Paul C. Diggles, whose expert knowledge of the English language helped me to improve many a rough and obscure sentence.

To Professor Lyon N. Richardson, my adviser when this book was in the stage of a Ph.D. dissertation at Western Reserve University, and to the other members of the doctoral committee—Professors Edmund Chapman, George Kummer, Harvey Wish, and Newbell Niles Puckett—I wish to express my thanks for reading the manuscript and offering helpful suggestions. I am especially beholden to Professor Richardson for his abiding interest in my work, and it is a pleasure to be one of those familiar with his critical perception, high standards, and unfailing generosity.

Members of my family—especially William Wayne Callow, my father; Mildred Callow, my mother; and Mrs. Marilyn Bodenstedt, my sister—have enthusiastically supported this project. My wife, Patricia Ann Callow, not only has been a model of patience during these long years but has actively participated by typing nearly every draft of the manuscript and by helping in the research. Her index of the Sketch Club minutes has proved to be of immense value.

For their favors I am indebted to Professor Wayne Andrews and Mr. Garnett McCoy, of the Archives of American Art; Mrs. Jean Uniechowski, Associate Director of Libraries, University of Detroit; Professor Neil Harris, of Harvard University; Dr. Cortland P. Auser, of the Westchester Historical Society, Tuckahoe, New York; and the staff at The University of North Carolina Press.

The following individuals and institutions have generously allowed me to use unpublished materials in their possession or under their jurisdiction: Mrs. Philinda Rand Anglemyer; The Archives of American Art; The Henry W. and Albert A. Berg Collection of the New York Public Library; The Century Association; The Detroit Institute of Arts; Mrs. Laura Edwards; Mr. Conrad Goddard; The Historical Society of Pennsylvania; Mrs. Edith Cole Hill; The Henry E. Huntington Library and Art Gallery; The Library of Congress; The Massachusetts Historical Society; The New-York Historical Society; The New York Public Library; The New York State Library; The University of Virginia; Mrs. Mary Cole Van Loan; Yale University.

Drs. William Cullen Bryant II, Henry B. Caldwell, Kenneth J. LaBudde, Jules D. Prown, and Paul H. Shepard, Jr., have kindly given me permission to use their unpublished theses and dissertations herein.

Finally, I am pleased to acknowledge a grant from the University of Detroit Research Administration which helped in the publication of this book.

The University of Detroit

CONTENTS

ILLUSTRATIONS

ABBREVIATIONS

Due to the exhaustive annotation in this volume, footnotes are cited in abbreviated form in order to avoid unnecessary duplication. All references to books and periodical articles fully contained in the bibliography are cited thus in footnotes: author, title, page(s) for first reference; author, page(s) for further references. References in footnotes to volumes of letters, journals, and correspondence are to those editions cited in the bibliography.

A A-A A U-E R	Cowdrey, Mary Bartlett (comp.). *American Academy of Fine Arts and American Art-Union: Exhibition Record: 1816-1852.* New York: New-York Historical Society, 1953.
A A-A A U-I	Cowdrey, Mary Bartlett, *et al. American Academy of Fine Arts and American Art-Union: Introduction: 1816-1852.* New York: New-York Historical Society, 1953.
D I A	Detroit Institute of Arts
F A R L	Frick Art Reference Library
H H L	Henry E. Huntington Library and Art Gallery
K	*The Knickerbocker*
L C	Library of Congress
L W	*The Literary World*
M H S	Massachusetts Historical Society
N A D E R	Cowdrey, Mary Bartlett (comp.). *National Academy of Design Exhibition Record: 1829-1860.* 2 vols. New York: New-York Historical Society, 1943.

NYHS	New-York Historical Society
NYHSQ	*New-York Historical Society Quarterly*
NYM	*The New-York Mirror*
NYPL	New York Public Library
NYRAM	*The New-York Review and Atheneum Magazine*
NYSL	New York State Library
PAFA	Rutledge, Anna Wells (comp.). *Cumulative Record of Exhibition Catalogues: The Pennsylvania Academy of the Fine Arts, 1807-1870: The Society of Artists, 1800-1814: The Artists' Fund Society, 1835-1845.* Philadelphia: American Philosophical Society, 1955.
SIL	Smithsonian Institution Library
USRLG	*United States Review and Literary Gazette*
YUL	Yale University Library

KINDRED
SPIRITS

Knickerbocker Writers and American Artists, 1807-1855

CHAPTER I

THE NEW YORK BACKGROUND

New York As a Literary Center

Between 1807 and 1825 New York City became the literary capital of America. Since even Philadelphia and Boston, the former cultural centers, yielded to their Dutch neighbor, whose writers, magazines, and publishing houses exceeded all others in number and prestige, New York's literary pre-eminence was an indisputable fact,[1] but assigning exact dates to it is both impossible and useless. *Salmagundi,* a collection of witty prose and verse from the pens of Washington Irving, William Irving, and James Kirke Paulding, appeared in 1807; and certainly the decade to which it belonged marks the beginning of an unusual productivity among the "Knickerbockers," a name later given to almost any author working in New York. Before the first quarter of the nineteenth century elapsed, Washington Irving wrote four of his major books, William Cullen Bryant published a volume

1. See Frank Luther Mott, *A History of American Magazines: 1741-1850,* pp. 201-2, 375-77; Kendall Taft (ed.), *Minor Knickerbockers,* pp. xiii-xxvii; G. Harrison Orians, *A Short History of American Literature,* pp. 64, 76, 100.

of significant poetry, and James Fenimore Cooper achieved recognition with two important novels, *The Spy* and *The Pilot*. Thus by 1825 a "Knickerbocracy"[2] of letters, destined to last until mid-century, had been established.

These three authors—Irving, Bryant, and Cooper—all New Yorkers either by birth or adoption, were surrounded by a whole galaxy of lesser figures whose lustre has now faded.[3] Gulian Verplanck shone as a political satirist, a defender of religion, and an editor of Shakespeare. Robert Sands, whose practical jokes included publishing reviews of nonexistent novels, in his more serious moods found time to translate and imitate materials from five languages as well as to join his friend James Wallis Eastburn in composing a metrical romance of the Indian. A half-dozen novels, a play, several vitriolic tracts on John Bull, a biography of Washington, and well over a hundred miscellaneous tales and sketches were poured out by James Kirke Paulding, sometimes remembered as the popularizer of the tongue-twister "Peter Piper picked a peck of pickled peppers." The city abounded in essayists. Besides William Cox and Theodore Fay, there was Nathaniel Parker Willis, a writer of greater merit, whose prose, although collected under such titles as *Ephemera, Hurry-Graphs*, and *Dashes at Life*, reveals much careful workmanship. New York could also boast of its poets. Joseph Rodman Drake and Fitz-Greene Halleck specialized in witty satires filled with local allusions, and Halleck's "Marco Bozzaris" proved the bane of schoolboy declamators but delighted many adults. Wit of another kind, tinged with Byronism, came from McDonald Clarke, Broadway's Mad Poet, who wrote primarily of pretty girls and one-sided love affairs, his verse usually approaching the eccentricity of his tragic life. A couplet of Clarke's—"Now twilight lets her curtain down / And pins it with a star"—has entered the stream of tradition; and not long ago a version from an autograph book turned up in the University of De-

2. This word is borrowed from Nathaniel Parker Willis (*Out-Doors at Idlewild*, p. 376), who used it in a somewhat different sense.

3. Biographical sketches of these authors, selections from their writings, a thorough analysis of their work, and useful bibliographies are in Taft, *Minor Knickerbockers*.

troit Folklore Archives. Other Gothamites did not sleep in abandoned hearses or crown themselves with wreaths of roses as Clarke did, but some of these men wrote poems that are even better known than this couplet. Who does not recognize at least the titles, if not the authors, of "The [Old Oaken] Bucket" (Samuel Woodworth); "Home, Sweet Home" (John Howard Payne); "A Visit from St. Nicholas" (Clement Clarke Moore); and "Woodman, Spare That Tree!" (George Pope Morris)?

Together with Irving, Cooper, and Bryant, these writers comprised America's first group of literary romanticists. Although Halleck, Drake, Paulding, and others never completely abandoned the satirical techniques popularized by Irving in *A History of New York*, the neoclassic outlook behind these techniques had become a recessive trait by the second quarter of the nineteenth century. Romanticism quickly dominated Knickerbocker literature. Even before the 1840's, when New Englanders began to seize the intellectual reins, the New Yorkers had exploited nearly every aspect of its theory and practice by infusing such romantic forms as the sentimental lyric, the historical romance, and the personal essay with such romantic ideas as primitivism, democracy, and nature therapy. Only medievalism, soon to animate the works of Longfellow, was conspicuously absent in Gothamite literature.

Another sign of New York's pre-eminence was the success of its magazines. The best of these periodicals was *The New-York Mirror*, a weekly miscellany begun in 1823. Published under various titles for over thirty years, the *Mirror* was an exception in an era of short-lived magazines; much of its endurance must be traced to the high ideals of its chief editor, George Pope Morris. Its many fine engravings were a special attraction, as were the travel letters of Fay and Willis, and the essays of William Cox, who gaily exposed the evils of early rising and the follies of temperance societies. In popularity this journal was second only to *The Knickerbocker*, a monthly edited by Lewis Gaylord Clark. Translations of foreign literature, humor of all kinds, and the chatty, familiar tone of its "Editor's Table" helped "Old *Knick*" to accumulate a thirty-two-year history. Other magazines, edited by Sands, Bryant, Willis, and the Duyckinck brothers, sometimes achieved literary distinction but never longevity.

Meanwhile New York rapidly became a center of publishing. *Salmagundi* and *The Sketch-Book* made first appearances there, as did Cooper's *Precaution, The Spy, The Pioneers,* and *The Pilot.* Between 1820 and 1852 the city could boast of its 345 publishers, including the houses of Wiley and Putnam, C. S. Van Winkle, the Harper Brothers, Burgess and Stringer, Stringer and Townsend, Baker and Scribner, and D. Appleton and Company. Only Philadelphia had even half this number of publishers.[4]

In spite of this bustling activity Knickerbocker literature lost some of its superiority during the late 1840's. The most serious threats came from the East and the South in the writings of Emerson, Whittier, Longfellow, and Simms, as well as from New York itself in the work of Donald Grant Mitchell, Cornelius Mathews, and other young authors who won recognition but seldom matched the abilities of their predecessors. Although several members of the older group remained active in the 1850's, they had done most of their best writing in the previous four decades. New York's literary supremacy had definitely come to an end by 1855, the publication date of *The Knickerbocker Gallery*, a collection of stories, poems, and essays by the friends of Lewis Gaylord Clark. Its inferior letterpress, compensated somewhat by respectable engravings, gave little indication that a golden era had just passed.

New York As an Art Center

New York became the country's art capital during the second quarter of the nineteenth century,[5] at least ten years after the Knickerbockers had received national recognition. This difference of one decade was important. It meant that the New York writer was in a

4. Hellmut Lehmann-Haupt, Lawrence C. Wroth, and Rollo G. Silver, *The Book in America*, p. 120; William Charvat, *Literary Publishing in America: 1790-1850*, pp. 23, 26; David Kaser, *Messrs. Carey & Lea of Philadelphia*, pp. 25-27.

5. Samuel Isham and Royal Cortissoz, *A History of American Painting*, p. 182. New York was recognized as the art center of the U.S. by Samuel Morse, if not by others, as early as 1818. See MS letter, [Samuel] Finley [B. Morse] to Lucretia P. Walker, New York, Jan. 12, 1818, Samuel Morse Papers, Vol. V, LC.

position to help artists in many ways, chiefly by directing public attention to their works and by supporting their organizations.

As the city rose to cultural distinction the number of its artists and patrons grew. It had no truly masterful sculptors, but its leading architects, Ithiel Town and Alexander Davis, as well as the landscape designer Andrew J. Downing, possessed unusual merit. Its painters consistently excelled in every branch of their art but the historical. Hundreds of portraits were turned out by John Wesley Jarvis, Henry Inman, and Charles Elliott, whose studios were patronized by all kinds of sitters from the aspiring author to the naval captain, from the local belle to the eminent merchant, each bent on having an "admirable likeness." Elliott even obliged an embarrassed prizefighter by touching up his black eye with a dab of oil color.[6] In the field of genre, rustic scenes were arranged in spacious geometric designs by the Long Islander William Sidney Mount; fantastic, bulgy-eyed characters from Irving's works were painted by John Quidor, an eccentric genius who once decorated the backs of fire engines; and Henry Inman sometimes turned from portraiture to depict children tumbling out of a country schoolhouse or playing a leisurely game of mumblety-peg. New York was also renowned for its landscape painters, known today as the Hudson River School. Its reputation was national, and its subjects ranged widely from the pastoral to the picturesque, a contrast apparent in the works of Asher Durand and Thomas Cole, its leading members. Other painters defied neat classifications: Robert Weir, for many years Instructor of Drawing at West Point, is remembered today for a single historical picture, "The Embarkation of the Pilgrims," but he also painted landscapes, portraits, and genre scenes, some of them from the works of Shakespeare and Scott. More versatile was John G. Chapman—a competent painter, a successful etcher and engraver, as well as a famous illustrator whose *American Drawing Book* went through many editions. Samuel F. B. Morse was an inventor and an artist, but his friend William Dunlap was even more amazing: painter, naturalist, playwright, diarist, biographer, novelist, and his-

6. T[homas]. B[angs]. Thorpe, "Painters of the Century, No. IX; Characteristic Incidents—Cole and Elliott," p. 1.

7

torian, Dunlap wrote lengthy, firsthand accounts of the theater and the arts of design, books which students of American culture consider invaluable. New York had many stage designers, too, and miniaturists and landscape architects. In the second quarter of the nineteenth century skillful artists were as numerous as skillful writers.

These artists, like the Knickerbockers, were important disseminators of romanticism. The architects and landscape designers, freeing themselves from the restraint of neoclassic forms just as Bryant and other poets had thrown off the shackles of the heroic couplet, turned to oriental and medieval models, attaining ultimately an eclecticism that had always been a characteristic of romantic expression. The painters for their part mixed such romantic ideas as primitivism and nationalism by joining the cults of the picturesque and the common man, the concepts of which they demonstrated in landscape and genre pictures. Between 1825 and 1850 it was these artists from New York who painted and designed many of America's best examples of romanticism.

A growth in patronage was an integral part of this cultural ripening. Increased commerce, stimulated chiefly by the opening of the Erie Canal in 1825, brought great wealth to some New Yorkers, above all to the merchant class. Out of this group came those who bought paintings and statuary, sent artists abroad to study, built homes in Grecian or Gothic styles, and made it fashionable to patronize the arts.

The worst of these *nouveaux riches*—"gilded dunces propt by gold," as McDonald Clarke described them—[7] were almost totally devoid of taste. Self-educated, but only in the art of Midas, they insisted that any American "has the perfect right to think as he pleases and say what he pleases, as well about a picture as a President."[8] However, neither their wealth nor their theories protected these patrons against the satirical letter printed in the magazine *Yankee Doodle* and supposedly sent by a wealthy New Yorker to his son touring Italy:

7. [McDonald Clarke], "Written after Hearing a Lady in Broadway Observe, 'He Is Certainly Mad,'" *The Elixir of Moonshine*, p. 147.
8. "The Fine Arts," *Yankee Doodle*, I (Oct. 10, 1846), 5.

Dear Son.—Your last favor of June 2d, per Cambria, came duly to hand. Glad to hear you've growed your mustashes. Nobody that is anybody, goes without them. . . . Well, the house is done, and very fine it is too; A No. 1. . . . Now I want to fill it with pictures from the old masters and enclose you a draft for $150 to buy them. I like to patronize the arts, and I'd build a church, but that's got vulgar . . . .

But about the Pictures, I wish you'd send me three or four Raffeyells, Cartunes if you can get them, one or two Teeshuns, a Michael Ann Gelo, his last Judgement of Paris if possible, a couple of Gueedoes, including his Chen Chee,—a chinese subject I suppose,—three small Coreggeowes, a fine large Reuben's to hang in the dining-room, and a couple of Moorillyoes, matches, for the drawing-room. In the way of Landscape I should like some half-dozen; Puss Ans, Risedales, Clawds and Sall Vaters, just as you please, all in good order and condition. As I want the real originals out of the palaces I don't mind making the draft $200 instead of $150.

I wont have any statuary, for I could'nt bear any thing but the Medicinal Venus and I see they've got that at the Museum here, only that they call it the Anatomical Venus, but Medicinal and Anatomical is all the same. But be sure you bring me something out of the Pity palace. Good by. . . .

Your affectionate Father,

_____   _____

P.S.—Don't forget the Chen Chee.[9]

In spite of its distortions this comic letter underscored a real situation: far too many pseudo-connoisseurs in New York and elsewhere merely pretended to a knowledge of the arts.[10] As long as they believed that taste was an instinct needing no nourishment but coming to full bloom immediately in a climate of wealth, such patrons hindered the progress of American art.

In their ignorance these men were quickly duped by unscrupulous dealers abounding in this new art center. The practices of specialists in fake "old masters" were flagrantly sinful but sometimes amusing. For example, in a joke told by Thomas Bangs Thorpe, the Italian

9. _Ibid._ Another satire on a would-be patron is in L. Gaylord Clark, _Knick-Knacks from an Editor's Table_, pp. 83-84.

10. See the ending of a MS copy of a letter from J. Fenimore Cooper to the Rev. [Louis L.] Noble, Cooperstown, Jan. 6, 1849, Thomas Cole Papers, DIA.

immigrant Gerlando Marsiglia reportedly cut a "Susanna and the Elders" into two sections, "the 'Susanna' of which finally appeared as a 'Venus' by Rubens, and 'The Elders' as 'Plato and Friends conversing in the Academic groves.' "[11] After the worst of these dealers had manufactured or imported such masterpieces, they enticed the wealthy with a snob-appeal technique described by William Dunlap as "the true and only mode" of operation:

Employ an auctioneer, who must employ a picture-dealer, who must be a foreigner, and, if possible, one who can speak no language so as to be intelligible. A catalogue must be made out, and every No. must have a great name affixed to it. The auctioneer must read the title, praise the picture, and appeal to the foreign connoisseur, who stands ready to say "dat ish fine"—"dat ish original"—"dat ish superb"—for all which he is liberally paid, and the pictures are knocked down at prices, which would be contemptible if they really possessed merit or originality, but which give an ample profit to the dealer, after paying all concerned. It is thus, that avarice, ignorance and impudence combine to crush the growing taste of the country, and oppose the efforts of those who would cherish the liberal arts.[12]

Parvenu patrons were also apt to hoard their collections and to treat American artists, as one editor sadly reported, "like upholsterers, mere decorators of private apartments."[13] N. P. Willis complained that "New-York is rich in pictures and statuary, to which there is no access except by acquaintance with the proprietor," noting also that in Europe "there are days set apart, by every owner of a fine gallery, when the public can be admitted."[14] In the twentieth century the

11. T[homas]. B[angs]. Thorpe, "Painters of the Century, No. II; Birth of the National Academy of Design," p. 5.

12. [William Dunlap], "A Review of the Gallery of the American Academy of Fine Arts, as Now Opened for the Exhibition of Dunlap's Painting of 'Death on the Pale Horse,' " NYRAM, II (Dec., 1825), 74, attributed to Dunlap in William Cullen Bryant's marked copy of this magazine, Berg Collection, NYPL. For a more extensive and humorous treatment of art auctions, see Clark, Knick-Knacks, pp. 205-7.

13. Editorial Notes—Fine Arts," Putnam's Monthly Magazine, I (March, 1853), 351. For one patron's high-handed treatment of Cole, see William Cullen Bryant, Orations and Addresses, pp. 9-11.

14. N[athaniel]. Parker Willis, The Rag-Bag, pp. 114-16. Willis suggested that tickets to these collections be given to hotel managers for distribution to out-of-town visitors.

availability of photographic reproductions and the profusion of museums compensate somewhat for the evils attending private patronage,
but in the nineteenth century a lack of such facilities obligated the
collector to open his doors to outsiders. When he refused to do so, he
damaged the reputations of the artists he had commissioned, smothered
the spirit of competition necessary for excelling, denied painters and
sculptors the means of improving their own work by studying the
works of others, and slowed down the growth of public taste.

A few ideal patrons were beyond criticism. The Knickerbockers
might well think highly of Luman Reed, for example, the merchant
who kept his third-floor gallery open to the public once a week, sent
the artist George Flagg to study in Europe, and commissioned several
important paintings, including Mount's "Bargaining for a Horse,"
Cole's "Course of Empire" series, and Durand's "Wrath of Peter
Stuyvesant." Reed's business partner Jonathan Sturges also owned
works by these artists and had financed Durand's first trip to Europe
in 1840. Both Sturges and Charles M. Leupp contributed generously
to the National Academy of Design. The collection of Philip Hone,
once mayor of New York, contained paintings by Thomas Doughty,
Robert Weir, William J. Bennett, Charles Robert Leslie, and Gilbert
Stuart Newton. To this group of patrons might be added several
other men who also bought the works of native artists;[15] but when
compared to the "hundreds of New-York merchants" claimed by a
writer in the *Mirror* to be "richer than Italian princes,"[16] the number
of enlightened and liberal devotees of the fine arts was disappointingly
small, especially for the art capital of a new country.

The Bread and Cheese Club

As a cultural center noted for its conviviality[17] New York City

15. Peter G. Stuyvesant, Gouverneur Kemble, and Irving's friend Henry Brevoort,
for example. Some patrons and their collections are listed in "Private Galleries," *NYM*,
XVII (March 7, 1840), 294; John Durand, *A. B. Durand*, pp. 65-66, 125. For works
owned by John Wolfe, Jonathan Sturges, Abraham M. Cozzens, Charles Leupp, Mar-
shall O. Roberts, and Elias L. Magoon, see the series entitled "Our Private Collections"
in *The Crayon*, III (Jan., 1856), 27-28; III (Feb., 1856), 57-58; III (April, 1856),
123; III (June, 1856), 186; III (Aug., 1856), 249; III (Dec., 1856), 374.

16. "Inman's Portrait of Van Buren," *NYM*, VII (March 20, 1830), 291.

17. See Taft, *Minor Knickerbockers*, pp. xxv-xxvii; Bayrd Still, "The Personality of

provided several organizations for social intercourse between artists and writers. Two of the most notable were The Bread and Cheese Club (sometimes called The Lunch) and The Sketch Club, the ancestor of The Century Association. The Bread and Cheese Club, founded in the autumn of 1822,[18] included in its roster the writers Cooper, Bryant, Halleck, Sands, and Verplanck, as well as the painters Dunlap, Durand, Jarvis, and Morse; it is probable that John Vanderlyn, Robert Weir, and Henry Inman were in the group at one time or another. Although the rest of the members were doctors, lawyers, merchants, and scientists, the poets and artists had been some of the first to join, so that from the very beginning a social nexus was promoted between them. No formal minutes were kept but it is evident that Cooper was not only the founder of the club but also its leader; after he left for Europe in 1826, the society gradually disintegrated. Yet some of its effects were lasting and may be traced throughout the lives of the members. For example, Verplanck continued his acquaintance with Weir, and Bryant became a special friend of Durand, while Cooper remained close to Morse and Dunlap.

Membership in The Bread and Cheese Club was not, however, limited to artists and writers. Therefore, as the artists experienced a growing sense of identity through their part in forming the National Academy, they decided to create more intimate ties among themselves, art patrons, and literary men by establishing a new organization called The Sketch Club or, less frequently, The XXI.

The Sketch Club

The first meeting recorded in the extant minutes of The Sketch Club[19] was held on February 6, 1829; other evidence, particularly

New York City," pp. 86-87; Sarah Kemble Knight, *The Journal of Madame Knight*, p. 56.

18. The best study of this club is Albert H. Marckwardt, "The Chronology and Personnel of the Bread and Cheese Club," pp. 389-99. The club may have been founded as early as 1820. See *The Letters and Journals of James Fenimore Cooper*, I, 157, n. 1. Further references to the club are in *idem*, I, 139-41, 155-57, 180-81, 187-88, 245, 368.

19. See the bibliography below, under Century Association. As far as can be determined, the minutes for 1829-1830 were taken by John Inman; for 1831-March 8, 1832, by Thomas S. Cummings; for March 15, 1832-April 4, 1833, by William

a letter of Charles Cromwell Ingham, this organization's first and probably sole president, shows that it had actually been founded during the latter half of 1827, after the second exhibition of the National Academy. According to Ingham, "the first regular meeting took place at the rooms of Thomas Cole,"[20] but the first meeting in the minutes was held at John L. Morton's. The earliest minutes to survive—those of 1829—are therefore not an accurate clue to the origins of the club although John Durand seemed to think so when he wrote its history in 1882.[21] Minutes of the earliest meetings were probably never even kept or, if kept, have since been lost. How else could we explain the fact that in the very first recorded meeting of the club the members decided to "revise and remodel" its constitution and bylaws?

Despite its obscure beginning The Sketch Club enjoyed a long life of thirty-two years or more. Its last recorded meeting was held on April 9, 1869, forty years after its first, but there had been an eight-year hiatus between March 14, 1861 and March 24, 1869. On this latter date John H. Gourlie wrote in the minutes: "This is the first meeting of the Club since 1861, and was a pleasant gathering of members and guests [at William Cullen Bryant's house]. It is proposed to continue them as in former times[.]" But this attempt proved futile, for only one more meeting was held.

A few clear objectives characterized The Sketch Club.[22] Conviviality and productiveness were to go hand in hand, for the earliest members were mostly National Academicians who wanted not only to mingle with writers and patrons but also to perfect themselves in the art of drawing. This association, they hoped, would eventually lead to the publication of a literary annual written, illustrated, and sponsored by the club. They wished also to avoid the ostentation found in the gatherings of The Bread and Cheese, which had been held in

---

Emerson; for 1844-June 24, 1851, by John Neilson, Jr.; and for Sept. 27, 1851-1869, by John H. Gourlie.

20. Quoted in Tho[ma]s. S. Cummings, *Historic Annals of the National Academy of Design*, pp. 110-11. Cummings' reference to The Sketch Club "of 1826" (p. 202) is undoubtedly a mistake.

21. *Prehistoric Notes of the Century Club*, p. 9.

22. For two later clubs which in objectives as well as name were similar to this organization, see Cummings, pp. 175-76, 202.

a hotel. Members of The Sketch Club therefore decided to meet in each other's homes or lodgings and to serve only simple, inexpensive refreshments.

During its early years probably no more than twenty-one persons belonged to The Sketch Club at a time, and it was therefore known as The Twenty-One, but in the minutes for January 12, 1844 and February 18, 1858 we find this limit eased to twenty-five. In all there were at least sixty-six members.[23] Artists were especially numerous during the early period. Thomas Cole, Asher Durand, Henry Inman, Samuel Morse, William Dunlap, Charles Ingham, John L. and Henry J. Morton, William Guy Wall, William J. Bennett, Thomas S. Cummings, Robert Weir, Frederick S. Agate, and George W. Hatch had all joined before 1831. Of this group, however, only Durand and Ingham amassed impressive attendance records and remained active members through the fifties and into the sixties.[24] The rest either died or moved away, their places being taken by Daniel Huntington, John G. Chapman, John F. Kensett, Henry K. Brown, Felix O. C. Darley, Francis W. Edmonds, Luther Terry, and Henry Peters Gray. But Wall, Morse, and Weir, although dropped from active membership when they left the city, subsequently visited the club as guests. Weir and Morse were later made honorary members and, finally, regular members again.

The earliest literary Sketch Clubbers were John Inman, James Hillhouse, Robert Sands, Gulian Verplanck, and William Cullen Bryant. In 1832 they were joined by Charles Fenno Hoffman and John Howard Payne.[25] Sands died at an early age; Hillhouse was dismissed

23. The list of 60 members compiled by John Durand (*Prehistoric Notes*, pp. 21-22) is somewhat incomplete. James E. DeKay, Samuel L. Knapp, James A. Hillhouse, Robert Sands, Henry J. Morton, and William G. Wall are all found as members in the minutes for 1829-30 but are not listed by Durand.

24. The extant minutes, covering a 24-year period, list the attendance at 259 meetings. Durand attended 195 of these meetings; Ingham, 185.

Ingham was re-elected president on Jan. 18, 1861; but minutes for the remaining meetings do not mention him. He died in 1863. Durand remained active through the club's last recorded meeting, which he attended.

25. Hoffman was proposed for membership on Nov. 2, 1832 and elected on the following Nov. 8. The first roster to list Payne among the members is in the minutes for Oct. 19, 1832.

for entertaining too lavishly;[26] and Inman left the club prior to 1844;[27] but Verplanck and Bryant remained active through the last recorded meeting.[28]

A third group of members, neither artists nor writers, might be called "amateurs," to borrow a term in vogue at the time. No matter how disparate their occupations, these men showed a mutual interest in the fine arts. Some of them taught at the National Academy: James Jay Mapes, an inventor and manufacturer, lectured on the chemistry of colors; and Dr. John Neilson, for a time the club's secretary, gave courses in anatomy. Others, like Professor Henry J. Anderson, Dr. James E. DeKay, and the Reverend Orville Dewey, occasionally wrote on art for the local magazines[29] or, like the merchants Jonathan Sturges, Charles Leupp, and Luman Reed, were noted collectors of painting. In 1830 The Sketch Club contained almost four artists to every amateur, but by 1859 the number of amateurs equalled the number of artists. Although this gradual shift in personnel eventually led to a rearrangement of The Sketch Club's goals, the crossfertilization of art, literature, and other professions united artist and patron and forced each member to broaden his outlook, making it "impossible," as John Durand said of The Century Association, "for a one-idea man to live, move and have his being in this assembly."[30]

Guests were frequently invited to meetings, and a list of them compiled only from the extant minutes includes over 500 different

26. See Durand, *Prehistoric Notes*, pp. 15-16; Cummings, p. 111; Charles T. Hazelrigg, *American Literary Pioneer*, pp. 144-45. Hillhouse seems to have never been a very active member. According to the minutes, he attended meetings on Feb. 6 and March 6, 1829 and on Feb. 4, 1830 and was host only for the meeting on March 27, 1829.

27. He attended a meeting on Jan. 12, 1832. After that he is not mentioned, but he could have returned to the club from 1834 to 1843, a period for which no minutes have as yet been located.

28. During the 24 years covered by the extant minutes, Bryant attended 161 meetings; Verplanck, 129 meetings.

29. See, for example, Orville Dewey, "Powers' Statues," *The Union Magazine of Literature and Art*, I (Oct., 1847), 160-61; [H. J. Anderson], Review of *Address Delivered before the American Academy of Fine Arts*, by William B. Lawrence, *The New-York Review*, I (July, 1825), 125-29, attributed to Anderson in Bryant's marked copy of this magazine, Berg Collection, NYPL. For DeKay, see Cummings, p. 229.

30. *Prehistoric Notes*, p. 19.

names.[31] At times these visitors even outnumbered members, so that on January 6, 1854, members were asked to invite their "resident friends" to no more than "two meetings during the season." In the 1850's the reputation of this convivial society was carried beyond the city limits by such distinguished guests as Martin Van Buren, James Fenimore Cooper, Dr. Oliver Wendell Holmes, Ralph Waldo Emerson, and William Makepeace Thackeray.[32] Residents occasionally joined the club if, after being proposed by a member, they could escape the single blackball able to exclude a candidate,[33] but failure to be elected did not prevent them from being asked to later meetings. Thomas Hicks and Lewis Gaylord Clark were regular visitors for years after an unsuccessful attempt to elect them.[34]

The club met on alternate Friday evenings during a season which lasted from November through April,[35] and on the days of the meetings cryptic announcements were sometimes published in the newspapers.[36] "S. C., H. I. 49 Vesey street," a one-line notice appearing in the *Evening Post* for January 14, 1830, meant simply that Henry

31. For examples of written invitations, see MS letters, Daniel Huntington to Evert Duyckinck, n.p., Jan. 19, 1850, and 48 E. 20th, June 21, 1851, Duyckinck Papers (Literary Correspondence), NYPL.

32. See the minutes for March 28, 1856; March 28, 1851; Nov. 25, 1853; March 26, 1852; and Dec. 3, 1852, respectively.

33. As the club approached its final years, it was decided that two blackballs would be needed to reject a candidate. See the amendments to the constitution in the minutes for Feb. 18, 1858, which also read that "no election shall be held unless thirteen members be present." Usually candidates were proposed at one meeting and balloted for at the next. These elections were held at special business meetings, which guests never attended, or at regular meetings either before visitors arrived or after they left. Apparently this policy was violated at times: On Jan. 6, 1854, it was decided that "no candidate for membership shall be balloted for during the presence of guests at the meetings of the Club."

34. Proposed for membership on Nov. 30, 1855, Hicks was a guest at 29 meetings from 1850 to 1869. Clark was proposed by Leupp on Jan. 12, 1844, and was balloted for on Jan. 19 of the same year. Although not elected, he visited 10 meetings during the period from 1845 to 1852.

35. See undated MS "Rules and Regulations of the Sketch Club," two pages of a loose sheet at the end of MS "Minutes of the Sketch Club 1829." Also see the rules contained in the minutes for Jan. 12, 1844, and Feb. 18, 1858. At first, meetings were held on Thursdays.

36. This plan was not adopted until approximately the latter half of the year 1829. See MS letter, J. L. Morton to Thomas Cole, New York, Dec. 15, 1829, Cole Papers, NYSL.

Inman was to entertain. According to tradition, a reader once conjectured that these communications had been inserted by a gambling club in an attempt to reorganize; his letter to the editor supposedly provoked a witty rejoinder from one of The Sketch Club's members, who asked in cacographical puns:

Are we not Sober Citizens and Sincere Christians? Do we not Sleep Coundly, Sing Cheerfully, Separate Coberly, Speak Censibly, Suffer Courageously and Sup Comfortably? You seem to think we Shuffle Cards, too; but, upon the Spotless Character of an S. C. it is not so; and the man who says it utters a Scandalous Calumny.

Since you manifest so much anxiety on the subject, however, I will tell you the honest truth; we are, in fact, a Secret Combination of Sworn Conspirators; and Social Conviviality is but a Simulated Cover for the Sacred Cecrecy of our Solemn Cabal.[37]

Probably to increase excitement and speculation the members added other abbreviations to their notices in the *Post* for 1830: "S.C.—J. B. S. m. d. Bank Coffee House" appeared on March 25; "S. C.—J. N.—min. a. m.—22 Howard street" on April 1; and "S. C.—C. I. pr. ov. t. c. 69 Franklin" on April 8. The respective hosts were therefore Dr. John B. Stevenson, Dr. John Neilson, and Charles Ingham, the abbreviations after Ingham's initials probably standing for "president of the club."

Meetings devoted in part to impromptu drawing and writing distinguished The Sketch Club from other social organizations. It was the duty of the host to provide a subject upon which artists and writers could expend themselves for one hour, usually the first of the evening. When the time was up, the host collected the sketches, which he then kept.[38] Most of the subjects came from literature. For instance, on April 24, 1829, members at Bryant's house were asked to describe "the discomfiture of a party of pleasure, upon an island which was overflowed by the tide, their boat having thought proper to travel off without leave or license." Taken from George Crabbe's

37. Quoted in Durand, *Prehistoric Notes*, p. 10.
38. "Constitution and Bye-Laws," in MS "Minutes of the Sketch Club 1829"; Cummings, p. 111; minutes for Jan. 12, 1844.

Tales of the Hall, the passage was probably read aloud by the host to refresh the memories and stimulate the imaginations of the sketchers. General topics, such as "The Emotions" and *"the abduction,"* were outnumbered by incidents based on the works of Mrs. Hemans, Byron, Spenser, Goldsmith, Thomson, and Irving,[39] while Scott's poems furnished matter for three meetings in a row.[40] During the first year of the club's recorded history the writings of the members themselves were not used as sources. However, none of its rules excluded such inspiration; and in 1833 R. Ray Ward planned a meeting at which members would base their drawings on "Boyuca," a story by Robert Sands, who had died suddenly the year before.[41] The minutes kept by John Inman reveal several other sources of inspiration, but they were recorded with more wit than accuracy. On May 29, 1829, he wrote of a meeting at Thomas Cole's house: "Subject an Indian (from Amer Khan & other poems by Miss Somebody Somebody) in the act of jumping into the Sea—probably in an access of puerperal fever." On June 5 of the same year he was still playing the wag: "Subject Abel Killing Cain or Cain Killing Abel—I forget which, but it was one or the other."

The practice of drawing at these meetings was not long-lived, and its gradual abandonment may be traced even in the early minutes of the club. Because February 20, 1829 was "a most abominable night, prolific only in wind, snow, colds, coughs, and frozen ears," there was "no Drawing but of corks"; at two other meetings during the same year definite subjects were not prescribed, the choice of them being left instead "to the *discretion* and *fancy* of the paper-spoilers," as the sketchers were called.[42] The next step was a separation of drawing and writing: for example, on February 4, 1830, artists were given a topic from Byron's works, but literary members were asked to write

39. Feb. 27, March 20, Feb. 6, Feb. 13, March 6, March 13, May 1, May 22, 1829, respectively.

40. March 27, April 3, and April 10, 1829.

41. MS letter, Ward to Morse, New York, Jan. 22, 1833, Morse Papers, Vol. XI, LC.

42. April 17, 1829. On May 1, 1829, the "subject [was] ambulatory and optional." Also see the minutes for Jan. 21, 1830: They mention no subject but simply state that "multitudes of Sketches were made and many oysters eaten."

on "The Sublime."[43] In 1833 subjects were still chosen by the host,[44] yet within a decade impromptu drawing changed from a scheduled activity to an occasional diversion. The atmosphere of the meetings was not conducive to it. Memorable drawings were seldom made by fingers sticky from raisins, and minds startled by the sound of popping corks and cracking peanut shells.[45] An influx of guests and non-artist-members whose livelihood did not depend on a bulging sketchbook added further distractions. Probably as a result, on January 2, 1844, Cole, Ingham, Durand, Chapman, and several other members helped to found the Artists' Sketch Club, an association of confirmed and genuine "paper-spoilers."[46] Artists who were members of both organizations could now mingle with amateurs on one day and draw with professionals on another.[47] Rules adopted by The Sketch Club on January 12, 1844 reflected this new situation by requiring only that hosts should provide materials in case anyone might care to draw at the meetings. Impromptu sketching was no longer an integral part of the agenda. In 1846, when its "rival" was either dead or dying, The Sketch Club urged its own members to bring finished drawings to the meetings.[48] But work once done in public was now done in private, and the club had been transformed from an artists' workshop into a very sociable gallery, where members could find sketches but not sketching.

Impromptu writing, never actually demanded by The Sketch Club's constitution, had been "frequently" practiced at the early meetings by those who could not draw but wished to amuse themselves while the artists drew.[49] Sometimes these compositions were transcribed in the minutes, and passages from one of them, a "penance" imposed on Sands, Neilson, and Inman "for certain contempt," have

43. Also see the minutes for Jan. 28, 1830.

44. See MS letter, Ward to Morse, New York, Jan. 22, 1833, Morse Papers, Vol. XI, LC.

45. For an example of such distractions, see the minutes for March 13, 1829.

46. Cummings, pp. 175-76, describes the club and lists its members but does not give reasons for its founding.

47. In 1844 the following artists were members of both clubs: Chapman, Ingham, Cummings, Durand, Gray, Cole, Morton, Edmonds, Shegogue, and Agate.

48. See the minutes for Jan. 9, Jan. 23, and Feb. 6, 1846.

49. Cummings, p. 111.

already been printed.[50] Though marred by crudities of thought and expression, all of these verses are remarkable not only for their humor but also for their communal authorship since at least three writers collaborated on each poem. At the meeting for February 4, 1830, Bryant, Sands, and the secretary, John Inman, were asked to write on "The Sublime." Together they composed the sixteen stanzas which follow:

SANDS

Ye everlasting hills that tower sublime
Grand as eternity and old as time
The greatest objects to be seen in nature—

SEC

Your glories in my soul are deeply graven
Since that blest day when first in old New Haven
I learned your qualities and nomenclature.

BRYANT

Ye piles of granite, basalt & grey wacke [soacke?][51]
That bear the umbrageous forests on your back
And carry clouds and tempests on your forehead.

SANDS

Gypsum & slate, asbestos, pudding stone,
Whoever fall your flinty ribs upon
Are very likely to come off with soreheads—

SANDS

Oh Chimborazo, Pyrenees and Alps
That into heaven thrust up y^r daring scalps
Cloud kissing Pyramids—Ye breasts of Isis.

SEC

My thoughts ye have a power to compel
And fix on Liberty and William Tell
And other grave & perilous devices.

50. Jan. 21, 1830, printed in Durand, *Prehistoric Notes*, p. 18.
51. As in Sawatch?

SECRETARY

From your eternal summits, vast & hoar
The Lauwine tumbles with outrageous roar.
And sometimes bothers those who travel under—

BRYANT

And without saying "By your leave" it slides
Crushing the bushes on yʳ ragged sides
And making all the old women scream like thunder.—

BRYANT

When'eer I gaze upon you, big and blue,
I feel myself almost as big as you,
And swell with proud emotions of sublimity.—

SANDS

I think Goliah was a fool to me
That Magog could not reach up to my knee
Or Sampson rival me in magnanimity.

SANDS

And oh ye great volcanos spitting coal
Pumping Earths entrails from the lowest hole
Vesuvius[,] Stromboli & mighty Etna—

SECRETARY

If twixt two of you I could raise a wedding
And be permitted to behold the bedding
I'd pay the expenses of yʳ jaunt to Gretna.

SECRETARY

But wo is me, your hearts are very hard
Ten thousand things yʳ union would retard
Your mighty bowels are so very stony—

SANDS

The car that carried Ammon would be broke
By carrying you a rod, in every spoke,
And it would cost a dreadful sight of money—

21

SANDS

So stand still all ye mountains for the present
Removing you would prove a job unpleasant
And dirt might become scarse in after ages.

SECRETARY

The roads too would perhaps be apt to suffer
And cry oh Lord, what everlasting Buffer
Is this that travels by such easy Stages.

Equally spirited verse had arisen out of a meeting on January 28,
1830. Instructed to write on "Character," Sands, Bryant, Neilson, and
the Inman brothers composed a narrative sketch of Xantippe, Socrates'
wife. The poem begins:

SANDS

In the reign of King Nebuchadnezzar
There lived an old maid named Zantippe,

SECRETARY

[John Inman]
She was more of a bitch than old Djazzar
When he drank up the great Mississip[p]i.

_____

_____

(Some rivers have queer names; I heard
of a stream that is christened Tonbigbee)

BRYANT

To her lord she behaved quite asburd [sic]
And never would let his old wig be—

_____

_____

She was cursed with a very bad character
A thing which was sadly unlucky;

SANDS

Though for modest pretences a fair actor
When her spouse with a gimlet she struck he[.]

. . . .

SECRETARY

The doctor was summoned but came not
Because of her bad reputation;

BRYANT

Says her husband, your gimlet I blame not
But I hate your damned vociferation.

Eighty lines of name-calling follow, and the poem ends with
Xantippe's final outburst:

SECRETARY

But tis useless to add to the list—
I've an argument here that is sounder;
So she up with her damnable fist
And knocked him as flat as a flounder.

The entire twenty-six stanzas, mere doggerel, to be sure, should at
least prove that the Sketch Clubbers were not the sedate, white-bearded
luminaries often pictured as typical American poets.

Analysis of the preceding poems reveals that the participants in
these verse-rounds had to be adept at rhyming, for, although there
was some variation in the pattern, in both poems each member was
forced to match the sounds furnished by the preceding member and
then furnish new sounds for the next member. A poem found in the
minutes for November 15, 1832 represents an even greater challenge
but a less successful outcome. Actually it is a wild attempt at blind
composition, i.e., composing the last line of one couplet and the first
line of the next without knowing what the preceding member has
composed. To explain this game and to recapture the mood in which
it was played, we must quote William Emerson's record of the entire
meeting:

Club met at the house of Dr Neilson in Stuyvesant St.; present, Mr
Ingham, president, Messrs Mapes, Sands, Neilson, W. W. Verplanck,
Payne, Gimber, Stevenson, Bennett, Hatch, Weir & the secretary. We
were also favored with the company of Col. Stone & Dr. Leo Wolf, as
guests. Another guest & a beautiful one too, danced in and out with light

and joyous skip, & set all our poets at their wits' end to determine whether
it were cherub or sylph. The majority were of opinion that she was a
lineal descendant of queen Mab; but one who stole a kiss swore that she
smacked of the angel. Whether or not it was through fairy influence, I
will not take upon me to say, but can only state the fact, that an un-
common vivacity of conversation prevailed throughout the evening. At
one period, indeed, the conversational mania did so rage, that not content
with one tongue the members burst forth into several, & the languages of
Gaul & Germany were poured forth as merrily as our own vernacular.
Some check was given to this loquacity by the announcement of a subject
for sketches, & all pencils were put in requisition to immortalize Celadon
& Amelia; & it being universally conceded that he of "The Seasons" had
made but a humdrum affair out of the adventure, the poets of the club
undertook to make each a couplet, knowing nothing of the preceding
except the word to which they must rhyme, & to Thomson's undying
shame the following exquisite morceau was the introduction of his un-
coalescing coalition.

> I guess the lightning Miss Amelia killed,
> And her fond daddy with deep grief was filled;
> But when the news unto her mammy came,
> Wrapt in a sheet of red & fiery flame,
> With rumbling thunder also, a great sight—
> I find it quite impossible to write;
> And oh! may he, who follows me, succeed;
> In ancient time, fair glory was the need
> Each bard desired; of late he seeks but gold,
> And other curses blast his head; but hold—
> Now sing of barring notes, not notes of hand—
> A most ignoble & unvaliant band
> Of yellow Philadelphia negroes—
> This mingled yarn! how quickly he or she grows!
> But now let's bring this metre to a finish;
> To end it here its merits won't diminish.

After this tremendous effort of poetic talent, it may well be supposed
that the club needed some refreshment & the doors of the supper-room
being thrown open they partook of our host's excellent oysters, & wine
of the vintage of /97 with extraordinary zest. On returning to the draw-

ing room, we were entertained with a comic opera on that most comical subject, the Cholera, & altho' the dish was spiced rather too hot with the vulgar & the profane at the same time it had no lack of the redeeming relish of wit. Shortly thereupon, artists, poets, editors, doctors, & lawyers with our consent adjourned, & all, so far as heard from, arrived safe at home, a contingency, which, considering the length of the journey, would have been quite remarkable, had not our good host, perhaps anticipating the effects of the vintage of '97 taken care to furnish us all with charts of the route.

Wm. Emerson, Sec^y

This impromptu writing and sketching must have sharpened the talents of those members who collaborated on such books as *The Talisman*, a literary annual started in 1827 by Sands, Bryant, and Verplanck. From time to time the club appointed committees to plan these works,[52] and it is quite possible that not only *The Talisman* series but also *The American Landscape* (1830) and *Tales of Glauber-Spa* (1832) were their official but unacknowledged publications. Each of the three *Talisman* volumes reflected some collaboration, but the last volume, issued on November 10, 1829, gave an especially important role to the artist-members, for their illustrations were closely integrated with poems and stories.[53] In fact, as a letter from Bryant to Verplanck indicates, traditional sequences were reversed when this issue was planned: "The necessity of putting the designs immediately into the hands of the engravers," Bryant cautioned his friend, "will oblige us rather to illustrate their designs than to have designs illustrating what we write."[54] The best of the twenty-five engravings in the series were Weir's "Red Jacket"; Inman's "William Tell"; Cole's "View near Ticonderoga"; and Neilson's drawing of "The Devil's Pulpit," a prototype of Durand's "Kindred Spirits." Every plate was small, but many were superior to those which later became standard gift-book quality. Some of the matching text, notably Bryant's sonnet to Cole, Halleck's verse portrait of "Red Jacket," and Verplanck's

52. See, for example, the minutes for March 15, April 26, and Dec. 6, 1832; Cummings, p. 150.
53. See William Cullen Bryant II, "Bryant: The Middle Years," p. 155.
54. MS letter, New York, Feb. 9, 1829, Berg-Bryant, NYPL.

"Gelyna," a prose tale, was also above average. "The oppressive sentimentality of the time" was replaced by a "gentle masculinity and
humor" which made this annual a respectable tribute to the genial
atmosphere of The Sketch Club.[55] But *The Talisman* would have
been more brilliant had some of the wild wit of John Inman's minutes
sparked its pages.

The most characteristic activities of The Sketch Club were verbal.
Lively conversations and sometimes discourses on all manner of topics
were to be expected "where so many of the speech-gifted race were
gathered together," and as a result there "was quite a hubbub, but
then it was none of your fierce, braggadocio, hurly burly hubbubs,"
wrote William Emerson, "but a peaceful, social, laughing, chatting
hubbub."[56] Colonel Trumbull and his American Academy were ridiculed;[57] a mock-vote of thanks for commanding high prices was even
extended to him although it was not sent in "an old gally pot," as
John Inman at first hoped it would be.[58] Members talked of politics,
argued over words, and contributed information on such grave topics
as the "domestic economy . . . of Bull-frogs."[59] Cole explained the
"combustion of pea nut shells"[60] and joined Ingham in discussing the
"nature and operations of clouds";[61] Verplanck described "antediluvian
butter churns";[62] and Bryant proved conclusively that diving into a
snowbank is the "perfection of bathing."[63] Although members were
encouraged to talk about anything, we find them penalizing Bryant
in the minutes of May 8, 1829 for "having given an excellent criticism
on a College oration, which he had not heard & an admirable account
of a dinner which he had not been within scent of." He was

55. Ralph Thompson, *American Literary Annuals & Gift Books*, p. 61.
56. March 29, 1832.
57. March 27, May 15, 1829.
58. March 13, 1829.
59. March 27, 20, 6, 1829, respectively.
60. March 13, 1829. Cole was "vehemently opposed" by Neilson and Ingham.
The ensuing argument tricked the artist Hatch, bent on drawing a scene from "The
Deserted Village," into "sketching nothing but pea nuts and sweet almond shells
instead of Sweet Auburn."
61. Feb. 20, 1829.
62. May 1, 1829.
63. May 1, 1829.

Asher B. Durand
KINDRED SPIRITS (1849)
(*The New York Public Library*)

Thomas Cole
VIEW NEAR TICONDEROGA
(*The Talisman* for 1830)

therefore ordered "to write & publish an account critical, poetical, ethical, didactic[,] metaphysical of the Exhibition of the Nat[ional] Ac[ademy] of Design before seeing the same"—actually an easy feat for a man who had probably viewed most of these pictures before they were hung. On the next day the *Evening Post* carried a full but unsigned review of the exhibition.

Other activities of the club were varied. There were excursions to Hoboken[64] and on July 4, 1848, an overnight visit to Roslyn, Bryant's Long Island home, which proved interesting enough to be recounted in the otherwise economical minutes kept by John Neilson: "A Sail . . . in the morning, a ramble through the beautiful grounds . . . & a display of fireworks in the evening rendered the day a very pleasant one, and after a night passed under the hospitable roof of their host the members returned to the city on the next morning." At other meetings they planned an exhibition of Thomas Cole's paintings,[65] exhibited their own works,[66] watched demonstrations of phrenology,[67] and engaged in a great deal of singing.[68] Magic was practiced by Henry Inman, who, "having taken private lessons of Dr Faustus," ate candle ends and "amazed" the club.[69] Another attempt at deception, the appearance of the Prince of Orange, was obviously more amusing than amazing. The event took place at R. Ray Ward's on January 24, 1833; the members, having worked up their appetites by sketching with extraordinary zeal, had just sat down to supper when, according to William Emerson, the secretary,

. . . a very distinguished guest was unceremoniously announced, being no less a personage than the *Prince of Orange*! I was not a little scandalized at the freedom with which all the company uttered their remarks upon him, directly before his face. There were certainly some striking peculiarities about the prince, & not the least was his decided Sicilian complexion,

64. June 13, June 20, Oct. 24, 1829; MS letter, Ingham to Verplanck, New York, June 22, 1832, Verplanck Papers, NYHS.

65. Feb. 18, 1848.

66. May 15, 1829; Nov. 5, 1847.

67. Feb. 16, 1844.

68. April 17, 1829; March 25, April 1, April 8, 1830; March 24, 1869. On March 1, 1844, there was "some fine singing by [the] Glee Club."

69. May 15, 1829.

altho' the most sceptical did not deny that we saw before us a legitimate scion of the house of Orange. At length one, ruder than the rest, chucked his highness under the chin, & observed that he was "a very fruitful subject." The prince ought doubtless to have replied that he was no subject at all, but he remained utterly mute, confounded, no doubt, by the affrontery of the remark.

Much more spectacular was the raising of a "legitimate & veritable ghost" at Robert Weir's house on April 17, 1829:

The door of the room slowly opened itself; strange noises were heard, seeming to consist of mingled thunder[,] groans, screeches, whistling and cracking of egg shells or pea nuts—A dim blue light pervaded the adjoining apartment which gradually increased in brilliancy until every object in the room was plainly perceptible, and at last the shadowy form of an unsubstantial figure was seen to rise through the floor extending its arms towards us, with a gesture of entreaty or remonstrance, as though blowing us up, for troubling its slumbers.

We were somewhat moved at the sight but on the whole retained our composure pretty decently well; nobody fainted or ran out of the room, although Messrs DeKay and Morse did turn a little pale—We were given to understand before we commenced that it would not perhaps be expedient to address the vision at this time, . . . for this reason we held our peace, and so, in a few minutes, the figure vanished away; then the light faded, the noises grumbled once more, the doors closed themselves again and the affair was ended.[70]

Luckily this ghostly guest stayed away from ensuing meetings, and the bedlam that continued for several decades was not of a supernatural kind.

The history of The Sketch Club indicates that romanticism could have a gay, light side. The members—America's first significant group of romantic writers and painters—were by no means the solitary, brooding melancholiacs popularly associated with this movement in England and on the Continent. Even Bryant, Cole, and Durand, whose works were often philosophical and contemplative, sometimes mystical, could mix wholeheartedly week after week in the sportive

70. May 15, 1829.

doings of their club. How much of this eagerness for artistic companionship was due to environment we shall never know, but certainly some credit must go to New York City itself, as famous then as now for its gregariousness. Whatever the source of The Sketch Club's congenial atmosphere, there is abundant evidence in *The Talisman* series and in examples to be discussed later that the members greatly benefited from it by sharing their best theories and techniques.

The Academies

Less playful organizations than The Sketch Club, namely, two academies and the American Art-Union, also gave artists and writers a chance to work together. These societies were extensively noticed in magazines and newspapers edited by Knickerbockers, and much of the best art criticism in the early nineteenth century appeared as reviews of their exhibitions. But here we are concerned not so much with the aesthetic judgments they evoked as with the Knickerbockers' part in their management.

New York City had two academies for artists. The first of these, incorporated in 1808 and called the American Academy of the Fine Arts, lasted until 1840.[71] The other, founded in 1825 as the New York Drawing Association but from 1826 called the National Academy of Design, is still in existence.

Certain defects in the management and operation of the American Academy caused its gradual downfall. In the first place, artists were not given a large enough part in its government, this role being taken primarily by the president, stockholders, and directors, most of whom were wealthy and aristocratic laymen—diplomats, statesmen, attorneys, jurists, doctors, bankers, merchants, capitalists, and philanthropists. Not until 1817, when Colonel John Trumbull succeeded to the presidency (an office he held until 1836), was the academy led by an artist.

Secondly, as Bryant observed, its exhibitions were "barren."[72] Most of the pictures shown were attributed to "old masters," but their

71. Its history is in Theodore Sizer, "The American Academy of the Fine Arts," in *AA-AAU-I*, pp. 1-93.
72. Bryant, *Orations*, p. 12.

authenticity was frequently denied by nineteenth-century reviewers, whose skepticism seems justified.[73] Other paintings were, by admission, only copies of "old masters." In 1828 a correspondent to the *Evening Post* reflected public feeling as he aptly characterized the academy's exhibition for that year: ". . . there are *huge* copies, and *little* copies, and *whole* copies, and *half* copies, and *good* copies, and *bad* copies; indeed, it is a sort of Noah's ark, in which were things of every kind, *clean* and *unclean, noble animals,* and *creeping things.*"[74] The academy's exhibitions were lacking not only in originality but also in variety.[75] Year after year the same paintings were hung, and bored New Yorkers yearned for novelty. It came in 1826 when the National Academy, a group of rebel artists, inaugurated a series of exhibitions limited to contemporary works by native painters, sculptors, and craftsmen. When this enlightened policy won public approval, the American Academy finally opened its own shows to fresh talent. But this change came too late, and after fourteen years of trying to compete with a younger and stronger organization, the American Academy died, neglected and forgotten.

With a few exceptions the Knickerbockers had taken little interest in the American Academy. Clement Clarke Moore was listed as one of its patrons, and Washington Irving was an honorary member, but only Gulian Verplanck was active in its affairs. Verplanck served as director of the academy from 1819 to 1824 and as vice-president from 1825 to 1828. He even delivered one of its annual addresses, and his speech on this occasion has proved to be an important document in the history of American architectural theory. But Verplanck's services to the American Academy were somewhat curtailed by his eight years in the House of Representatives, which required his presence in Washington. Thus when a merger of the American and National academies was attempted, he was not in town to help. His office in the

73. See "The Fine Arts," *K*, V (May, 1835), 465-68; Sizer, in *AA-AAU-I*, p. 50.

74. Denon, "The Two Academies," *New-York Evening Post*, May 17, 1828.

75. Humorous comments on this sameness are in [William Dunlap], "American Academy of the Fine Arts," *NYM*, X (June 15, 1833), 398. Joseph Rodman Drake satirized other aspects in his poem "To the Directors of the Academy of Arts," collected in *The Poetical Writings of Fitz-Greene Halleck,* pp. 336-39.

former and his friendly connections with the latter (through The Sketch Club) made him the logical agent to effect this merger, so that William Dunlap was indulging in no mere flattery when he wrote: "I presume Morse has informed you of the proposed junction of the artists and the American Academy, a failure which I think would not have happened if you had been here."[76]

It was the National Academy which afforded genuine opportunities for writers to work side by side with artists. True, it had been founded and was managed, not by laymen, but by professional painters, architects, sculptors, and engravers. Yet some of the Knickerbockers held honorary membership in this academy,[77] and two of these writers were even appointed to its faculty. Verplanck was Lecturer of History in 1831 and Professor of History from 1832 to 1838, but he probably never delivered a lecture although he was invited to do so on more than one occasion.[78] His friend Bryant was much more active. In 1828 Bryant was notified that he had been unanimously elected Professor of Mythology and Antiquities,[79] and in the same year, although greatly occupied with his duties as assistant editor of the *Evening Post*, he began a series of five lectures on the mythology of ancient Greece and Rome.[80] According to Thomas Cummings, these talks were "filled with a fervid poetic fire, that interested all."[81] Until these lectures are published,[82] this "fervid poetic fire" cannot be

76. MS letter, Dunlap to Verplanck, New York, Jan. 26, 1826, Verplanck Papers, NYHS.

77. Bryant (1833-78), Cooper (1831-51), Irving (1841-59), Halleck (1841-67), and Verplanck (1830-70). See Eliot Clark, *History of the National Academy of Design*, pp. 249, 251, 257, and 273, respectively. Each of these men held the title of "Honorary Member, Amateur" until his death, even though this classification was discontinued in 1863.

78. Letter from Vernon C. Porter, Director, National Academy of Design, New York, March 27, 1959. Verplanck was invited to lecture at his convenience in MS letter, Dunlap to Verplanck, New York, Oct. 24, 1835, Verplanck Papers, NYHS. Also see Cummings, pp. 173-74.

79. MS letter, John L. Morton to Bryant, New York, Jan. 5, 1828, Bryant-Godwin Collection, NYPL. He retained this title until 1830; from 1831 until 1838 he was called "Professor of Mythology."

80. Bryant II, p. 141, corrects the dates given in Parke Godwin, *A Biography of William Cullen Bryant*, I, 224.

81. Cummings, p. 125.

82. "Research in Progress," *American Literature*, XXXV (Jan., 1964), 576, lists Robert B. Silber's "William Cullen Bryant's 'Lectures on Mythology'" (unpublished

verified, but the fact that Bryant repeated the series in 1829 is certain proof of his popularity with the academy.

Bryant's many services made him, of all the Knickerbockers, its most cherished lay member. When the National Academy fought a paper war with John Trumbull and his followers, correspondence from both camps was printed in the *Evening Post*, but Bryant, its assistant editor, favored the newer organization[83] and, according to his own testimony, "lent its founders such an aid as a daily press could give."[84] During and after this period he made friends with many of the rebel artists and became an intimate of their first two presidents, Samuel Morse and Asher Durand. In 1845 the academicians invited him to deliver a eulogy on Thomas Cole, another of his friends,[85] and in 1865 to speak at the opening of their new building.[86] With Bryant's death a relationship that had lasted over thirty years was ended, and the academy passed several resolutions of mourning for this distinguished member.[87]

The American Art-Union

Another organization served by the Knickerbockers and thus forming a link between artists and writers was the American Art-Union, begun in 1839 as the Apollo Association. In accordance with its plan each member paid five dollars a year, for which he received several publications, including an illustrated *Bulletin*, annual *Transactions*, and a large engraving of an American painting. With most of this money the Art-Union bought from a low of seven to a high of four hundred and sixty original, contemporary works of art, exhibited them in its "perpetual free gallery," and at the end of the year raffled them

---

Ph.D. dissertation, Iowa, 1962), apparently based on the MSS of these lectures; but I have not been able to examine this work.

83. Bryant II, p. 147.

84. Quoted in Cummings, p. 341.

85. *Ibid.*, p. 205.

86. Delivered on April 28, 1865, and printed as "The Academy of Design," *Prose Writings of William Cullen Bryant*, I, 230-36. When the cornerstone of this building was laid (Oct. 21, 1863), Bryant also gave a short address, which is printed in Cummings, p. 341.

87. "Mr. Bryant and the National Academy," New York *Evening Post*, June 14, 1878.

off to its members, each of whom had been given one lottery ticket for his five dollars. The Art-Union was popular chiefly because it served and usually satisfied four classes of people: the winners of coveted works by many of the nation's best painters; those members who did not win but were consoled with excellent engravings; the public who attended the exhibitions; and, finally, the artists whose paintings were bought for distribution. As its operations spread all over the United States and into Canada and England, the Art-Union was obliged to pay certain secretaries, agents, and supervisors. Its president and Committee of Management, however, worked for nothing, so that in spite of its businesslike characteristics it was almost wholly a philanthropic venture.[88]

Although this institution was directed largely by businessmen (professional artists having been purposely barred from its management), some of its offices were held by writers. Bryant was president for the years 1844, 1845, and 1846. He was followed from 1847 through 1850 by Prosper Montgomery Wetmore, author of *Lexington, with Other Fugitive Poems*. The Art-Union's Committee of Management, the group that chose the paintings to be distributed, and determined the prices to be paid for them, usually numbered at least one writer among its thirteen members. Since Wetmore and Bryant as well as George W. Curtis and Evert A. Duyckinck served this committee at one time or another, from its beginning until its demise in 1852 the Art-Union always had an author or an editor among its administrators.

It is difficult to isolate the contributions of these Knickerbockers to the Art-Union. The Committee of Management acted ultimately as a group, and individual members who might have made themselves felt in its meetings were soon reduced to anonymity in its actions and reports. For example, although we know that the Art-Union bought four of Christopher Pearse Cranch's paintings soon after he had asked Evert Duyckinck to influence the Committee of Management,[89] we

88. Charles E. Baker, "The American Art-Union," in *AA-AAU-I*, pp. 103, 107-9, 161.

89. MS letter, Cranch to Duyckinck, Fishkill Landing, Sept. 1, 1849, Duyckinck Papers: Literary Correspondence, NYPL.

cannot with real certainty attribute Cranch's good fortune to Duyckinck's intercession; while such a causal relationship is quite possible, other factors must be considered—such as the fact that during the previous four years Cranch had already sold twelve of his works to the Art-Union.

The president achieved more identity than did any member of the committee; on the other hand, his job was less important than theirs. It involved "presiding at the meetings of the Association, and of the Committee of Management," watching "over the interests of the Institution," and recommending "such measures as he . . . deem[ed] expedient."[90] He chose and bought paintings only when he functioned as a member of the Committee of Management; then like the others he was swallowed up in the group.

Nevertheless, one may at least briefly evaluate the presidential careers of Bryant and Wetmore without ignoring the corporate nature of the Art-Union. Bryant's three terms as president represent a middle period in the history of this institution. When he began his first term in 1844 there were only 1,452 members and income was a paltry $7,129; when he retired in 1846 membership had jumped to 4,457, and income to $22,293. But the mammoth proportions that the Art-Union was yet to attain can be seen in the figures of 1849: a membership of 18,960 and an income of $73,857.[91]

Bryant was not especially responsible for this growth, but he was responsible for avoiding friction with the National Academy,[92] for lending dignity to his office,[93] and, most of all, for making the Art-Union a symbol of the public's triumph over private patronage. In his annual addresses at the December lotteries he insisted that the value of the Art-Union lay in its direct relationship with the people. He was suspicious of the wealthy patron and connoisseur and remarked that a love of art, like charity, "is not after all found amongst

90. Charles E. Baker, "Constitution of the American Art-Union," in *AA-AAU-I*, p. 119.

91. Mary B. Cowdrey, "Publications of the American Art-Union," in *AA-AAU-I*, pp. 243-52.

92. Durand, *A. B. Durand*, pp. 168-69.

93. American Art-Union, "Report of the Nominating Committee," *Transactions of the American Art-Union, for the Year 1846*, p. 24.

34

the most opulent." By "collect[ing] small contributions into large masses, and direct[ing] them to great results"[94] the Art-Union was able to bypass the caprices of the wealthy and still keep the arts on a financially sound course. At the end of his third term Bryant therefore traced the Art-Union's progress to a perfect meeting of minds: "The plan of our Institution is precisely what the people of our country want, . . . [and] it commends itself to their good sense, that when you offer them a method of encouraging the Fine Arts, suited to their means, and to the equal condition of society among us, they adopt it readily and support it zealously."[95] The subtle note of democracy introduced by the phrase "the equal condition of society among us" further enhanced the symbolism, so that with Bryant's help the Art-Union looked as indigenous as the clapboard house.

Prosper Montgomery Wetmore was a less successful president than Bryant had been. Under Wetmore the Art-Union grew both in membership and income, reaching the "peak of its development" in 1849, his last term;[96] at the same time relations with the National Academy, whose annual exhibitions were seemingly threatened by the Art-Union's "perpetual free gallery," were strained to the breaking point. An officer in the state militia for many years, Wetmore bullied artists as he would soldiers. He and his managers ignored their own amateur status to analyze the work of professionals in painful detail, then issue reports bristling with insolent remarks on the faults of these artists. Young and old were advised not only what to paint but also how to paint. A number of unhappy incidents resulted, and not until Wetmore was succeeded by Abraham M. Cozzens, a member of The Sketch Club "who could talk to artists in their own tongue,"[97] did the National Academy and the Art-Union become friendly again. But neither Wetmore's arrogance nor Cozzens' diplomacy could stave off the fierce attack of the painter Thomas W. Whitley, a non-academician who in a prolonged fit of pique over the Art-Union's rejection

94. From a speech delivered at the annual meeting, Dec. 19, 1845, quoted in American Art-Union, *Transactions . . . 1845*, pp. 4-5.

95. From a speech delivered at the annual meeting, Dec. 18, 1846, quoted in American Art-Union, *Transactions . . . 1846*, p. 6.

96. Cowdrey, in *AA-AAU-I*, p. 252.

97. Baker, in *AA-AAU-I*, p. 173.

of his pictures, carried on a malicious campaign to destroy that institution. Ironically enough, Bryant had once recommended that the Art-Union buy Whitley's paintings.[98] No doubt Bryant was shocked as he learned that the chain of events leading to the Art-Union's collapse in 1852 had been forged by this friend in need.

In retrospect, the Knickerbockers joined or were invited to join the art movements of New York City for three main reasons: to associate with men who shared their interests either as professionals or amateurs, to patronize the artists, and to educate the public. The Sketch Club best fulfilled the first objective; the Art-Union made realities of the second and third objectives. The American Academy was an obvious failure, and the National Academy afforded only limited opportunities to a few laymen since it was operated solely by artists. In fact, much of the early history of New York as an art center is one of changing ratios between artists and amateurs. Laymen predominated in the American Academy; the artists won out in the National Academy and in the early Sketch Club; but the laymen again outweighed the artists in the later Sketch Club and in the Art-Union. When the amateurs of any one organization were comprised of Knickerbocker writers or such distinguished patrons as Reed, Sturges, and Leupp, friction was usually at a minimum; artists were understood; their works were not only bought but appreciated; and there was affability, co-operation, and progress.

In this account of institutions supported by Knickerbockers the names of certain writers are noticeably absent. Where was Irving and where, for example, were Willis, Fay, Street, and Paulding when The Sketch Club and the National Academy were developing? For one thing, some of these writers were not joiners; for another, a few of them were not especially well liked. Many were out of town when members were elected or committees formed. Irving and Willis spent several years abroad and, as a result, temporarily lost contact with art movements in New York. Theodore Fay lived almost two-thirds of his life in Europe; Alfred Billings Street made Albany his permanent

98. This interesting story is told in E. Maurice Bloch, "The American Art-Union's Downfall," pp. 331-59.

residence; and Paulding spent much of his time in Tarrytown, Washington, and Hyde Park. But although these writers were neither members of The Sketch Club nor active participants in the affairs of the Art-Union or the National Academy, they all contributed in some way to the growth of the fine arts in America. They will therefore appear in later chapters, together with Bryant, Verplanck, and Cooper, whose connections with artists have so far been only partially revealed.

CHAPTER II

THE WRITERS' FRIENDSHIPS

WITH

AMERICAN ARTISTS

Before analyzing the art-material in Knickerbocker literature, which is the purpose of the next chapters, we must examine the close personal ties between the artists and the authors; for in most cases these friendships not only prompted the Knickerbockers to write about the fine arts but also gave them enough familiarity with their subject to write with confidence and perception. In the previous chapter relatively large groups of friends were seen working together in clubs and other organizations; in this chapter we narrow our focus to pairs— to Irving and Allston, Cooper and Greenough, Bryant and Durand, and to some combinations of writer and artist which, though important, have been neglected for almost a century.

Washington Irving

Washington Irving should be treated first, for he was the oldest of the major Knickerbockers. Moreover, his connection with the fine arts began early and lasted long.[1] In his pre-teens he received drawing instructions from Archibald Robertson, a Scottish immigrant, who later became a director of the American Academy. At this time Irving's interest was bolstered by his admiration for the artists John and Alexander Anderson, family friends, one of whom, John, was the unsuccessful suitor of Irving's sister Catherine. Stimulated by the sketch books of these men, Washington kept up his own drawing. This practice afforded him amusement on trips to the North in 1802-1803, and he continued it long after his first visit to Europe in 1804, the beginning of his extensive relationships with American painters studying and working overseas.[2]

IRVING AND ALLSTON. Of the painters who became Irving's friends after his arrival in Europe only one achieved a reputation close to his own. This was Washington Allston, remembered today, like Irving, as a leader in the development of romanticism. In Rome during the spring of 1805 Irving met Allston for the first time. He was immediately impressed with the young painter's genius, and an intimacy between them was nurtured by frequent visits to art galleries, where Allston taught Irving to concentrate on one masterpiece at a time.[3] Then but twenty-one years old and not yet settled in a career, Irving began to think of becoming a painter himself. "I mentioned the idea to Allston, and he caught at it with eagerness," Irving later recalled. "Nothing could be more feasible. We would take an apartment together. He would give me all the instruction and criticism in his power, and was sure I would succeed." But after a few days Irving

1. For an extensive study of this subject see Jules D. Prown, "Washington Irving's Interest in Art and His Influence upon American Painting," pp. 5-45.

2. See Donald A. Shelley, "American Painting in Irving's Day," p. 19; William Dunlap, *A History of the Rise and Progress of the Arts of Design in the United States*, II, 79-88; Stanley T. Williams, *The Life of Washington Irving*, I, 17-18; Pierre M. Irving, *The Life and Letters of Washington Irving*, I, 42. For reproductions of Irving's drawings, see *The Journals of Washington Irving*.

3. Washington Irving, "Washington Allston," in *Biographies and Miscellanies*, pp. 143-44; Williams, I, 65, 165, 394; P. M. Irving, I, 108-111; Jared B. Flagg, *The Life and Letters of Washington Allston*, p. 61.

declined the proposal, "doubts and fears" having turned him to "sterile reality";[4] for he saw, as Stanley Williams suggests, more potential in his notebooks, systematically filled with observations on the scenery, history, and character types of Europe, than in his charming but casual drawings.[5]

When Irving left Rome in April of 1805, Allston stayed on. They did not meet again until both had returned to America—and then they met but infrequently. Later, when they found themselves together in England, their friendship reached its greatest intensity. In his essay on Allston Irving described their relationship during this period, which began in 1815 with his arrival in London and ended three years later with Allston's departure for the United States: "I used to pass long evenings with him and [Charles R.] Leslie; indeed Allston, if any one would keep him company, would sit up until cock-crowing, and it was hard to break away from the charm of his conversation. He was an admirable story-teller; for a ghost-story none could surpass him."[6] Allston and Irving respected each other's abilities. Irving waxed enthusiastic over Allston's work and was especially pleased with his illustrations for a new edition of Knickerbocker's *History of New York*. Allston himself always eagerly awaited Irving's comments on his paintings and once expressed disappointment that Irving could not furnish "hints" for his "Belshazzar's Feast." After 1818 when Allston returned to America to waste away his life on this ill-fated picture, their paths seldom crossed, and their friendship became little more than a pleasant memory. Irving mentioned only one meeting with Allston after that. The painter was then "in the gray evening of life, apparently much retired from the world."[7] He died in 1843, more than a decade before Irving, who during his own last days, upon hearing Allston's name mentioned, was "set . . . all glowing with tender, affectionate enthusiasm."[8]

4. Irving, *Biographies*, p. 145.
5. Williams, I, 45-46.
6. *Biographies*, p. 146. Also see P. M. Irving, I, 297.
7. W. Irving, *Biographies*, p. 150.
8. William G. Dix's account of a call on Irving, given in P. M. Irving, III, 386. Also see III, 313; Williams, II, 237, 401.

LESLIE'S CIRCLE. Allston's departure for the United States had been the occasion for a deepening friendship between Irving and Charles R. Leslie, an American painter who lived in England nearly all of his life.[9] Upon first meeting Leslie in 1817, Irving had been "somewhat pleased, and more amused" with the young artist;[10] but their mutual love of painting, Allston, and England kindled their friendship into a lifelong fervency which such a mild beginning would hardly seem to foreshadow. Soon they were breakfasting with Walter Scott, attending the coronation of George IV, calling on Samuel Rogers, dining at the York Chop House, and taking enjoyable excursions to Greenwich and Richmond. As Leslie remarked: "The harmony that subsisted among us was uninterrupted."[11]

Another member of this circle was Gilbert Stuart Newton, also an American, and a relative of Gilbert Stuart.[12] Having come to England after a period of halfhearted study in Italy, Newton was introduced to Irving by Leslie; and the three soon made a gay trio. Irving stayed at Newton's apartment for a time, and Newton painted Irving's portrait, which the author's friends pronounced the best likeness of him.

Irving followed every step of Newton's career, taking special delight in Newton's rapidity of execution and uncanny eye for color but acknowledging his lack of skill in drawing. All these things Irving wrote to Dunlap for publication, noting further that the current estimate of Newton as an arrogant and irascible puppy was not correct. Dunlap was forced to conclude that any artist who was a friend of Irving and Leslie must be blessed with "good sense" and "an amiable disposition."[13] Furthermore, when Newton became a successful genre painter, Irving could take part of the credit, for he had persuaded Newton to shun portraiture for this less remunerative branch of art.

9. See P. M. Irving, I, 297, 379, II, 43; Prown, p. 138, n. 2; Charles R. Leslie, *Autobiographical Recollections*, pp. lii, 42.

10. Quoted in P. M. Irving, I, 284.

11. Leslie, p. 42.

12. Dunlap, *Arts of Design*, III, 80-84; P. M. Irving, I, 298, 323, 340, 371-72, II, 42-43, 53-55, 195; Williams, I, 203, 498, II, 16; Prown, pp. 142-43, n. 16.

13. Dunlap, *Arts of Design*, III, 83.

Other peripheral members of this circle were William Edward West, an American who became famous for his portrait of Byron, and David Wilkie, a Scottish painter. Irving and West spent a great deal of time together in Paris and London, occasionally meeting later in New York, Boston, and other parts of the eastern United States.[14] Wilkie's connection with Irving seems more important, encompassing the years 1827 and 1828, when Irving was in Spain.[15] Having just finished *The Life and Voyages of Columbus*, he was able to luxuriate in the more enjoyable task of studying early Spanish art with Wilkie. Irving regarded his friend as a kind of heaven-sent teacher and once remarked, "I would not give an hour's conversation with Wilkie, about paintings . . . for all the enthusiastic and rapturous declamations of the common run of amateurs and artists."[16] Just how extensive this Spanish experience was can be found in Irving's notebook—filled with jottings about a tour to Toledo, the bull fights, excursions to museums, churches, and vaults, all undertaken by that inseparable trio of Irving, Wilkie, and Prince Dolgorouki, a Russian attaché. On the whole, it was a valuable experience, too. Irving learned about painting from an expert, and the expert in turn acquired a new facility and freedom in his art. No one would praise him more for this than his friend Irving who, in a sketch of the painter written probably for a Spanish newspaper, claimed that Wilkie excelled even the Flemish masters in style, taste, and imagination.[17]

There was a certain reciprocity in Irving's relationship with Leslie and his fellow painters, who have been accused by no less an able critic than James Thomas Flexner of exerting "a depressing influence" on Irving's work.[18] Dunlap once wrote: "Washington Irving . . . has told me . . . that while he was writing his 'Sketch Book,' he saw every step they [Leslie and Newton] made in their art, and they saw

14. Williams, I, 283; P. M. Irving, II, 65; N. P. Dunn, "An Artist of the Past: William Edward West and His Friends at Home and Abroad," pp. 661-62.

15. The best treatment of this friendship is in Prown, pp. 23-32, 148-56. Other references are in Williams, I, 283, 325, 335, 482, 485, 495; P. M. Irving, II, 90, 123, 195, III, 338.

16. Quoted in Williams, I, 327.

17. The entire sketch is transcribed in Prown, pp. 114-17.

18. James T. Flexner, *The Light of Distant Skies*, pp. 189-90.

every line of his writing."[19] The same thing held true for some of Irving's other works in which the artist-influence is strong though not immediately apparent. For instance, Leslie advised Irving to omit "Buckthorne and His Friends" from *Bracebridge Hall*; he did so, substituting the "Student of Salamanca" in its place—"an ill-judged change, as he afterwards regarded it, but he was prone to yield too readily to the suggestions of others," wrote Pierre Irving.[20] Because Leslie had not seemed pleased with "Mountjoy," Irving threw the manuscript aside; and it remained unfinished until it was published as a fragment in a magazine.[21] And Irving's lamentable inferiority complex over what he thought to be the crudities in Knickerbocker's *History of New York*, stemmed at least partly from Leslie's comments: "I enjoyed very much the renewal of my acquaintance with my old friend 'Diedrich.' I have the highest respect for the old gentleman . . . , but I must say that in some of *his jokes* he goes near to be thought a little indelicate. . . . I really think he would not suffer by dispensing with them in the future."[22] Irving did dispense with them, and he even traced these refinements to Allston's and Leslie's illustrations, which had set his mind on a new track.[23]

It is improbable that Leslie, Newton, Allston, and the other artists influenced Irving much beyond the matter of eliminating a few crude jokes. They have been accused of carrying "Irving away from the American themes that produced his most vital work into rhapsodies to English gentility."[24] Yet such observations deserve to be qualified. Irving's curiosity for things English and European had been developed before his intimacy with these painters, as is indicated in his prefaces to *The Sketch-Book* and *Bracebridge Hall*. Leslie, Allston, Newton, and Wilkie were only the means through which he expressed this interest, not the cause of it. Moreover, it is possible to demonstrate on the contrary that artist-influence could actually benefit Irving's work.

19. *Arts of Design*, III, 13.
20. Williams, I, 204, 438, II, 289. The quotation is from P. M. Irving, I, 381.
21. P. M. Irving, III, 268.
22. Leslie, p. 227.
23. P. M. Irving, I, 270.
24. Flexner, pp. 189-90.

Stanley Williams shows, for example, that the best stories in *Brace-bridge Hall*—and this includes the famous "Stout Gentleman"—were derived from the association between Irving and Leslie.[25]

If Leslie over-advised Irving, he was paid back in kind; for Irving seldom hesitated to tell him what and how to paint. Yet for this service Leslie was ever grateful. "I not only owe to you some of the happiest social hours of my life," he wrote to Irving, "but you opened to me a new range of observation in my art, and a perception of qualities and characters of things which painters do not always imbibe from each other."[26] Irving in turn considered Leslie an excellent artist and on more than one occasion praised those powers which, according to Leslie, he had helped to mature.[27]

IRVING'S LIFELONG INTEREST IN ART. This intimacy between Irving and the Leslie circle, as well as acquaintance with other artists (listed in Appendix I), constantly stimulated Irving's interest in art-matters. We are not surprised, therefore, to find him under the pseudonym of Geoffrey Crayon, or to discover him naming one of his works *The Sketch-Book*; helping William Dunlap to gather material for a history of American art;[28] recommending the painter William H. Powell for a government commission;[29] making frequent visits to cathedrals, castles, museums, mosques, and manor houses; planning the remodeling of his home at Sunnyside;[30] accepting special invitations to judge newly finished paintings;[31] and in general devoting his life to the fine arts in their various forms.

25. Williams, I, 204-205, II, 280.
26. Quoted in P. M. Irving, I, 297.
27. *Ibid.*, I, 298, II, 42, 175, 179, 223.
28. See *Diary of William Dunlap*, III, 772, 776, 816, 819, 822.
29. See photostatic copies of MS letters, Henry Brevoort to Irving, New York, May 26, 1844; Irving to The Library Committee of Congress, Sunnyside, Jan. 7, 1847, William H. Powell Miscellaneous Papers, NYPL; Prown, pp. 37, 159. For an anonymous expression of disappointment over the selection of Powell for the Rotunda commission, see "The Fine Arts," *LW*, I (Nov. 20, 1847), 159. Irving is excused for influencing this choice in "Editorial Notes—Fine Arts," *Putnam's Monthly Magazine*, III (Jan., 1854), 118.
30. Washington Irving, "A Letter from Irving to His Architect," p. 47.
31. P. M. Irving, III, 355. Durand, *A. B. Durand*, p. 174; Prown, pp. 39, 160, n. 32.

Gulian Verplanck

Besides writing political satires, legal and religious tracts, a collection of discourses on literature, history, and the arts, as well as miscellaneous tales and essays in the *Talisman* series and *The New-York Mirror*, the versatile Gulian Verplanck was a professor at the General Theological Seminary, a vestryman of Trinity Church, and a member of Congress, where he introduced an improved copyright law. He achieved, moreover, some local reputation as an art critic and collector,[32] but he best served America's painters and sculptors through his role as chairman of the Committee on Public Buildings for the House of Representatives. In this capacity he dispensed lucrative commissions to Inman, Weir, Frazee, and Greenough, who together with several other artists, including Allston, Cole, and Dunlap, were his friends or acquaintances.[33]

The story of these favors, marking the first era of public patronage in the United States, revolves around Verplanck's relationship with Washington Allston, an intimate friend since 1815.[34] Verplanck not only publicized Allston's paintings and obtained him an honorary membership in the New-York Historical Society but also offered him an enviable commission from the government.[35] It was Verplanck's duty as chairman of the Committee on Public Buildings to see that all eight of the panels in the Rotunda of the Capitol were filled. John Trumbull had done four of them, yet these pictures failed to impress the Knickerbockers. Joseph Rodman Drake, in fact, roundly abused "The Signing of the Declaration of Independence" in a vicious poem

32. Bryant's praise of Verplanck's critical ability is in James G. Wilson, *Bryant and His Friends*, p. 87. Items in Verplanck's collection, highly esteemed by Dunlap (*Arts of Design*, III, 277), are given in "A Review of the Gallery of the American Academy of Fine Arts," *NYRAM*, II (Jan., 1826), 157; Harold E. Dickson, *John Wesley Jarvis*, p. 161; "Private Galleries," *NYM*, XVII (March 7, 1840), 294; *AA-AAU-ER*, pp. 207, 264, 413, 417-20; *NADER*, II, 191.

33. Those friendships not analyzed in this section are documented in Appendix I.

34. Verplanck and Allston became close friends while in Europe. See MS letter, Bryant to Verplanck, Cummington, Aug. 26, 1826, Bryant-Verplanck Correspondence, Berg Collection, NYPL.

35. Robert W. July, *The Essential New Yorker*, p. 117; Flagg, pp. 153, 229-39, 287-89.

entitled "The National Painting" (1819). Bryant was also obviously dissatisfied with Trumbull's work, for in 1828 he cautioned Verplanck "not [to] let Col Trumbull paint the other 4 national pictures." After all, he continued, "the Col has got 32000 dollars already for his copies. Give one to Allston while he is not only alive but in the vigor of his genius. Give one to Morse who is going abroad next spring—to Rome —who will study it there, and give 5 years of his life to it. Give one to Sully—and if the Col cannot do without the remaining one, let him have it as a matter of grace."[36] Two years later Verplanck followed at least some of Bryant's advice by offering the job to Allston, but this choice eventually proved ill-fated. In their lengthy correspondence Verplanck and Allston tried to find a subject that would meet the approval of Congress. Allston did not wish to paint episodes from military and naval history because he felt himself to be weak in this sphere and believed that such materials could be more impressively recorded by poets and historians, and by novelists like Cooper, than by painters, in whose medium it was especially difficult to represent the blasts of trumpets and the clatter of arms. Hoping that Biblical subjects would prove suitable in the Rotunda, Allston suggested painting the three Marys at the tomb; but Verplanck, knowing the preferences of Congress, wanted him to select the landing of the Pilgrims. Not finding this subject to his liking, Allston suggested Columbus' first interview with Ferdinand and Isabella, a topic which Irving had by then successfully introduced in literature. Delays followed; and Allston finally announced, after six years of indecision and excuses, that he could not accept the commission.

Meanwhile, taking more interest than Allston in governmental patronage, Verplanck's other friends asked for commissions in letters remarkable for a variety of approaches. Cole wrote in veiled terms tinged with hopelessness: "I wish you to understand that in respect [to] the *large pictures* I am by no [means] so confident in my own capacity as to pretend to compete with the artists we spoke of this

36. MS letter, Bryant to Verplanck, New York, Dec. 29, 1828, Bryant-Verplanck Correspondence, Berg Collection, NYPL.

morning—."[37] But Morse bared his soul. He had lived, he wrote Verplanck, for years in the expectation of painting in the Rotunda; he had gone abroad to ready himself, and he had ignored the needs of his purse and heart to reach the climax of his professional career. Yet he was beginning to lose hope.[38] John Frazee, more belligerent than Morse, used another type of approach. Wishing to make statues of Washington[39] and Jefferson,[40] Frazee resorted to an imprudent attack on the "Chanting Cherubs," a work by his strongest competitor for governmental favor, the foreign-trained Horatio Greenough. He noted that Greenough's marble group was an offense against classical tradition, for the legs of its smallest figure obscured each other at one point. He also thought it absurd that the cherubs had not been made to look to heaven while they sang: Were they supposed to be inspired angels praising their God? They looked more like schoolboys at their lessons.[41] Then, after broadly hinting that Greenough needed the help of Italians in his work and was therefore not the man to be commissioned by the United States government,[42] Frazee declared himself most able to carve a truly native masterpiece, and he warned Verplanck not to underestimate his powers.[43] In direct contrast to Frazee's bold approach were the humble letters of Robert W. Weir, who, although advised by George P. Morris to apply for a panel in the Rotunda, hesitated to seek recommendations. For example, he did not want to ask Washington Irving for a letter because, if he then received the commission but failed to execute it successfully, Irving

37. MS letter, Cole to Verplanck, 20 Greene St. [New York], Wednesday [ca. 1834], Verplanck Papers, NYHS.

38. MS letter, Morse to Verplanck, Paris, Jan. 2, 1832, Verplanck Papers, NYHS. Also see MS letter, Morse to Verplanck, New York, Dec. 21, 1826, Verplanck Papers, NYHS.

39. MS letter, Frazee to Verplanck, New York, Feb. 18, 1832, Verplanck Papers, NYHS.

40. MS letters, Frazee to Verplanck, New York, April 14, 1832; Jan. 16, [18]33, Verplanck Papers, NYHS.

41. MS letter, Frazee to Verplanck, New York, Feb. 18, 1832, Verplanck Papers, NYHS.

42. MS letter, Frazee to Verplanck, New York, April 14, 1832, Verplanck Papers, NYHS.

43. MS letter, Frazee to Verplanck, New York, April 27, 1832, Verplanck Papers, NYHS.

would appear to be a poor judge of talent. This was why at first he declined to let even Verplanck see his eagerness for a panel.[44] Weir changed his mind, however, and within a year was directly approaching Verplanck,[45] explaining that he had no other friends in Washington.[46] Another member of The Sketch Club, Henry Inman, also asked Verplanck for a chance to paint one of the panels;[47] it is probable that a similar request came from John Vanderlyn, who had already relied on Verplanck, a fellow member of the American Academy, for assistance in other matters.[48]

When most of the commissions were settled Verplanck was no longer on the committee, but his influence was apparent;[49] for his friends Weir, Inman, and Vanderlyn each received a panel,[50] the other panel going to John G. Chapman, soon to become a member of The Sketch Club. The artists were given $10,000 apiece for their work, but an even larger commission had been awarded Horatio Greenough, whom Allston had recommended to Verplanck.[51] Over a fifteen-year

44. MS letter, Weir to Morris, West Point, Jan. 20, 1835, Verplanck Papers, NYHS. Yet Weir did show his eagerness to Morris and in this letter admitted that he had once asked Morris to help him get the commission. John Quincy Adams had suggested that the job of filling these panels in the Rotunda could best be handled by foreign artists. Apparently Morris had written to Weir that someone should publicly reprimand Adams for ignoring native talent. But Weir was quite objective in his answer, pointing out that Adams could very well be right, that such commissions would be extremely difficult to fulfill, and that only Washington Allston could successfully execute them, although many other American painters would be willing to try.

45. MS letter, Weir to Verplanck, West Point, Jan. 2, 1836, Verplanck Papers, NYHS.

46. MS letter, Weir to Verplanck, West Point, June 12, 1836, Verplanck Papers, NYHS.

47. See MS letter, Inman to Verplanck, U.S. Hotel, Phila[delphia]., no month given, 1834, Verplanck Papers, NYHS.

48. See MS letters, Vanderlyn to Verplanck, New York, Aug. 25, 1829; New York, July 18, 1834, Verplanck Papers, NYHS.

49. See MS letter, L. Jarvis to Verplanck, Washington, March 1, 1834, Verplanck Papers, NYHS.

50. Because of Verplanck's influence Vanderlyn was also commissioned by Congress to paint a full-length picture of George Washington. See July, p. 134. Soon after receiving the commission to fill a panel in the Rotunda, Weir asked Verplanck to help in choosing a subject for the picture, eventually called "The Embarkation of the Pilgrims," and in 1834, when the painting was completed, to defend it against certain critics. See MS letters, Weir to Verplanck, West Point, Dec. 20, 1836; March 15, 1837; Baltimore, Dec. 15, 1843[?], Verplanck Papers, NYHS; Irene Weir, *Robert W. Weir, Artist*, p. 75.

51. July, p. 134.

period Congress spent a total of $49,100 on Greenough's colossal statue of George Washington.[52]

Yet these governmental favors proved to be full of disappointments. The paintings now in the Rotunda, whether the efforts of Weir and his fellows or of Trumbull, have generally been regarded as second-rate affairs by modern critics; and Greenough's semi-draped figure of Washington has been ridiculed ever since the day of its unveiling. The feeling has prevailed that Congress might have employed better, more mature artists. A commission should have been voted certainly to Samuel Morse, who as a painter of historical pictures had shown more promise than any of his contemporaries with the possible exception of Allston. When Inman died not long after receiving a panel, Verplanck and other citizens signed a petition to have the commission transferred to Morse;[53] but the petition failed, and the panel was awarded to William H. Powell, an inferior artist. By this time Morse had not only given up painting but also successfully demonstrated the telegraph, an achievement that earned him more lasting fame than a panel in the Rotunda, no matter how beautifully decorated, could have done. Much different was the case of John Frazee, who had hoped for the commission finally given to Greenough. Although no doubt keenly disappointed, Frazee never willfully abandoned his art, remaining a sculptor and an architect until ill health prevented him from working any longer. Verplanck had secured for him only a relatively small commission to carve a bust of John Jay, for which Frazee received $400 from Congress. Perhaps he was consoled somewhat by the fact that this was the first Congressional order given to an American for statuary to be placed in the Capitol. In this it preceded Greenough's Washington commission by nearly one year.[54]

52. Glenn Brown, *History of the United States Capitol*, I, 110.

53. Presented in 1846, this petition is quoted in Charles E. Fairman, *Art and Artists of the Capitol*, pp. 106-7. It should not be confused with the subscription of 1837 which is mentioned below in the section of this chapter devoted to Cooper and Morse.

54. Henry B. Caldwell, "John Frazee, American Sculptor," pp. 29, 34, 39, 79, n. 109, 96. Cf. John Frazee, "The Autobiography of Frazee, the Sculptor," p. 18, in which the amount of the commission is given as $500.

Verplanck should be neither praised too highly nor censured too severely for his part in these governmental commissions. In the first place, responsibility was divided: Verplanck was not the only member of his committee although he was apparently the most powerful; moreover, the committee was limited merely to advising Congress, with whom the final choice of artists rested. Secondly, Allston's vacillations as well as the scattered resentment toward Morse, factors which kept the best native artists from being selected, were beyond Verplanck's control. Thirdly, in the nineteenth century, historical painting was one of America's youngest arts, its development having been retarded by a lack of great public buildings with large wall areas needing decoration, by a dearth of original historical paintings imported from Europe to serve as models, and by a general reluctance on the part of local and national government to pay for murals or paintings of monumental dimensions. Most artists in the United States made a living chiefly by painting portraits; none could afford to specialize in historical pictures, and only a few tried to make such painting a side line, so that even the best native artists showed only "promise" in this field. Hiring any of them to decorate the Capitol was risky indeed. Nevertheless, most of Verplanck's fellow Congressmen were as eager as he to patronize American talent. Unable to procure Allston, they selected men whom they considered next best. The results of this decision were hardly ideal, but Verplanck and his committee must be commended at least for giving historical painting a chance to develop in the New World.

VERPLANCK AND ROBERT WEIR. Verplanck also served his friends in other ways, apparent, for example, in his dealings with Robert Weir, who regarded him as the epitome of kindness and good judgment.[55] Their association had begun in The Sketch Club, on whose *Talisman* series both men worked, and in the National Academy of Design, which

55. MS letter, Weir to Col. Geo. P. Morris, West Point, April 14, 1835, Miscellaneous Letters, NYHS. Weir even named one of his sons after Verplanck. See MS letter, Weir to Verplanck, West Point, Feb. 19, 1838, Verplanck Papers, NYHS, and I. Weir, p. 99. Other evidence of this friendship is in MS letters, Weir to Verplanck, West Point, July 22, 1837 and Nov. 12, 1849, Verplanck Papers, NYHS.

they served as faculty members. Seventeen years younger than his friend, Weir naturally enough sought Verplanck's advice on both personal and professional matters, and frequently invited Verplanck to see his paintings before releasing them to the public.[56] Sometimes Verplanck found buyers for these pictures, as in the case of "Santa Claus," which Weir considered "one of the best things" he had ever painted.[57] Since Verplanck himself owned several of Weir's paintings, notably "Bourbon's Last March," "Landing of Hendrick Hudson," and "Washington's Head-Quarters," he must be regarded as a patron as well as an agent.[58]

In 1834 Weir was made Teacher of Drawing at the United States Military Academy. The appointment itself and, indeed, much of his subsequent career at West Point owed a great deal to the interest and influence of Verplanck,[59] whom Weir thanked with the utmost humility in 1835, expressing the fear that Verplanck had perhaps overestimated his talents.[60] Had Weir known that he would shortly be training some distinguished men of the future—the artist Whistler as well as Generals Grant, Lee, and Sherman—he might have felt even more inferior. But he soon became occupied with other problems, especially with his lot as a lowly teacher (even though he was in effect the head of his department, being its only member). His annual salary was $900, and house and fuel were free; but prices were higher than in the city, and he had a large family. Moreover, during the two months of summer vacation, an opportune time for him to devote

56. See MS letters, Weir to Verplanck, West Point, Dec. 23, 1837, Feb. 26, 1838, April 8, 1845, March 17, 1854, Verplanck Papers, NYHS.

57. MS letter, Weir to Verplanck, West Point, Feb. 21, 1837, Verplanck Papers, NYHS. See R. W. G. Vail, "An Encore for Santa Claus," pp. 327-30. Another letter indicates that Verplanck had discovered a purchaser for one of Weir's landscapes: MS letter, Weir to Verplanck, West Point, Jan. 17, 1835, Verplanck Papers, NYHS.

58. See July, p. 118; MS letters, Weir to Verplanck, West Point, June 17, 1834; Oct. 4, 1834; Dec. 11, 1835; Jan. 2, 1836; Sept. 6, 1849, Verplanck Papers, NYHS.

59. Weir accepted this post, which Verplanck wrote him of on January 2, in MS letter, Weir to Verplanck, New York, Jan. 5, 1833, Verplanck Papers, NYHS. Verplanck also attempted, but failed, to procure this appointment for William Dunlap, his close friend. See July, p. 117, and MS letter, Dunlap to Verplanck, New York, Jan. 11, 1833, Verplanck Papers, NYHS.

60. MS letter, Weir to Verplanck, West Point, Jan. 17, 1835, Verplanck Papers, NYHS.

himself to painting, he was forced to work in a hot attic studio. He began to resent, besides, the subordinate position given to his department in the academy; he contended that drawing was absolutely essential for a military education because it trains the eyes of those who as officers need to exercise good judgment in the field. With these complaints, most of which he attributed to his low rank, he again turned to Verplanck for help. But not until 1846, twelve years after his appointment to West Point, was Weir raised from Teacher to Professor of Drawing. Verplanck probably deserves some of the credit for this change of rank and for the Congressional act which in 1855 added $500 to Weir's salary by putting the Department of Drawing on a level with other departments of the academy.[61]

This somewhat detailed treatment of Verplanck's kindness toward one painter has been made possible simply because of some unusually full letters preserved in the Verplanck Papers owned by the New-York Historical Society. It is quite likely that a dozen or more artists besides Weir received miscellaneous favors from this influential Knickerbocker; but since the correspondence necessary to document this conjecture has not been found, the particulars of his part in Congressional patronage and of his friendship with Weir must be used to suggest Verplanck's further influence on the course of American art.

James Fenimore Cooper

Less versatile than Verplanck but certainly more celebrated, James Fenimore Cooper enjoyed associations with a small group of artists, one of whom, Samuel Morse, nearly outshone him in fame. These associations are clearly revealed in Cooper's letters and, to a lesser extent, in his many novels and travel books. The total picture is of a man strongly influenced by the world of art.

Yet this world had only a small role in shaping Cooper until he passed the age of thirty. His life as a boy on the frontier was one of

61. I. Weir, p. 66; MS letters, Weir to Verplanck, West Point, Jan. 2, 1836, Baltimore, Dec. 15, 1843[?], West Point, Jan. 14, 1850, Jan. 8, 1851, Dec. 23, 1851, Feb. 6, 1855, Verplanck Papers, NYHS. Weir asked Verplanck for various other favors in MS letters, Weir to Verplanck, West Point, Aug. 22, 1849, Dec. 5, 1849, Verplanck Papers, NYHS.

adventure far outweighing intellectual pursuits although he did become familiar with the engravings in his family's home[62] and with a distinguished portrait of his father painted by Gilbert Stuart.[63] Unlike Irving, Cooper is not known to have been instructed in drawing; and his brief career at Yale, where "little learning of any kind found its way into his head,"[64] left him with less interest in the fine arts than in the scenery of New Haven's countryside. Service aboard various ships, the next passage in Cooper's life, also furthered his acquaintance with nature, but only during leaves ashore could he have found opportunities to look at well-known paintings.[65] In London, for example, he may have seen some portraits by Joshua Reynolds, whom he mentions in his first novel.[66] Cooper left the Navy in 1810 and for a decade engaged in various non-artistic pursuits, such as farming, outfitting a whaling ship, and trading land. Then in 1820 he began his literary career. Up to this time, he was barely familiar with painting, sculpture, and architecture; among their practitioners he had few, if any, friends, his first extant letter to mention an artist being written in 1823, his thirty-fourth year.[67]

COOPER AND SAMUEL MORSE.[68] Approximately between 1820 and 1825 Cooper met the American artists who joined him in The Bread and Cheese Club. He took a particular liking to Samuel Morse, two years his junior but his equal in reputation. When Cooper left for Europe in 1826, their friendship was interrupted, only to be renewed at Rome during 1830. For ten consecutive months out of the next two years

62. [James Fenimore Cooper], *Gleanings in Europe: Italy*, I, 36.
63. Cooper later attempted to add this painting to his collection. See Cooper to Richard Cooper, Spa, Belgium, Aug. 5, 1832, in Cooper, *Letters and Journals*, II, 295.
64. Thomas R. Lounsbury, *James Fenimore Cooper*, p. 7.
65. Cf. Cooper, *Letters and Journals*, I, 95-96.
66. J[ames]. Fenimore Cooper, *Precaution*, I, 226.
67. Cooper asked to be mentioned to Washington Allston, "a stranger to me, in every thing but reputation" (letter to Richard Henry Dana, New York, April 14, 1823, Cooper, *Letters and Journals*, I, 94).
68. *Ibid.*, I, 395, 397, n. 4, 433-34, n. 2, II, 163, 167 n., 172, 183 n., 323, 328, 375, 381 n.; Samuel F. B. Morse, *Letters and Journals*, I, 263-64, 338, 419-20, 427, II, 304-5, 314-15; Cooper, *Correspondence*, I, 292-93, 311, 354-55, 358; Carleton Mabee, *The American Leonardo*, pp. 160-61; Lounsbury, pp. 76-77; James F. Beard, Jr., "Cooper and His Artistic Contemporaries," p. 115.

they saw each other daily in Paris;[69] so closely were they associated that Morse was even rumored engaged to Cooper's daughter Susan, a promising young amateur artist.

It was partly through Morse's aid that Cooper became an art patron and collector during this time. "Though possessing the trifling advantage of a few thousands the most," Cooper admitted, "I am not yet thank Heaven, Ass enough to believe I have the best taste";[70] therefore, most of his gifts to the National Academy, including a number of casts from the antique, had been selected by Morse. When choosing paintings for his own collection, moreover, Cooper again relied on Morse, and once even thought of "invading Italy" with him "on a picture speculation." "I mean seriously," Cooper wrote, "with a view to put money in our pockets, while we befriend the arts—."[71] These plans never materialized, but Cooper did buy a Rembrandt, a Holbein, and, with Morse standing beside him, a Teniers.[72]

Believing that Morse was "just as good a fellow as there is going,"[73] Cooper commissioned him to copy Rembrandt's "Tobit and the Angel" and later offered him similar jobs just to keep him from returning to America. In the meantime Morse turned to painting one of his largest canvases, "The Gallery of the Louvre." Cooper saw this picture develop step by step. Deeply convinced of Morse's growing stature as an artist, and eager to watch him at work, the novelist made a visit to the Louvre part of his daily schedule. As he wrote to his friend William Dunlap,[74]

69. Beard gives the dates of this period as Sept. 28, 1831, to July 18, 1832, in Cooper, *Letters and Journals*, II, 183 n. For Willis' impressions of this Paris friendship, see N[athaniel]. P[arker]. Willis, *Pencillings by the Way*, p. 22.

70. Cooper to Dunlap, Paris, March 16, 1832, Dunlap, *Diary*, III, 608.

71. Cooper to Horatio Greenough, Paris, Dec. 24, 1831, Cooper, *Letters and Journals*, II, 165.

72. *Ibid.*, II, 172, 179, 239-40, 266, 312, 372, 374. Cooper's humorous account of buying the Teniers was written in a letter to Horatio Greenough, Paris, Dec. 24, 1831, in *idem*, II, 163-64. At the present time the authenticity of these three pictures cannot be determined. Apparently the experts who examined them considered them genuine. Cooper also mentions having sold a "beautiful Breughel"—"an original . . . beyond question"—to Henry Brevoort (*idem*, II, 372).

73. Cooper, in Dunlap, *Diary*, III, 608.

74. Beard summarizes Cooper's relations with Dunlap in "Cooper and His Artistic Contemporaries," pp. 114-15, and in Cooper, *Letters and Journals*, II, 240-41 n.

I get up at eight, read the papers, breakfast at ten, sit down to the quill at 1/2 past ten—work till one—throw off my morning gown, draw on my boots and gloves, take a cane that Horace Greenough gave me, and go to the Louvre, where I find Morse stuck up on a high working stand, perch myself astradle of one of the seats, and bore him just as I used to bore you when you made the memorable likeness of St. Peter. "Lay it on here, Samuel—more yellow—the nose is too short—the eye too small— damn it if I had been a painter what a picture I should have painted."— and all this stuff over again and which Samuel takes just as good-naturedly as good old William. Well there I sit and have sat so often and so long that my face is just as well known as any Vandyke on the walls. Crowds get round the picture, for Samuel has quite made a hit in the Louvre, and I believe that half the merit is mine. So much from keeping company with ones [sic] betters. At six we are at home eating a good dinner, and I manage to get a good deal out of Morse in this way too.[75]

Cooper's great interest in this painting reportedly led Morse to offer it to him for about $2,500, but for some reason Cooper never bought the picture.[76] This did not dampen their friendship, however.

Morse returned to America first and soon was urging Cooper to follow him. On November 5, 1833, the novelist and his family arrived in New York, settling temporarily in a house that Morse had found for them on Bleecker Street. Soon Cooper hoped to make a Gothic mansion of Otsego Hall in Cooperstown, so he naturally persuaded Morse to help with the plans. And when Cooper's journalistic disputes began to multiply, Morse again came to his friend's aid,[77] although already engaged in heated battles of his own with the enemies of the National Academy.

These were trying times for Morse: Not only had he failed in his campaign to be elected Mayor of New York City but he was also finding it impossible to realize his dream of many years—to paint great historical pictures for the Capitol. Confronted with "some tough stumps to pry up, and heavy stones to roll out of the way," he had

75. Cooper to Dunlap, Paris, March 16, 1832, Dunlap, *Diary*, III, 608.
76. Mabee, pp. 160-61; Morse, *Letters and Journals*, I, 426; Cooper, *Correspondence*, I, 320; Beard, in Cooper, *Letters and Journals*, II, 236, n. 1.
77. Lounsbury, p. 76; Beard, in Cooper, *Letters and Journals*, II, 381 n.

written to Cooper: "I should like a little of your sinew to come to my aid . . . as it was wont to come at the Louvre."[78] According to Edward Lind Morse,[79] Cooper's response was so far-reaching that it actually caused Morse to perfect his telegraph before others did and thus establish American priority in its invention. The story centers in a letter which Cooper is said to have written to John Quincy Adams, then on the committee to choose painters for the Rotunda commissions. The letter, signed "An Amateur" and published in the New York *Evening Post* for December 23, 1834,[80] takes Adams to task for opening the job to foreign artists and questions his judgment in having granted governmental patronage to E. Luigi Persico. Supposedly Adams was so offended by this attack, which he attributed to Morse rather than to Cooper, that he completely ruined any chance of Morse's receiving a panel. The ultimate consequence of this letter was therefore the perfection of the telegraph, for not long after his failure to gain this commission Morse gradually gave up painting and began to spend more and more time on his invention. Had he waited longer, i.e., had he received the Rotunda commission, credit for inventing the telegraph would have gone to others who were already only a short distance behind him in perfecting this instrument. When we look over Cooper's letter, however, it does not seem vicious enough to have caused that much anger in a seasoned statesman. Furthermore, opposition to Morse for the commission was probably caused by more than one letter, one man, or one event.[81]

In 1837 Cooper joined George Pope Morris, John G. Chapman, and others in collecting a subscription for their disappointed friend. Each contributor was to pay fifty dollars in installments of five dollars per month, to commission Morse to paint a historical picture as large as the panel denied him by the government. But having become so active otherwise, Morse was unable to work on this painting; he eventually returned the money to his well-meaning patrons.[82]

78. Letter dated New York, Feb. 28, 1833, Cooper, *Correspondence*, I, 311.
79. In Morse, *Letters and Journals*, II, 25-34.
80. Reprinted in Cooper, *Letters and Journals*, III, 79-80.
81. A passage in Cooper's *Sea Lions* (I, 140) upholds Morse's priority in inventing the telegraph.
82. See MS letters, John G. Chapman to Cooper, New York, March 21, 1837; A. B.

This friendship between Cooper and Morse, lasting until the former's death in 1851, was cemented not only with reciprocal favors but also with mutual interests. Both men became immersed in political matters, meeting often with Lafayette in Paris, forming a society to aid the Poles, and speculating on the destinies of governments and the progress of revolutions. Each was concerned with the other's reputation and was quick to defend it in public or private. Although their prejudices were not identical—Cooper being severe with Yankees and Puritans, Morse with Catholics—this difference proved harmless to their friendship. After Cooper's death, Morse recalled that their long intimacy "was never for a moment clouded by the slightest coolness."[83]

COOPER AND GREENOUGH. Another unclouded relationship existed between Cooper and the sculptor Horatio Greenough.[84] Sixteen years younger than Cooper, Greenough naturally turned to him for advice and, since he was a man of wealth and influence, for other help as well. Cooper responded "with a generosity that would bind the coldest mortal."[85] In the first place, he persuaded Lafayette to sit to Greenough for a portrait bust. Secondly, he "laid out several anchors"[86] in the way of securing governmental patronage for Greenough, recommending him not only to Louis McLane, the Secretary of the Treasury, but also to President Andrew Jackson, as capable of executing the proposed statue of George Washington. Thirdly, believing that "a trifling loan to a friend must not be dealt by like a broker's ac-

---

Durand to Cooper, New York, Sept. 4, 1837, Cooper Collection, YUL; Mabee, pp. 245-46.

83. Morse, *Letters and Journals*, II, 314.

84. Cooper, *Letters and Journals*, I, 368-72, 390, 397 n. 1, 399, 402, 403-4, 406-7, 389-92, 394-400, 402-8, 412-14, 430-33, II, 44-45, 53-55, 61-62, 76-77, 114, 116-18, 144-45, 162-68, 233-36, 244-45, 267-69, 322, 334-35, 367-73, 383-84, III, 219-21, 232-34, 328-32, IV, 389-90; Dunlap, *Arts of Design*, III, 227-31; Horatio Greenough, *Letters of Horatio Greenough to His Brother*, pp. 47, 87; Cooper, *Correspondence*, I, 264, 284; Nathalia Wright, "The Chanting Cherubs: Horatio Greenough's Marble Group for James Fenimore Cooper," pp. 177-97; Henry T. Tuckerman, *A Memorial of Horatio Greenough*, p. 208; Lounsbury, p. 115.

85. Horatio Greenough to Henry Greenough, Paris, Oct. 3, 1831, in Greenough, *Letters*, p. 87.

86. Cooper to Greenough, Paris, July 4, 1831, Cooper, *Letters and Journals*, II, 117.

count,"[87] he lent Greenough at least 1600 francs, interest-free; and, fourthly, he commissioned Greenough to carve the "Chanting Cherubs," a marble group based on a picture supposedly by Raphael. Moreover, although he dispensed these favors during a very short time, from 1829 to 1832, it was probably the most critical period of his friend's career; for, in Italy prior to meeting Cooper, Greenough had received "few or no orders."[88] "Fenimore Cooper saved me from despair . . . ," the sculptor wrote to Dunlap: "He employed me as I wished to be employed. . . ."[89]

The "Chanting Cherubs" was in several ways Greenough's most important commission up to 1832 (when the United States government began to patronize him). In a letter written for publication in the *New-York American*, Cooper explained the historical significance of these thirty-inch-high angels, calling them "probably the first groupe ever completed by an American sculptor."[90] They have also been termed "the first work in marble of proportions larger than a bust to be executed by one American at the order of another."[91] Furthermore, Greenough had carved them himself from living models. Even this was a departure from usual procedures, "for among sculptors of the current neoclassical school the common practice was to model according to ideal dimensions and to delegate the marble work to assistants."[92] Having already agreed to pay Greenough two hundred dollars for the "Chanting Cherubs," Cooper also allowed him to exhibit the group in the principal cities of the United States and to keep the profit from three months' receipts. These exhibitions, combined with the statue's novelty and Cooper's frequent mention of its merits in letters to his influential friends, made the "Chanting Cherubs" one of the most publicized works to come from the chisel of an American before the Civil War. Reactions were varied: *The New-York Mirror*

87. Cooper to Greenough, Paris, June 13, 1833, Cooper, *Letters and Journals*, II, 384.
88. Dunlap, *Arts of Design*, III, 222.
89. *Ibid.*, III, 226.
90. Cooper, *Letters and Journals*, I, 431.
91. Wright, "The Chanting Cherubs," p. 179.
92. *Ibid.*, p. 181. Cf. Cooper to Greenough, Sorrento, Sept. 15, 1829, Cooper, *Letters and Journals*, I, 389.

John Goffe Rand
WILLIAM CULLEN BRYANT
(*unrestored portrait*)
(*The New-York Historical Society, New York City*)

American School, 19th cent.
MCDONALD CLARKE
(*The Long Island Historical Society and the Frick Art Reference Library*)

Chester Harding
NATHANIEL PARKER WILLIS
(*The Brook and the Frick Art Reference Library*)

Charles Loring Elliott
LEWIS GAYLORD CLARK
(*The Knickerbocker Gallery, 1855*)

Charles C. Ingham
GULIAN C. VERPLANCK
(*The New-York Historical Society, New York City*)

praised this statue as "a specimen of art probably never surpassed by any American";[93] others were shocked by the nudity of the angels or were disappointed that they did not sing; still others thought them lacking in artistic merit. Nevertheless, Greenough was shoved before the public. The "Chanting Cherubs," already an important chapter in the history of American sculpture, became also the preface to his statue of Washington. Certainly the publicity that he received from the first commission helped at least in a small way to get him the second. In fact, this was the result anticipated by Greenough and Cooper when they entered into "an innocent little conspiracy . . . that this group should pave the way to a Washington for the capitol."[94]

One of Cooper's efforts to promote another work of Greenough's was less successful, serving only to provoke a bitter attack on the novelist by John Frazee or one of his adherents. At the beginning of a long letter published in Dunlap's history of American art Cooper had praised Greenough's bust of Lafayette as equal in merit to the Frenchman Pierre Jean David's treatment of the same subject. As far as Cooper could remember—and it proved unfortunate that his memory was not better—no other sculptors "of any eminence" had successfully carved a likeness of this distinguished statesman.[95] Hoping to stir up more business for Greenough, Dunlap turned this letter into a sly bit of propaganda by calling for a larger work, this time to be commissioned presumably by Congress: ". . . America must have a statue of Lafayette," he wrote; ". . . [and] Greenough has a claim to the execution of this statue. . . ."[96] But an equally valid claim belonged to the sculptor John Frazee. Having already carved a bust of Lafayette which, according to a testimonial letter from Lafayette's son, was an incontestable likeness, Frazee was another candidate to make the statue proposed by Dunlap, who, with Cooper, had forgotten or ignored this fact in his zeal to befriend Greenough. The mistake was soon uncovered in a thoroughly documented, vigorously phrased arti-

93. Remarks by the editors introducing a correspondent's letter in praise of "The Chanting Cherubs," NYM, IX (June 30, 1832), 411.
94. Cooper, quoted in Dunlap, *Arts of Design*, III, 230-31.
95. *Ibid.*, III, 228.
96. *Ibid.*, III, 227.

cle published by *The North American Magazine* in January, 1835.[97]
Written probably by Frazee himself,[98] the article began with an attack
on Dunlap for devoting more space to Cooper's letter ("a very museum of curious matter") than "to the entire history of many of the first
artists of our country!" Then the author turned directly on Cooper:
"We know not why Mr Cooper deemed himself a dictator in the
Fine Arts, as well as an Apicius in edibles and a Caesar in politics:
but this we know, we are not bound to bend in awe to his opinion."
After expressing the hope "that Frazee will soon be appreciated as a
native artist," the writer asked his readers to "cherish and caress our
own [artists] in our own land, and leave all foreigners and residents
in foreign countries to the enjoyment of their transatlantic fame!"
His readers, knowing full well that Greenough and Cooper had lived
abroad for the greater part of a decade, could hardly have missed the
point.

In spite of the fact that Cooper's generosity had occasional ill
effects, Greenough always regarded him as a benefactor, "a father . . .
in kindness."[99] To repay this debt of friendship Greenough performed
such services as proofreading one of his works and acting as an agent
to his foreign publishers. Above all, when Cooper was alienating the
American public with his outspokenness, Greenough offered moral
support not only by defending the novelist's right to criticize America
but also by insisting that he would have been less a man had he not
expressed himself sincerely and freely. Greenough was Cooper's
staunchest defender. Their friendship, beneficial to both parties, ended
only with Cooper's death in 1851. Greenough died a year and three
months later, while planning a monument to the "glorious Fenimore."[100]

Cooper's purse was never quite full enough to make him a renowned patron of artists. He could afford a few orders from Morse
and Greenough and a copy of Guido Reni's "Aurora" from John G.

97. "American Statuaries," *The North American Magazine*, V (Jan., 1835), 204-7.
98. Caldwell, pp. 82-83, n. 135.
99. Greenough, quoted in Dunlap, *Arts of Design*, III, 224.
100. Greenough, quoted in Beard, p. 115. A full description of this projected
monument is in MS letter, Greenough to Bryant, Cambridge, Mass., Feb. 5, 1852,
Bryant-Godwin Collection, NYPL.

Chapman, but Thomas Cole seems to have been the only other important American to receive a commission from him. Writing from London to New York in May of 1828, Cooper asked his friend Charles Wilkes to "tell Cole to take a subject of his own . . . and put something into it, that he may call the Leatherstocking, and paint the thing in the course of the summer. I do not want the autumn leaf. A little sunshine and shadow are more to my taste."[101] Whether Cole followed these instructions is uncertain, because the finished painting, apparently a scene from *The Prairie*, has not been located. Like the "Chanting Cherubs," it resulted in wider contacts for its artist. Cooper gave it, as he had intended all along, to Samuel Rogers, the English poet. Rogers was also a renowned patron, and Cooper obviously hoped that he would do something for Cole when the artist came to England. Rogers did take an interest in Cole, as two short letters among the Cole Papers attest. In one Rogers invited Cole to dinner, and in the other he expressed his debt to Cooper for sending him this new friend.[102] Although Wilkes later complained that the painting had not moved Rogers to "patronize" Cole,[103] the artist himself thought that Rogers "behaved in a very friendly manner"[104] and was altogether "a valuable acquaintance."[105]

In spite of this commission, Cole should not be ranked with Greenough and Morse as one of Cooper's close friends. The temptation to do so is, of course, very strong: Cooper and Cole were both members of The Bread and Cheese Club; they both specialized in depicting scenery; they both exploited the cycle-of-nations theme, Cole in "The Course of Empire," Cooper in *The Crater*; Cole drew and painted scenes from Cooper's novels; Cooper praised Cole in print. Yet, in the opening lines of a letter to Louis Noble, Cole's biographer, Cooper made it clear that he and Cole had never had a chance to become more than acquaintances, for they were seldom living in the same

101. Cooper, *Letters and Journals*, I, 263.

102. MS letters, Rogers to Cole, n.p. [Dec. 31, 1829], May 16, 1830, Cole Papers, NYSL.

103. Wilkes to Cooper, New York, July 29, 1830, Cooper, *Correspondence*, I, 182.

104. Cole, quoted in Louis L. Noble, *The Course of Empire*, p. 112.

105. Quoted in Dunlap, *Arts of Design*, III, 152.

place at the same time.[106] Noble omitted this part of the letter but printed later passages, containing extravagant applause for "The Course of Empire." As a result, Cooper and Cole seem to be closer than they actually were.

This misunderstanding serves to remind us that Cooper was acquainted with a number of native and foreign artists,[107] but only two or three knew him well. It was they who brought out the best in him. How else, for example, can we explain the genuine and frequent humor in his letters to them? Nothing like this appears in his novels or travel books or in the bulk of his correspondence. To most of his contemporaries Cooper seemed overbearing and cranky, but to his closest artist-friends he was truly noble. As Thomas Lounsbury has observed: "Intimate acquaintance was sure to bring to Cooper respect, admiration, and finally affection. Few men have stood better than he that final test of excellence which rests upon the fact that those who knew him best loved him most."[108] Greenough and Morse would have agreed heartily.

William Cullen Bryant

William Cullen Bryant probably knew more American artists than did any other Knickerbocker writer.[109] In the first place, he outlived not only Irving, Cooper, and Verplanck, but also some of the younger authors, such as Morris and Willis. Secondly, during his eighty-four years he achieved a social and professional status that provided many opportunities to mingle with large numbers of artists. He held regular memberships in The Bread and Cheese Club, The Sketch Club, and The Century Association, as well as an honorary membership in the National Academy of Design. He was the third president of the American Art-Union and the first vice-president of the Metropolitan Museum of Art. Moreover, as editor of the New York *Evening Post*

106. MS copy of a letter from Cooper to the Rev. Noble, Cooperstown, Jan. 6, 1849, Cole Papers, DIA.

107. For the native artists, see Appendix I. Cooper's acquaintances among foreign artists may be sampled in his *Letters and Journals*, I, 202, 254, 347, 356, II, 269-70, 283, 285, 290-91, III, 175.

108. Lounsbury, p. 82.

109. Unless analyzed in this section, these friendships are documented in Appendix I.

for forty-nine years, he was able to keep abreast of art matters on both sides of the Atlantic. A hardy traveler, he saw many parts of America and made six trips to Europe, carefully recording visits to museums, private galleries, and studios in detailed letters to his wife and his newspaper.

BRYANT'S FELLOW CLUB MEMBERS. For over a half-century Bryant continued his friendships with members of The Sketch Club and The Bread and Cheese Club, in whose meetings he had experienced his first extensive contacts with American artists.[110] Even those painters and sculptors who went abroad were not lost to him: he looked them up in Europe, finding John Vanderlyn and Daniel Huntington in Paris, Henry Kirke Brown and John G. Chapman in Rome, and, after much searching, William G. Wall in Dublin. At home he corresponded and exchanged visits with Robert Weir, "a man of great simplicity of character and depth of feeling"[111] who shared his passion for landscape.[112] On one occasion, a July afternoon in 1836, they rode horseback "to a solitary lake among the mountains about seven miles distant" from West Point. "The view was very striking," Bryant recalled:

We stood on a steep precipice several hundred feet above it—the rocks about us were black as ink with a peculiar kind of moss, and were crowned with rough looking pitch pine trees full of large cones and black as the rocks; below us lay the lake, quiet and glassy, with large patches of of [sic] the broad-leaved water-lily on its amber coloured waters; . . . and to the west rose mountain behind mountain all covered with the natural forest. In returning we were soon overtaken by the rain which gave us

110. When he first came to New York, Bryant met Morse and Cole not only at meetings of The Lunch but also at the homes of Henry and Robert Sedgwick. See William Cullen Bryant, "Reminiscences of Miss Sedgwick," p. 441.

111. MS letter, Bryant to Richard H. Dana, New York, Aug. 4, 1843, Dana Papers, MHS.

112. MS letters, Weir to Bryant, West Point, March 18, 1851, March 17, 1863, Aug. 22, 1865, Bryant-Godwin, NYPL; Bryant to Mrs. F. F. Bryant, New York, July 20, 1836, July 6, 1837, Goddard-Roslyn, NYPL. In 1866 Weir gave a painting to Bryant. See MS letter, Weir to Bryant, West Point, May 18, 1866, Goddard-Roslyn, NYPL. Bryant's description of Weir's "Embarkation of the Pilgrims" was reprinted in "Weir's Great National Painting," NYM, XIX (Aug. 21, 1841), 271. Their friendship is also mentioned in Wilson, p. 97.

a terrible drenching, and we reached Mr. Weir's house as wet as a pair of drowned rats. Mr. Weir gave me dry clothes, a huge jacket and a pair of pantaloons half a foot too long for me, in which I cut a queer figure. I caught a cold in my limbs, and the next Sunday had a slight attack of something like the cholera morbus[.] I am now in excellent health again.[113]

An amiable man, as this quotation shows, Bryant easily remained on good terms with the other club-members, especially Dunlap, Morse, Inman, Allston, Gray, Kensett, and Ingham—many of whom he praised in speeches and articles.

Thomas Cole and Asher Durand were Bryant's closest friends among the artists of The Sketch Club. Arriving in New York City during the same year, 1825, the twenty-four-year-old Cole and the thirty-one-year-old Bryant easily began their acquaintance in gatherings at the homes of the Sedgwicks and in the meetings of The Lunch; and together they played important roles in the early development of The Sketch Club and the National Academy. With this solid foundation strengthened by a mutual love of landscape, their friendship lasted for twenty-three years, until Cole's death in 1848.

During approximately four-fifths of this time, however, Bryant and Cole were separated. In the first place, as the dates of their European trips indicate, they never went abroad at the same time, much less together. Cole was out of the country from 1829 to 1832, Bryant from 1834 to 1836, Cole from 1841 to 1842, and Bryant in 1845. In the second place, even when they were both in the United States they were hardly next-door neighbors. In 1836 Cole moved to Catskill, New York, and this was to be his permanent residence for the rest of his life. That he visited his friends in New York City cannot be denied, but if we may use the minutes of The Sketch Club as evidence, these visits became less and less frequent. In 1844 he is listed as having attended six of its meetings; in 1845, three; in 1846, one; in 1847, one; and in 1848 (the year of his death), none. These dates and

113. MS letter, Bryant to Mrs. F. F. Bryant, New York, Aug. 15, 1836, Goddard-Roslyn, NYPL.

figures may be somewhat misleading. For example, although Bryant went to Europe in 1845, he did not leave until April and was therefore able to attend the three Sketch Club meetings which Cole also attended that year. But one conclusion is certain: Bryant and Cole lived simultaneously in New York City for only five years; thus the opportunities for contact between them were more limited than scholars have usually implied.

At present little can be added to the details of their association,[114] which is well-known among historians, but its popularity may be analyzed to some advantage here.

The friendship reached print very early when Bryant wrote his sonnet "To Cole, the Painter, on His Departure for Europe," published in *The Talisman* for 1830, only four and one-half years after he and Cole had first met. Hortative in tone and animated by a nationalistic primitivism, the poem distinguishes the wild, pristine American scenery from the humanized landscape of Europe and then advises Cole to "keep that earlier, wilder image bright." In spite of its sincerity and its superiority to typical gift-book verse, there are faults in this sonnet. Two of its word-pictures—"savannas where the bison roves" and "Skies, where the desert eagle wheels and screams"— supposedly describing American scenes deeply etched on Cole's memory, were actually components of landscapes quite alien to his paintings—or to those of any professional American artist in 1829. Technically, too, the poem is inferior even to most of Bryant's other sonnets (which as a group are considered among his poorest efforts), its

114. Both men were accomplished walkers and together enjoyed "many delightful rambles among the Catskills" (Godwin, II, 34, and I, 384). Bryant wrote several letters of introduction to friends overseas when Cole went to Europe. Cole did the same for Bryant. See, for example, MS letters, Cole to an unidentified correspondent, New York, April 18, 1845, Bryant to Cole, New York, July 11, 1841, Bryant to G. C. Grandi, New York, July 6, 1841, Bryant to Julia Hepp, New York, Aug. 6, 1841, Bryant to Professor Rosini, New York, Aug., 1841, Cole Papers, NYSL; Bryant to Monsieur Barrault, New York, July 6, 1841, Cole Papers, DIA. Bryant revised at least one of Cole's poems (see MS letter, L. Gaylord Clark to Cole, 2 Park Place, June 1 [1841], Cole Papers, NYSL) and, in the columns of the *Evening Post*, kept Cole's name before the public (see MS letter, Bryant to Cole, New York, Dec. 21 [22?], 1843, Cole Papers, NYSL; William Cullen Bryant, *Letters of a Traveller*, p. 24). Unless otherwise noted, all references to *Letters of a Traveller* are to the Putnam edition, 1850. Bryant's other services to Cole are treated in Bryant II, pp. 223-24.

awkward punctuation and mongrel rime scheme doing little to convey his deep feelings for the topic.[115]

The public was again reminded of this friendship of painter and poet when, in 1848, shortly after Cole's death, Bryant delivered a eulogy on him before the National Academy of Design.[116] Although this oration met with varying reactions from Bryant's friends, it was nevertheless a balanced estimate of Cole's accomplishments,[117] indicating that Bryant rather than Louis Noble should have been Cole's biographer. If Bryant entertained any notions of writing such a full-length study, however, he dismissed them under pressure from Noble, who made it known that as Cole's former pastor he expected to write the authorized biography.[118] From that time on, the two writers cooperated on this project,[119] Noble even dedicating his work to Bryant.[120] In spite of Noble's enthusiasm, Bryant could have written a more accurate biography. Noble misedited Cole's journals and, by truncating a letter from Cooper, left his readers with the erroneous impression that Cole and Cooper had been intimate friends.[121] Furthermore, Noble never recorded Cole's great discontent with his career as a painter and with the subordinate role given to the fine arts in America. Only recently have these dark sides of Cole's personality been exposed.[122] Had he not yielded to Noble's aggressive-

115. Quotations from this poem are taken from *The Poetical Works of William Cullen Bryant*, I, 219. Bryant's sonnets are criticized in Gay Allen, *American Prosody*, pp. 44-45.

116. Bryant, *Orations*, pp. 1-41.

117. Comments from Samuel Rogers and Richard H. Dana, plus Bryant's answer to Dana's criticism, are in Godwin, II, 36-37. Today's critics might find it difficult to condone Cole's allegorical bent or to call his moralizing unobtrusive, as Bryant did. See *idem* and Bryant, *Orations*, pp. 20-25, 34. But such judgments were quite consistent with Bryant's critical standards. See James T. Callow, "William Cullen Bryant: Literary Critic," pp. 27-36.

118. MS letter, Noble to Bryant, Catskill, April 4, 1848, Bryant-Godwin, NYPL. Bryant had asked Durand to gather information from Cole's family and friends.

119. See *ibid.* and MS letter, Noble to Bryant, Catskill, Nov. 18, 1851, Goddard-Roslyn, NYPL.

120. Noble first asked permission in MS letter, Noble to Bryant, Catskill, March 31, 1851, Bryant-Godwin, NYPL.

121. See Kenneth J. LaBudde, "The Mind of Thomas Cole," p. 100, and cf. Noble, p. 224, to MS copy of a letter from Cooper to the Rev. Noble, Cooperstown, Jan. 6, 1849, Cole Papers, DIA.

122. LaBudde, pp. 135-80, has convincingly demonstrated Cole's disappointment.

ness, Bryant might have written a biography needing fewer revisions; instead his tribute was limited to a forty-one-page eulogy.

Asher Durand's "Kindred Spirits" (1849), commissioned by the patron Jonathan Sturges "as a token of gratitude" for this eulogy,[123] was the third reminder of Bryant's friendship with Cole. It was also the most forceful. A dramatic picture, it shows Cole pointing with his cane to the beauties of a silvery landscape while Bryant stands next to him. Interest is enhanced by various contrasts between finely wrought leaves and massive rocks, between the soft, hazy, simple background and the hard, clear, detailed foreground, and between the two human intruders and the unspoiled landscape, looking as if it had never before known the gaze and feel of man. Moreover, there is a delicate balance of space and light, position and proportion, giving one the impression of a perfect compromise between man and nature. Bryant and Cole are on the edge of the strongest light in the picture, so that the trees to their right and the rocks behind them are more clearly revealed than they. Again, the two figures are not perfectly centered in this view, and they occupy less than one-thirtieth of the canvas. Nevertheless, they remain the most important elements of the picture—as in real life neither the masters nor slaves of nature, but its favored intimates. "Kindred Spirits" has been called an "unforgettable" painting.[124] For these subtleties alone it deserves to be remembered.

Not only "Kindred Spirits" but also the sonnet to Cole are, in fact, well-known today. "The light of distant skies," a phrase from the sonnet, has been used as the title of a book by James Thomas Flexner; and the sonnet, despite its shortcomings, has found its way into anthologies of American literature, either because of its brevity or the opportunity it gives editors and teachers to relate romanticism to painting and poetry. "Kindred Spirits" has also been reproduced in these anthologies, and it was even used as the cover of the Summer, 1959 issue of *Art in America*, dedicated to parallels between literature and the fine arts. Although the painting once hung in a rather inaccessible

123. See the letter from Sturges to Bryant quoted in Godwin, II, 37.
124. E. P. Richardson, *Painting in America*, p. 169.

office of the New York Public Library, it has subsequently been seen by many people; for over two months in 1959 it was exhibited at the Detroit Institute of Arts.

As a result of the popularity of "Kindred Spirits" and the sonnet "To Cole" Bryant's friendship with Cole has been celebrated more than any author-artist relationship in America. These documents have not only served as reminders of this association but have also provided corroborative evidence of a certain similarity in the thinking and methods of these two men. Together Bryant and Cole depicted the mingling of the picturesque and beautiful in native scenery, stressed its virgin character, worked from firsthand observation, and were fond of extracting allegory from nature.[125] Later chapters in this study will demonstrate that these attitudes and techniques were shared by other painters and writers, many of whom were also friends, but this fact should not make us less thankful that these complex relationships have been simplified into the popular linking of Bryant and Cole in the minds of the educated. Here is a symbol to remind us of the potential for unity in the arts.

Lacking this publicity, Bryant's relationship with Asher Durand should be heavily weighed to restore the historical balance. Cole died in middle age, but Durand lived to be ninety; consequently his friendship with Bryant lasted thirty years longer than Cole's. For fifty-three years Durand and Bryant were closely associated. They met not only at the various functions of The Sketch Club and the National Academy but also at Bryant's home, where Durand was frequently entertained.[126] Drawn together by a love of nature, they undoubtedly accompanied each other on hikes in search of the picturesque; and in 1830 they collaborated in producing *The American Landscape*, a periodical devoted to native scenery. In fact, their attitudes toward nature were so alike that Durand based at least five of his pictures on themes from Bryant's verse.[127]

125. Evelyn L. Schmitt, "Two American Romantics—Thomas Cole and William Cullen Bryant," pp. 61-68.

126. See Godwin, II, 58, and Durand's entry dated May 13, 1855, in the MS "Guest Book at Roslyn, L. I.," Bryant Family Papers, NYPL.

127. Bertha M. Stearns, "Nineteenth-Century Writers in the World of Art," pp. 31-32; Durand, *A. B. Durand*, p. 174.

Perhaps because it produced no famous testimonials—no sonnets, no memorial addresses—this friendship has been neglected. Bryant's printed works contain only incidental references to Durand;[128] his "graceful address" upon the occasion of Durand's seventy-sixth birthday[129] was unfortunately never printed, and since Durand outlived him, Bryant never celebrated their friendship with the customary oration. Furthermore, Durand's portrait of Bryant, who considered it one of the best likenesses,[130] has received little publicity. The greatest tribute to this friendship is actually the well-known "Kindred Spirits."[131] Upon seeing the full-length figures of Bryant and Cole standing alone amid this spectacular landscape, one should not forget that its painter was Durand, whom Bryant called "the shyest of men."[132] Although Durand left himself out of this picture, he had every right to be in it, for he was just as much Bryant's kindred spirit as Cole.

BRYANT AND JOHN RAND. Bryant was acquainted with many artists who were not members of The Sketch Club. Certainly the most unusual of these associations was his friendship with John Goffe Rand, the painter who invented the screw-top, collapsible tin tube at first intended primarily to contain paint, but now used also to hold glue, toothpaste, food, medicine, and many other substances. Although generally overlooked by historians, Rand's invention was an important

128. See, for example, Bryant's letter to Richard H. Dana, quoted in Godwin, II, 37. At the request of E. Anna Lewis, Bryant sent some remarks on Durand and Cole to be published by *Graham's Magazine*; but the passages which were printed contained Bryant's opinion of Durand as a painter, not as a friend. See MS letter, E. Anna Lewis to Bryant, Brooklyn, July 11, 1854, Goddard-Roslyn, NYPL, and Bryant, quoted in E. Anna Lewis, "Art and Artists of America: Asher Brown Durand," p. 322.

129. Durand, *A. B. Durand*, p. 201. It was delivered in the presence of such notables as Thomas Hicks, Eastman Johnson, William Page, and Erastus D. Palmer at a surprise party for Durand in 1872.

130. This portrait (*ca.* 1856) is much later than one by Inman (1835), which Bryant also prized. See Wilson, p. 114. Durand discussed his painting of Bryant at some length in MS letter, A. B. Durand to John Durand, Shokan [New York], Aug. 6, 1854, Durand Papers, NYPL.

131. See letter from Sturges to Bryant, quoted in Godwin, II, 37. Bryant's wife thanked Durand for this painting, which she praised, in MS letter, F. F. Bryant to Durand, Roslyn, Jan. 1, 1855, Durand Papers, NYPL. Bryant had done the same in MS letter, Bryant to Durand, New York, Feb. 26, 1849, Durand Papers, NYPL.

132. MS letter, Bryant to R. H. Dana, New York, April 8, 1851, Goddard-Roslyn, NYPL.

contribution to the fine arts; as Maurice Grosser has proved, it shared with the camera the distinction of having "changed the whole character of painting."[133] Patented in 1841, the tin tube was at first intended to preserve artists' paints. In this use lay its significance. First, this invention liberated the artist from the irksome task of grinding his own colors. Secondly, it enabled him to paint landscapes directly from nature. Equipped with the new portable paint, he could abandon his former routine of outdoor sketching and indoor painting and, thanks to Rand, could perform both operations in the open air. On the other hand, the tin tube had certain drawbacks. Since it was not perfectly airtight, manufacturers filled it with slow-drying paints. The results were multiple: the artist began to replace the old method of underpainting, which now took too long to dry, with the practice of direct painting, "where each tone is put down as it is intended to appear in the picture";[134] since the new paint contained a reduced amount of pigment and was therefore more transparent, artists took to applying it thickly. This was one reason for the "loaded brush stroke" of the late nineteenth century.[135] Thus John Rand's invention was in a large measure responsible for the earmarks of modern painting, much of which embodies direct, outdoor finishing, lack of underpainting, and thick gobs of color placed side by side without blending.[136]

Because even less is known of John Rand than of his invention, his personal history can be outlined quickly. He was born on January 27, 1801, in Bedford, New Hampshire. There he spent his early years on the farm of his father, Deacon Jonathan Rand, and later worked as a house and sign painter as well as a cabinetmaker. Around the year 1825 he supposedly received some training in art from Samuel Morse. After leaving Bedford, Rand studied briefly under Chester Harding in Boston and then opened a studio of his own on Brattle Street but, acquiring some renown as a portrait painter, soon established himself in Charleston, South Carolina, where he met and married Lavinia

133. Maurice Grosser, *The Painter's Eye*, p. 62.
134. *Ibid.*, p. 66.
135. *Ibid.*
136. The effects of Rand's invention are explained in detail by Grosser, pp. 62-67.

Brainerd. In 1833 he was living in New York City. Within the year, however, he sailed for England, arriving on December 30th with a portrait of Bryant which he had apparently just finished. London then became his home for nearly fourteen years although he went to Paris occasionally and in 1840 made a short visit to the United States. After completely failing in his business ventures, which included manufacturing his inventions as well as painting portraits, he returned to America in the fall of 1847 and soon settled in New York City. At this time his reputation was limited, but he exhibited in the shows of the National Academy, and his studio was considered well worth visiting. One of its attractions was a portrait of Bryant, rendered with great "geniality and poetic expression,"[137] perhaps the same painting that Rand's great-grandniece recently donated to the New-York Historical Society.[138] Toward the end of his life Rand painted very few pictures. He died, poor but respected, in 1873.[139]

Bryant's connection with the man whose invention revolutionized the techniques of painting has been almost completely ignored in the past and could hardly be reconstructed today were it not for twenty-one unpublished letters from Rand to Bryant. These manuscripts, usually containing four pages of cramped writing, are in the Bryant-

137. "Art and Artists," *The Home Journal*, May 31, 1851, p. 2.

138. In a letter to the author (Washington, D.C., Aug. 19, 1958) the donor, Mrs. P. R. Anglemyer, dates this painting *ca.* 1846. Therefore, it is probably not the same portrait that Rand took to England in 1833.

139. This sketch—an outline for my projected biography of Rand—has been compiled from several sources: Mary Elizabeth Franklin, "John Goffe Rand," typewritten monograph in the collection of Mrs. P. R. Anglemyer; [Ellen Campbell], "A Forgotten New England Artist and Inventor," typewritten monograph in the files of FARL; "Arts and Artists in Manchester: By a Staff Contributor," *Manchester Historic Association Collections*, IV (1908), 110-11; *NADER*, II, 88; George C. Groce and David H. Wallace, *The New-York Historical Society's Dictionary of Artists in America, 1564-1860*, p. 523; C. W. Wallace, "John Rand," pp. 1-5. SIL, FARL, and Mr. George A. Stauter, public relations counsel for the Industrial Products Group of Minneapolis-Honeywell, have provided useful information. Mrs. P. R. Anglemyer has kindly answered many questions concerning Rand and has shown me some of his paintings. Members of her family, including her sister, the late Miss Jean C. Rand, have also been helpful. It has been generally supposed that Rand left New York for England in 1834, but Rand gives the date of his arrival in London as December 30, 1833, in MS letter, Rand to Bryant, London, Jan. 6 [or 5], 1834, Bryant-Godwin, NYPL. The date of his return to the U.S. in 1847 has been established through MS letter, Bryant to Mrs. F. F. Bryant, New York, Oct. 19, 1847, Goddard-Roslyn, NYPL.

Godwin collection at the New York Public Library; but Parke Godwin for some undisclosed reason never used them in his life of Bryant.
Yet this correspondence[140] forms a miniature autobiography of Rand
and fully describes his activities in London from 1834 to 1838, facts
otherwise not readily available. What is more important here, the
letters, if used in conjunction with other sources, demonstrate that
Bryant aided Rand throughout the inventor's lifetime.

Bryant directly and indirectly contributed to Rand's temporary
success as a portrait painter abroad. In the first place, Bryant lent
Rand money to become established in London. The exact amount
of this loan, not revealed in the correspondence, must have been substantial if Rand's gratitude and extreme deference may be used as
clues. Ten days after arriving in England, he thanked Bryant "for
favours received": "What shall I say? I did write several epistles on
that subject, but destroyed them as being silly. I know you despise a
silly thing—If I *say I am your most obedient* and *humble servant* it
would be nothing. These words are ruined . . . . I ha[ve] only one
way to express my sentiments which is to improve the opportunity I
now enjoy."[141] Later, impressed with an increasing number of sitters,
Rand promised repayment in monthly installments of ten pounds, and
wrote with enthusiasm: "My Dear Mr. and Mrs. Bryant you have
made us the happiest people on earth, your astonishing generosity
has been crowned with success. We are now out of the fear of want,
and situated in a very pleasing and respectable circle of acquaintances,
all of which we must attribute to no other cause under heaven than
your generosity."[142] Even though during his first three years in England Rand was able to return some of the money,[143] he had not

140. Only two of Bryant's letters to Rand have been found, but in other collections:
MS letters, Bryant to Rand, Paris, July 20, 1834, YUL; Bryant to Rand, New York,
Aug. 13, 1838, BR Box 270, HHL. Rand's letters indicate that Bryant frequently
replied. In a letter to the author (Washington, D.C., Nov. 13, 1956), Mrs. Anglemyer
suggests that Bryant's letters could have been among the papers of Rand that were
destroyed by fire.

141. MS letter, Rand to Bryant, London, Jan. 6 [or 5], 1834, Bryant-Godwin,
NYPL.

142. MS letter, Rand to Bryant, London, July 23, 1834, Bryant-Godwin, NYPL.

143. MS letters, Bryant to Welles and Co., Pisa, Feb. 4, 1835; Bryant to Madame
Bryant, Paris, Jan. 30, 1836, Goddard-Roslyn, NYPL.

erased the debt by June of 1842,[144] and one suspects that it was never liquidated while Rand stayed in Europe, for what he and his wife interpreted as signs of prosperity[145] proved only to be omens of penury. The debt may have shaken this friendship sometime between July, 1838, and June, 1842, a period for which no letters from Rand have been found,[146] but the interruption was only temporary. In 1845 during his second visit to Europe, Bryant called on the Rands several times, finding Mrs. Rand "in delicate health," her husband "quite well and quite poor, and quite active."[147] They talked of Rand's latest inventions, and Bryant wrote a letter to the *Evening Post* praising him as "one of the most ingenious mechanicians in the world."[148] Mrs. Rand bought a gift for Bryant's wife[149] and took Bryant to Sunday service in a crowded London chapel;[150] her husband gave Bryant a useful letter of introduction to a Parisian acquaintance.[151] In short,

144. Rand wrote to Bryant of making business transactions "as soon as it is in my power." These in turn would enable him "to pay a certain debt" (MS letter, Rand to Bryant [London], June 19, 1842, Bryant-Godwin, NYPL). Bryant had asked for payment at least once. See MS letter, Rand to Bryant, n.p., n.d. [probably 1838], Bryant-Godwin, NYPL. Writing to Bryant at New York, Rand opened his letter with this acknowledgment: "Your last letter has given me great pain, not on account to an allusion to the loan, but that circumstances required you to make such an allusion."

145. See MS letter, Bryant to Mrs. F. F. Bryant, New York, July 22, 1841, Goddard-Roslyn, NYPL.

146. This conjecture would explain a curious passage in one of Rand's letters: "I have been very much rejoiced by receiving a letter from you . . . [because of] the liberty it gives me to write to you again, which priviledge [*sic*] I feared I had certainly lost" (MS letter, Rand to Bryant [London], June 19, 1842, Bryant-Godwin, NYPL). In MS letter, Bryant to Mrs. F. F. Bryant, New York, July 22, 1841, Goddard-Roslyn, NYPL, Bryant transcribed a letter from Mrs. Rand to Mrs. Bryant which was dated April 20, 1841. Mrs. Rand promised repayment of the loan within a year and noted the coming of good fortune. Knowing that the vague language of this letter would mystify his wife, Bryant tried to explain: "Miss Robbins says that Rand has invented some machines and taken out patents, by which he expects to make himself very rich. Perhaps this is the key to the meaning of Mrs. Rand's letter." Although Bryant may have talked to Rand in 1840, when the latter visited New York, Bryant's reliance on Miss Robbins for news of Rand suggests an estrangement.

147. MS letter, Bryant to Mrs. Frances F. Bryant, London, June 1, 1845, Goddard-Roslyn, NYPL.

148. Bryant, *Letters of a Traveller*, p. 218.

149. See the sections dated June 14 and June 17 in MS letter, Bryant to Mrs. F. F. Bryant, London, June 1, 1845, Goddard-Roslyn, NYPL.

150. MS letter, Bryant to Mrs. F. F. Bryant, Paris, Aug. 4, 1845, Goddard-Roslyn, NYPL.

151. MS letter, Bryant to Mrs. Frances F. Bryant, Paris, Aug. 5, 1845, Goddard-Roslyn, NYPL.

the unpaid debt had no serious consequences; the relationships between the Rands and the Bryants were very cordial in spite of it.

Not only Bryant's money but also his reputation contributed to Rand's experiences abroad. Rand had brought his portrait of Bryant to London, and by using it to prove that Bryant was his friend he acquired a number of important sitters.[152] "I dont flatter you when I say that your portrait is universally admired," Rand wrote in 1834; he then acknowledged Bryant's unconscious part in a chain reaction of contacts finally leading to commissions from the nobility:

Mrs. Rand went to deliver letters from Mrs. Bethune to a Miss Rolleston—found Miss Rolls. a real blue who knew much respecting American literature, on being told I was an artist she at once asked why I did not bring a likeness of our poet Bryant. Lavinia [Rand's wife] sprang up and clapped her hands, and said "So we have[.]" Miss Roll[e]ston then repeated some of your poems and Mrs. Rand came home so excited we hardly knew her. The next day we had a call from Dr. Shee [Sleigh] a friend of Miss Roll. who seemed fully satisfyed with the expectations that were raised of your portrait[.] Dr. Shee [sic] will give me letters to a *Duke* and severall other distinguished characters.[153]

152. Thus he wrote enthusiastically of his acquaintance with a Mr. Rich, "a very cautious and judicious gentleman [who] advised me to take the advantage of any avenue to the wealthy. He also kindly proposed to assist me to approach Bishop Bromfield and asked me to call on him for any advice I might want. . . . I have shown Mr. Rich one of the papers you gave[.] It had great weight with him, as he advised me to publish myself saying it would move [prove?] to my advantage. Mr. Rich spoke very highly of your volume of poems before I told him I was acquainted with you.—Said it was as much read as any poetry at present—that no poetry went off well at present" (MS letter, Rand to Bryant, London, Jan. 6 [or 5], 1834, Bryant-Godwin, NYPL). According to a bit of gossip recorded in N[athaniel]. P[arker]. W[illis]., "Pencillings by the Way," *NYM*, XII (April 4, 1835), 317, Rand was currently writing a book on the philosophy of painting. However, when Willis collected his *Pencillings* in "The First Complete Edition" (1844), this rumor—and indeed the entire passage on Rand—was omitted, leading us to doubt that Rand even started such a book.

153. MS letter, Rand to Bryant, London, Jan. 25, 1834, Bryant-Godwin, NYPL. This letter contains four sections, each with a different date: Jan. 25, 1834; Jan. 30; Feb. 4; Feb. 7. Rand corrected his misspelling of Dr. Sleigh's name in the section dated Feb. 7. In the same letter (section dated Jan. 30) Rand told of attending a party at which a "gent. who sung a song, on being told I was an American, asked me if I had ev[er] seen Mr. Bryant the poet. I told him I had a por[trait] of Mr. B. and gave him my card.—asked if you tal[ked] of coming to Eng. Ans. Nothing more likely—he wished to be introduced in case such an event should happen[.]"

By cutting off "the bottom part" of a letter Rand was able to give Miss Rolleston her idol's autograph. She in turn promised to introduce the Rands to "a brother of Miss Edgeworth" and to several other celebrities.[154] A similar incident relating Bryant's overseas reputation to Rand's career has been recounted by the inventor's descendants. Two English ladies, upon learning that the poet Bryant was a friend of the Rands, whom they had chanced to meet at church, were so impressed and excited that they immediately told their brother, Lord Bexley, of their discovery. He in turn arranged to sit to Rand for a portrait.[155] From that time on, Rand became a favorite with the nobility and, as N. P. Willis remarked, was "up to the lips in success" and "in a fair way" to realizing "a fortune."[156] Unconsciously but in a real sense Bryant had launched Rand on this promising career.

But Rand was soon plagued with bad luck; and while continuing to rely on Bryant's help, he was never able to stop misfortunes from accumulating. Mrs. Rand fell ill for many weeks; Rand himself caught smallpox and narrowly escaped death from it; during his sickness he incurred more debts; he was continually injured by the vagaries of his sitters and would-be patrons and was slandered by his fellow artists and countrymen. Problem after problem he poured into his copious and complicated letters,[157] which Bryant must have found as difficult to follow as to answer. One of his replies, apparently to a letter dated July 17, 1838, was as encouraging as possible under the circumstances; but he warned Rand to pay no heed to increasing debts and malicious gossip. As an editor, Bryant noted, he himself was slandered every day, and his debts were far greater than Rand's; yet he had learned to retain his peace of mind in spite of such irritations.[158] Meanwhile Rand had been thinking of giving up his profession and returning to America. In desperation he asked Bryant's advice. Should he raise silk worms? Should he "get some old pictures

154. *Ibid.*, section dated Jan. 30.
155. [Campbell], p. 3; Franklin, p. 9.
156. Willis, "Pencillings by the Way," *NYM*, XII (April 4, 1835), 317.
157. See MS letters, Rand to Bryant, London, March 28, 1835, Feb. 6, 1836, Sept. 23, 1837, and especially July 17, 1838, Bryant-Godwin, NYPL.
158. MS letter, Bryant to Rand, New York, August 13, 1838, BR Box 270, HHL.

in trust" and exhibit them in the United States? Or could he become an author?

In my leisure moments I have been writing letters of a fictitious traveler in England. The traveler is an unsophisticated Yankee who by his simplicity brings out the follies . . . and inconsistencies of mankind, at the same time supposing it all to arise from his own ignorance. If I could get them through a literary paper in america [sic] . . . I could sell an edition here under the title of A Volume of blunders.

However you will be a better judge of this than myself[.]

ANOTHER PLAN

Could you get some wild land in the *far West* and let me go on to it and increase its value by improving it. [sic] I never did any thing else till I was 20 years old, besides I have almost every useful trade for such an enterprise[.][159]

These suggestions were the frantic gropings of a man about to go under, and in an undated letter that must have been written at this time, we see him reach the depths of his despair: "I was in hopes something favourable would occur but my matters [are] . . . worse and worse and I now tell you as a point of duty, if you cannot give me a situation about the office in which I can get a living and be gradually paying you something, it is not likely that you will hear of me much longer in the land of the living."[160]

At this point we must turn to other sources to continue the history of this friendship, since no letters have been found for 1839, 1840, and 1841. It is important, therefore, to recall that during these years Rand gave up painting and invented the collapsible tube, which he patented in France, England, Belgium, and the United States.[161]

The few remaining letters, beginning in June of 1842, indicate that Rand solicited Bryant's help during a trying period in which he was never rewarded for his own genius. The first setback at this time

159. MS letter, Rand to Bryant, London, May 20, 1838, Bryant-Godwin, NYPL. The above quotation is dated July 19. In 1836 Bryant had thought of settling in the west. See Godwin, I, 322.
160. MS letter, Rand to Bryant, n.p., n.d., Bryant-Godwin, NYPL.
161. MS letter, Rand to Bryant, [London], June 19, 1842, Bryant-Godwin, NYPL.

started with a confusion of patentees. Although all of the patents for the tube had been taken out in Rand's name, the expenses incurred in applying for them had been paid by a Mr. Brown, who in turn received a moiety of the rights to the invention. Later, Brown not only refused to sell his half but also insisted on advertising the tubes as "Brown's Patent." When, under the same label, he began to export the tubes to the United States, Rand objected, claiming an equal right to sell them under his own name. As early as 1842 Rand asked Bryant to insert in the *Evening Post* and other newspapers a notice stating that the tin tube would soon appear in England and the United States under the name of John Rand, the rightful patentee. Rand promised to cover the expense of these advertisements but admitted his inability as yet to repay Bryant's loan.[162] Four years later, beset with an increasing number of counterfeit tubes, Rand not only made a similar request for advertising but also asked Bryant to find a lawyer competent enough to straighten out confusion over his American patent.[163] Meanwhile, bad luck seemed to multiply itself. Its newest shape was described by Bryant, writing to the *Evening Post* from London in July, 1845:

The musical world here are talking about Colman's improvement in the piano. I have seen the instrument which the inventor brought out from America. It is furnished with a row of brass reeds, like those of the instrument called the Seraphine. These take up the sound made by the string of the piano, and prolong it to any degree which is desired. It is a splicing of the sounds of one instrument upon another. Yet if the invention were to be left where it is, in Colman's instrument, it could not succeed with the public. The notes of the reeds are too harsh and nasal, and want the sweetness and mellowness of tone which belong to the string of the piano.

At present the invention is in the hands of Mr. Rand, the portrait painter, a countryman of ours, who is one of the most ingenious mechanicians in the world. He has improved the tones of the reeds till they rival, in softness and fullness, those of the strings, and, in fact, can hardly be

162. *Ibid.*

163. See respectively *ibid.*, and MS letter, Rand to Bryant, Paris, Feb. 28, 1846, Bryant-Godwin, NYPL.

distinguished from them, so that the sounds of the two instruments run into one another without any apparent difference. Mr. Rand has contrived three or four different machines for making the reeds with dispatch and precision; and if the difficulty of keeping the strings, which are undergoing a constant relaxation, in perfect unison with the reeds can be overcome, I see nothing to prevent the most complete and brilliant success.[164]

But success was not for Mr. Rand, in spite of this free publicity furnished by Bryant. Rand no sooner poured his money into manufacturing the Eolian attachment than one of his American employees stole the plans and patented the invention in the United States. The expense of resultant legal proceedings and of manufacturing the invention itself ultimately forced Rand to sell most of his patents in the tube although he never relinquished his American patent.[165] By 1846 Rand foresaw the ruination of both his business ventures and his health as well:

. . . I am so completely disheartened by the failure of the Eolian Pianoforte that I have no means or courage to attempt anything els[e] in this world. To me it has worse than failed, as it has involved the interest I had in the Tube business in such a manner that I would be glad to give it all up without any consideration to escape from the care and anxiety which has already impaired my health to such a degree that I am daily working in immediate danger of suddenly being taken off with the apoplexy.

I only put off the fatal moment by taking strong doses of calomel every few weeks.[166]

It took a year for Rand to disentangle himself from affairs in Europe. He had suggested to Bryant the possibility of opening a color shop in New York,[167] but after returning to America in 1847, broken in health and spirit, and forced to rely on friends to pay his customs duties,[168] he again took up portrait painting in New York City.

164. Bryant, *Letters of a Traveller*, pp. 217-18.
165. "Death of John Gough Rand," New York *Evening Post*, Jan. 23, 1873.
166. MS letter, Rand to Bryant, London, Oct., 1846, Bryant-Godwin, NYPL.
167. See *ibid*.
168. [Campbell], p. 4; MS letter, Bryant to Mrs. F. F. Bryant, New York, Oct. 19, 1847, Goddard-Roslyn, NYPL.

His relationships with Bryant during later years continued to be friendly. Around 1861 Bryant tried to interest "some members of the War Department" in Rand's "plan for assisting the speed of certain projectiles used in warfare,"[169] but the plan was never adopted. At this time the Rands visited Bryant at Roslyn for several months. When Rand died in 1873, Bryant served as one of the pallbearers at his funeral.

The light which Rand's letters throw on the friendship between these two men still fails to penetrate many dark corners. Further research may clarify, for example, their relations prior to 1833, during the period between 1838 and 1842, and in the years after 1848, but enough evidence has been collected by now to prove that Rand and Bryant were close friends for over half of their lives.

Although only one of Bryant's many associations with artists who were not members of The Sketch Club, his friendship with Rand is quite important because it raised Bryant to the rank of patron. Whether Bryant actually commissioned and paid for Rand's portraits of him is uncertain, but there is no doubt that he lent money to Rand and that with the aid of this loan Rand was able to establish himself as a portrait painter. Bryant gave Rand, just as Cooper gave Greenough, money to become known by and therefore deserves to stand with Cooper as a patron of the fine arts.

BRYANT'S MISCELLANEOUS FRIENDSHIPS.[170] Without fear of hyperbole, one might say that Bryant knew, besides Rand, over one hundred American artists who did not belong to The Sketch Club. His correspondence and Godwin's biography of him reveal the names of at least thirty native painters, sculptors, and architects with whom he came in contact throughout his long life; but his five-year service with the American Art-Union would certainly more than triple this list. Only a few of these artists were Bryant's close friends, however:

169. [Campbell], p. 4. In 1850 Rand had disclosed another one of his inventions to Bryant—a way of easily discovering a desired page in a reference book. See MS letter, Rand to Bryant, New York, Feb. 11, 1850, Goddard-Roslyn, NYPL.
170. See Appendix I.

"As I advance in life," he once observed, "the world widens in some respects and contracts in others; I have more acquaintances and fewer intimates."[171]

Bryant knew a large number of sculptors, more, in fact, than his fellow Knickerbockers could have claimed as friends or acquaintances. This is not surprising since most of the Knickerbockers died before sculpture became an established art in the United States. Furthermore, many American sculptors lived and worked abroad for the greater part of their careers. Thus only authors like Bryant, who lived to see this craft come into its own at home and who traveled enough to become familiar with its practitioners elsewhere, could have known as many sculptors as he did. Bryant's closest friends among these artists were Horatio Greenough and Henry Kirke Brown. He also knew John Frazee, Hiram Powers, Joseph Mozier, Thomas Crawford, Richard S. Greenough, and William Wetmore Story—all born before 1820. His acquaintances in the younger group included Edward S. Bartholomew, Randolph Rogers, John Rogers, and Harriet Hosmer—all born after 1820. Although he never wrote any important essay on the art or history of sculpture, his thumbnail analysis of John Rogers' achievement is well worth preserving: "You have succeeded in a higher degree than almost any artist of any age in making sculpture a narrative art, and giving to motionless and speechless figures the power to relate their own adventures."[172]

Besides native sculptors, Bryant knew the landscape designer Andrew Jackson Downing and a host of painters, many of whose names are memorable in the development of American art: William S. Mount, Eastman Johnson, George Loring Brown, Emanuel Leutze, Albert Bierstadt, John James Audubon, Thomas Sully, Thomas Hicks, William Page, and William Morris Hunt.

Bryant's wide acquaintance among American artists was recognized by the Century Association in 1864 at a festival celebrating his seven-

171. Quoted in Godwin, I, 382.
172. MS letter, Bryant to Rogers, Long Island, Oct. 18, 1869, Miscellaneous Letters, NYHS. Rogers' letters to Bryant accompanied his sculptural groups which he sent as gifts to the poet: MS letters, Rogers to Bryant [New York], Dec. 24, 1862; New York, Oct. 11, 1869, Bryant-Godwin, NYPL.

tieth birthday. A portfolio of over forty pictures, including drawings, watercolors, and oils, was given to the poet—a lavish and impressive gesture since they were the works of such notables as Durand, Kensett, Gifford, Church, Bierstadt, Hicks, and Darley, who contributed them for the occasion.[173] In making this presentation, Daniel Huntington, president of the National Academy, told Bryant: "Of the vast multitudes who with ever-growing delight bend over your pages, there are none whose hearts glow with deeper joy and pride than those of the artists . . . ." Bryant in turn clarified motives which for thirty-nine years had led him to court the society of American painters and sculptors: "Among the artists of our country are some of my oldest and best friends. In their conversation I have taken great delight, and derived from it much instruction. In them the love and study of nature tend to preserve the native simplicity of character, to make them frank and ingenuous, and to divert their attention from selfish interests. I shall prize this gift, therefore, not only as a memorial of the genius of our artists, but also as a token of the good-will of a class of men for whom I cherish a particular regard and esteem."[174] Bryant remained true to these friendships during the rest of his life, five years of which he devoted to helping establish and guide the Metropolitan Museum of Art, incorporated in 1870, eight years before his death.[175]

173. See Godwin, II, 214-20. This collection, later given to the Century Club by Julia S. Bryant, is described in Charles D. Lay and Theodore Bolton, *Works of Art, Silver and Furniture Belonging to the Century Association,* pp. 43-46. Although Robert Weir had been a member of The Sketch Club while he lived in New York, he later moved to West Point and therefore never joined the Century. Apropos of the festival Weir wrote to Bryant: "Since my partial recovery from a painful illness I have amused myself with painting a little picture for you with the hope that you will give it a place among those presented to you by the artists of the Century Club" (MS letter, Weir to Bryant, West Point, May 18, 1866, Goddard-Roslyn, NYPL).

174. Quoted in Godwin, II, 220.

175. Bryant was elected to preside, on November 23, 1869, at the first public meeting in which the Metropolitan Museum was planned. See Bryant, *Prose Writings,* II, 261-66, for his excellent speech on this occasion. The appropriateness of selecting Bryant to preside at this meeting is noted by Winifred E. Howe in her *History of the Metropolitan Museum of Art,* p. 106. Bryant served as one of the museum's vice-presidents from 1870 to 1874. An expression of appreciation for his services may be found in New York Metropolitan Museum of Art, *Annual Report* (1877-78), pp. 103-4.

Nathaniel Parker Willis

Of the younger Knickerbockers, Nathaniel Parker Willis deserves treatment in some detail, for he utilized art-material in more literary genres than did any of his contemporaries. His first travel book, *Pencillings by the Way*, abounds in descriptions of studios and galleries; his collections of familiar essays, beginning with *A l'Abri* and ending with *The Convalescent*, frequently mention artists of his acquaintance; his poetry was sometimes written to accompany engravings; and he composed most of the letterpress for William Bartlett's popular views of American, Canadian, and Irish scenery. Moreover, he used artists as the major characters in much of his fiction, including a play, *Tortesa, the Usurer*; a novel, *Paul Fane*; and such short stories as "The Icy Veil," "A Revelation of a Previous Life," "The Countess Nyschriem, and the Handsome Artist," "Light Vervain," "Those Ungrateful Blidgimses," and "Two Buckets in a Well." Exploiting this material long before Henry James began to do so, Willis was able to give it as much verisimilitude as fiction need have, simply by recalling many experiences shared with painters and sculptors both here and abroad.

WILLIS, HARDING, ALLSTON, AND ALEXANDER.[176] In 1827 Willis took the customary grand tour through New York State and Canada prior to graduating from Yale College, where he had already made a name for himself by publishing verses over the signatures of "Roy" and "Cassius." At Montreal he met Chester Harding, a very successful portrait painter at the time, having just earned $12,000 during a three-year stay in England. Harding was mostly self taught in his art; after spending some of his early years painting houses, he had toured the backwoods as an itinerant limner, charging $25 per likeness, and he claimed to have been the only artist to paint Daniel Boone from life. Until after his marriage Harding had read no other book than

---

176. Henry A. Beers, *Nathaniel Parker Willis*, pp. 63, 92; Chester Harding, *A Sketch of Chester Harding*, pp. 194, 205, 260-61; Kenneth L. Daughrity, "The Life and Work of Nathaniel Parker Willis," pp. 87-88, 96, 250-51.

the Bible, and that with great difficulty. All of these peculiarities made him a *rara avis* in the fashionable circles of England and certainly also in the refined atmosphere of Boston, his home from 1826 to 1843. Therefore, it was most unlikely that this frontiersman-turned-artist would become a fast friend of the dashing Nat Willis, who, if not the worldly fop that his critics thought him to be, was a highly literate example of city-bred elegance, and, besides was fourteen years younger than Harding. Yet these two opposites renewed their acquaintance in Boston and soon were the closest of friends.

Their relationship, lasting over thirty years, was based on their high regard for each other's talent and reputation. In Boston they had been members of a supper club with Washington Allston, then occupied with his twenty-five-year task of painting "Belshazzar's Feast."[177] When Harding mentioned this period in his autobiography, he wrote admiringly of Willis: "He was the 'lion' of the town; was young, handsome, and wrote poetry divinely. He often met Allston at my house, and, I trust, recollects how swiftly the hours flew by. . . . The friendship then formed between us has never for a moment been disturbed."[178] Harding also showed his great esteem for Willis by giving him a portrait of the Duke of Hamilton, a picture which Harding always regarded as the "crowning point" of his "success as an artist in England."[179] Actually, the duke was only one of many fashionable English patrons who entertained Harding in a very friendly manner—showing him their galleries, introducing him to other potential sitters, and teaching him the fine points of shooting partridges and pheasants on their estates. Harding had become so popular, in fact, that by habitually mentioning him as a friend Willis also

177. There is no evidence that Willis and Allston ever became intimate friends, but after the latter had died Willis wrote of him: "It is true, the personal and familiar character of all men of genius will not bear posthumous unveiling—but Allston's will. He was, in the phraseology of the old dramatists, 'a sweet gentleman.' God never wove the woof and warp of taste, feeling, and intellect, under a more clear and transparent surface than in the 'Paint King' of our country. You read his mind first, in seeing him. His frame was but the net that held it in. Everybody loved him" (*The Prose Works of N. P. Willis*, p. 602).

178. Harding, p. 194.

179. *Ibid.*, p. 261.

gained quick admittance to English society. In appreciation he made a policy of keeping Harding's name before the public.[180]

Perhaps he even used Harding as the model of Bosh Blivins, a fictional character providing comic relief in Willis' only novel, *Paul Fane* (1857). Like Harding, Blivins is a painter who has gone abroad after touring the frontier in search of commissions. There are also tempting parallels to Harding in Blivins' rustic speech and homely philosophy of art, accented by contrast with the sophisticated vocabulary and idealistic musings of Paul Fane, the hero of the novel. By creating this fictional likeness Willis may have been unconsciously repaying a favor, for Harding had once painted portraits of the author and his mother, Mrs. Nathaniel Willis.[181] Yet, as is fitting in a novel, the resemblance between Blivins and Harding is merely suggestive, not minutely detailed; furthermore, Willis had other friends, including his former schoolmate George J. Pumpelly and the artist Francis Alexander, who could have also served as prototypes for this character.[182]

Like Harding, Alexander was a rustic-turned-painter and several years older than Willis. They must have met sometime before 1827 in New York, but it was in Boston that their friendship ripened. Alexander painted Willis' portrait with a sure touch that belied his back country origins and recent entrance into the profession, and Willis in his turn wrote a sonnet entitled "To a Picture of 'Genevieve' by Alexander." Both men went to Europe in 1831, and with the painter John Cranch they took a trip from Florence to Venice—the story of which is delightfully told in Willis' *Pencillings by the Way.* Unfortunately, because our evidence gives out here, a reconstruction of their friendship after 1832 is at present impossible.[183]

180. See [Willis], "The Editor's Table," *The American Monthly Magazine,* II (May, 1830), 148; Willis, *Famous Persons and Places,* pp. 151-52; *A l'Abri,* pp. 46-47; *The Convalescent,* p. 367; *Pencillings,* pp. 32, 187.

181. Letter to the author from Mrs. Grinnell Willis, Greenwich, Conn., May 29, 1955.

182. Daughrity, p. 88, suggests that Pumpelly was the model not only of Blivins but also of Forbearance Smith and Job, two other characters in Willis' fiction.

183. Willis' sonnet and an undated letter from Willis to Alexander are in MS, YUL. Also see Daughrity, pp. 103-4, 114-15; Willis, *Pencillings,* pp. 47-52.

WILLIS AND THE GREENOUGHS. During his early years as an author Willis was associated with several members of the Greenough family. Undoubtedly his acquaintance with these artists began in Boston, where he lived primarily from 1812 until 1831 and edited two gift books, *The Legendary* and *The Token*, as well as *The American Monthly Magazine*, a periodical of only two years' endurance.

Willis launched the young Henry Greenough on a literary career by inducing him to write for the *American Monthly*. Henry had been designing buildings and teaching in Boston, but he left there in 1829 to study painting with Cole and Morse at Florence. Willis requested him to jot down his experiences in Italy: "Write me about these things. It is a fault in a traveller's book that first impressions are not arrested . . . . The first glance, the earliest sentiment awakened in the mind by beauty and grandeur, is worth all the tame after-philosophy of the best of observers."[184] Henry soon complied by writing an anonymous "Letter from Italy,"[185] in which he described the feast of Corpus Christi with the same impressionistic abandon that was soon to characterize Willis' own *Pencillings by the Way*. Greenough's subsequent career embraced both art and literature. He supervised the decoration of the Crystal Palace in New York and wrote two novels, *Ernest Carroll* and *Apelles*, both of which are seldom remembered today.

A more easily documented friendship,[186] marked by a number of reciprocated favors, existed between Willis and Henry's older brother Horatio. When Willis arrived at Paris in 1832, under contract to write travel letters for *The New-York Mirror*, he found Horatio fraternizing daily with Morse and Cooper, who was then planning to influence the government to order a statue of Washington from Greenough. Willis promptly wrote to his American readers: "For the love of true taste, do everything in your power to second such an

184. Willis to Henry Greenough, Boston, March 28, 1830, in Greenough, *Letters*, p. 60. Also see Alfred Greenough to Henry Greenough, *idem*, p. 26.

185. *The American Monthly Magazine*, II (Aug., 1830), 345-48. Also see Greenough, *Letters*, p. 66.

186. Willis, *Pencillings*, p. 46; Beers, p. 121; Greenough, *Letters*, pp. 90-91; Daughrity, pp. 42, 304.

appeal when it comes."[187] During the summer and autumn of 1832 Willis was in the northern part of Italy. Horatio had come there from Paris, and at Florence Willis lived right above him in a room last occupied by Thomas Cole. Soon Greenough molded a bust of Willis, later reproducing it in marble cut, by coincidence, from the same block that he had used for a full-length statue of Willis' future wife, Cornelia Grinnell, then only five years old.

Besides furnishing this romantic incident for Willis' already romantic life, Greenough proved to be a good friend in other ways as well. For example, in Rome he introduced Willis ". . . to Gibson, the English sculptor, who presented him with a cast of his bas-relief, Cupid and Psyche. Under the guidance of the two, Willis amused himself by trying his hand, in an amateurish fashion, at moulding in clay. He was flattered by their assurances that he had a good touch, and felt half inclined, for a moment, to exchange his dilettantish pursuit of letters for an equally dilettantish pursuit of art. His dreams of the possibilities of such a career took shape long after in the novel of 'Paul Fane.' "[188] Greenough was not entirely satisfied with Willis' manner of adjusting to the social and artistic life of Italy,[189] but he was nevertheless willing to acquaint Willis with as much of it as he could. In this way he did his friend a great favor, for Willis was able to use this milieu in a novel, in many short stories, and in *Pencillings by the Way*, the cornerstone of his reputation. But he had paid for this material in advance, so to speak, by introducing Greenough to readers of his travel letters, printed not only by *The New-York Mirror* but, according to George P. Morris, by five hundred newspapers as well.[190]

187. Willis, *Pencillings*, p. 8.

188. Beers, pp. 120-21. Greenough gave news of Willis in MS letter, Horatio Greenough to Bryant, Florence, Feb. 24 [1835], Goddard-Roslyn, NYPL.

189. See MS letters, Horatio G[reenough] to Morse, Florence, May 31, 1832; Horatio Greenough to Morse, Florence, June 3, 1832, Morse Papers, Vol. X, LC.

190. Beers, p. 116. When it was first installed in the Capitol, Willis vigorously defended Greenough's statue of Washington, insisting that its merits would never be appreciated fully unless it was placed under better lighting. See Willis, *Rural Letters*, pp. 170-71.

WILLIS AND OTHER ARTISTS. Harding, Allston, Alexander, and the Greenoughs were only a few of Willis' many friends and acquaintances among artists. Others included Samuel Morse, Asher Durand, Robert Weir, John F. Kensett, Andrew J. Downing, George Flagg, John Rand, Rembrandt Peale, William Bartlett, William A. Wall, and Thomas Hicks. Since much of Willis' correspondence has been burned,[191] his connections with these artists cannot be described in any detail, although he mentions many of them in his published writings, and it is known that Rand and Wall painted portraits of him. However, even this rather skimpy evidence indicates that, in spite of the fact that Willis was not a member of The Sketch Club, he had more artist-friends than any other Knickerbocker with the exception of Bryant.[192] These associations help to account for the numerous allusions to the fine arts and their practitioners in Willis' large output of prose and poetry.

Other Knickerbockers

Other writers from New York also made friends with American artists.[193] James Kirke Paulding, one of the oldest members of the Knickerbocracy, knew the sculptor Horatio Greenough and a few painters, but the record of these acquaintances is not so complete as we might wish. Thomas Sully, returning to America after a fifteen-year sojourn in Europe, was flattered by the welcome Paulding gave him. After he had seen Paulding's art collection, he candidly evaluated it in his journal, expressing his contempt for a bust of Washington but his admiration for a cast from the Magdalene of Canova. Two other busts, one of Columbus and one of Amerigo Vespucci, he noted without comment.[194] As Paulding's collection and his writings indicate, he was not only an Americanist but also very much an antiquarian and historian; besides, his cousin John had been one of the

191. Letter to the author from Mrs. Grinnell Willis, Greenwich, Conn., May 29, 1955.

192. See Appendix I.

193. Documentation for these friendships is given in Appendix I.

194. See the entries for Sept. 19, 21, 1829 and Sept. 24-25, 1831 in the typewritten copy of Thomas Sully's "Journal," NYPL. Paulding's collection is further treated in Wilson, p. 153; *NADER*, I, 36, 76.

principals in the famous capture of Major André. As a result Paulding was consulted by such artists as Asher Durand and Horatio Greenough when they were in need of background for their works. He is said also to have been interested in the career of John Quidor, and considering the dearth of sources for this eccentric painter's life, it is unfortunate that Paulding never published an account of the times he watched Quidor paint at John Wesley Jarvis' studio. Another artist befriended by Paulding was John G. Chapman, remembered today for his "Baptism of Pocahontas" in the Rotunda of the Capitol. Paulding commissioned him to paint nine scenes associated with the life of George Washington and, when artists were being chosen for the Rotunda job, recommended him to influential correspondents like Richard Henry Wilde and John C. Calhoun. Writing to the latter on July 1, 1836, Paulding claimed that Chapman had the "inventive genius" needed not only to conceive and arrange "a number of figures" but also to combine them "in one action, so as to produce one great effect."[195] Soon after this the two friends were collaborating on *A Christmas Gift from Fairy Land* (*ca.* 1838), a handsome book with quaint letterpress by Paulding and lively drawings by Chapman. Perhaps Paulding was recalling this work when in 1843 he recommended Chapman to the editor of *Graham's Magazine*: "Should you require any Pictures, or illustrations for your mag—there is an artist here of the name of John G. Chapman, a friend of mine, who for richness and facility of designing, and rapidity & punctuality in executing, is without an equal among living artists."[196] In his relations with these painter-friends Paulding could sometimes request favors as well as dispense them. This is apparent in the undated note which he scribbled to John Wesley Jarvis asking for "a few sketches, short stories & incidents, of Kentucky or Tennessee manners, and especially some of their peculiar phrases & comparisons. If you can add, or *invent* a few ludicrous Scenes of Col. Crockett at Washington, You will be sure

195. Quoted in Norman Kane, *The Americanist (Literary & Historical Americana): Number Twenty-Three* (Pottstown, Pa. [1964]), item 25. The recommendation to Congressman Wilde, dated Feb. 13, 1835, is in *The Letters of James Kirke Paulding*, p. 164.

196. Paulding, *Letters*, p. 325. See *idem*, pp. 165, n. 4, 169-70, 185, 192-93, for other aspects of this friendship.

of my everlasting gratitude."[197] Paulding had turned to the right person, for Jarvis was a celebrated raconteur conversant with life in the South; it is not known, however, whether he furnished the requested material—obviously meant for inclusion in *The Lion of the West*, Paulding's dramatic caricature of Davy Crockett.[198]

McDonald Clarke, the "Mad Poet of Broadway," is an exception in this chapter, for he received more from the artists than he gave. But Clarke's condition was atypical: he had little to give. He was without funds, without influence, and generally without sanity. He was incapable of taking care of himself, much less others. Asher Durand, probably hearing rumors that Clarke was sleeping beneath the flagpole at the Battery, took pity on this homeless poet and gave him a table in his studio where he could dash off wild "letters and verses, and come and go as he pleased."[199] There Clarke met Durand's pupils and co-workers—J. W. Casilear, Lewis P. Clover (who painted Clarke's portrait), and J. W. Paradise—and in his letters he begs to be remembered to them. There, too, he was rather harshly treated by William Page. Clarke had left his diary "lying about where any visitor so disposed could peruse its contents, consisting of dreams quite amusing, and occasionally, though rarely, very indelicate, along with unfinished scraps of poetry, wild visionary conceits, comments on books and pictures, without any idea probably that they would ever be read by anybody but himself—all recorded with a degree of faithfulness and honesty sometimes startling." As Clover recalled the incident:

One morning Mr. William Page, the artist, who knew Clarke well, and had doubtless heard of one of his recorded dreams, came in and asked to see the diary. It was handed to him; he read it over carefully, frowned, and, without saying a word, put it into the stove. Shortly after Mr. Page went out Mr. Clarke entered, and, looking around for his diary, complained that he could not find it. "Have you seen anything of it?" said he, addressing me. "Yes," I replied; "Mr. Page has just read it, and, being displeased with an indelicate reference to a member of his family,

197. *Letters*, p. 113.
198. For Paulding and Jarvis also see Dickson, pp. 137, 315; [Paulding], *Salmagundi, Second Series*, I, 143.
199. Durand, *A. B. Durand*, p. 87.

has burned it." "Oh," said Clarke, with the innocence of a child, "can that be possible! He should have remembered that it was only a dream."[200]

Later, right up to the final snapping of his mind, his removal to an asylum, and his tragic death, Clarke was subjected to much crueler treatment than this, but not by his artist-friends.

Such New Yorkers as John Howard Payne, Clement Clarke Moore, Fitz-Greene Halleck, Charles Fenno Hoffman, Theodore Fay, and Evert A. Duyckinck also associated with American artists; these friendships are documented in Appendix I. This survey must not end, however, without mentioning the elegant group pictured in Junius Brutus Stearns' "Fishing Party" (1857).[201] Seated at the right is Lewis Gaylord Clark, the well-known editor of *The Knickerbocker*. Standing beside him in the middle of the picture is the humorist Frederick S. Cozzens, author of the *Sparrowgrass Papers*. And at the left of the scene, looking perhaps too "posed" for the natural setting, is the portrait painter Charles Loring Elliott. Here is a symbol of artist-writer friendships that goes "Kindred Spirits" one better, for it shows *two* writers and a painter. Evidence of the relationship between Stearns and these writers has, unfortunately, not turned up, but that between Clark and Elliott is easily confirmed. When Clark wrote an article on Elliott for *Lippincott's*, he recalled "an acquaintance and friendship extending through a period of more than thirty years, and almost daily intercourse of intimacy."[202] He frequently mentioned Elliott in the "Editor's Table" of his own magazine, thus keeping the painter's name before the public, and when *The Knickerbocker Gallery* was published, Elliott's portrait of Clark was engraved as the frontispiece.

With such friends the Knickerbockers developed severe cases of art on the brain. As the following chapters will show, they praised artists in magazines, travel books, and novels; employed the techniques of landscape painters; analyzed architecture with the enthusiasm of devoted amateurs; and wrote letterpress for engravings in gift books and periodicals. Another symptom, more appropriately

200. Quoted in *ibid.*, p. 88.
201. Reproduced, discussed, and offered for sale in *Panorama*, II (Nov., 1946), 36.
202. L. Gaylord Clark, "Charles Loring Elliott," p. 652.

noted here, was their frequent use of figures of speech based on the visual arts. Cornelius Mathews called one of his works *A Pen-and-Ink Panorama of New York City*; other writers invented such titles as *Crayon Sketches, Drawings and Tintings*, and *Dashes at Life with a Free Pencil*. Many a Knickerbocker book, with or without such titles, was filled with other proof that the author saw the affinities between the verbal and the visual and often thought of himself as a painter, sculptor, or architect. In *Homeward Bound*, for example, Cooper promised "to touch in a few of the stronger lights of our picture, leaving the softer tints and the shadows to be discovered."[203] Other figures were based not on a knowledge of the craft itself but on a familiarity with its practitioners and their works. Thus Irving wrote of a woman's "hair . . . put up very much in the style of Sir Peter Lely's portraits";[204] Cooper of "Rembrandt-like hemlocks";[205] and Willis of objects and people too numerous to quote, all linked with the names of Raphael, Titian, Claude, Hogarth, Reynolds, Fuseli, or many another famous artist.[206] At their worst both types of figures were esoteric beyond intelligibility, but at their best they communicated universally. Whatever their merits, they proved that long and intimate acquaintance with artists affected even the vocabulary of the Knickerbockers.

203. I, 10. Also see J. Fenimore Cooper, *Home as Found*, I, iv, II, 14; *The Monikins*, I, 102. Cooper even thought of himself as a painter of New-World groups in the attitudes of Salvator Rosa's banditti. See J. Fenimore Cooper, *The Deerslayer*, II, 13. Washington Irving once confessed, "I am prone to paint pictures to myself . . ." (*Bracebridge Hall*, p. 93); and in "The Author's Account of Himself," his most famous preface, he wrote: "As it is the fashion for modern tourists to travel pencil in hand, and bring home their port-folios filled with sketches, I am disposed to get up a few for the entertainment of my friends" (*The Sketch-Book*, p. 18). Also see Williams, II, 318; Henry A. Pochmann, *Washington Irving: Representative Selections*, pp. lxxix-lxxx. Willis used the language not only of painting but also of photography to describe his own work. See his *Rural Letters*, p. viii, and *Hurry-Graphs*, p. 109.

204. Irving, *Bracebridge Hall*, p. 46. Also see *idem*, pp. 27, 189; William Irving, James Kirke Paulding, and Washington Irving, *Salmagundi*, p. 24.

205. Cooper, *Home as Found*, I, 224. Also see James Fenimore Cooper, *Gleanings in Europe: France*, p. 274; *The Deerslayer*, I, 32.

206. See Willis, *People I Have Met*, pp. 137, 142; *Pencillings*, pp. 54, 57, 90, 154, 212; *Hurry-Graphs*, pp. 16, 183; *Out-Doors at Idlewild*, pp. 142, 201, 504-505; *Famous Persons and Places*, pp. 159, 321, 415-16; *Rural Letters*, pp. 166, 238; *Fun-Jottings*, p. 145.

CHAPTER III

THE FINE ARTS

IN THE LITERARY MAGAZINES

OF NEW YORK

Before 1825 the fine arts received less frequent coverage in the literary magazines of New York City than did science, politics, economics, and religion. Even the annually bound volumes of these periodicals lacked one or more of the features which later characterized art magazines: news items; reviews of exhibitions; notices of art books; essays on painting, sculpture, and architecture; and illustrations engraved on wood, copper, or steel. Editors were not to be blamed for the absence of such material. Their magazines, written at first for a local audience, merely reflected the cultural status of New York City where the fine arts did not really flourish until the second quarter of the nineteenth century. As painting, architecture, and, to some extent, sculpture made significant advances after 1825, Gothamite editors began to acknowledge and facilitate this progress by increasing the scope of their maga-zines to include the fine arts.

From 1825 until the founding of America's first genuine art jour-nal, *The Crayon*, in 1855, the task of acquainting the public with the fine arts was energetically undertaken by literary magazines. The space devoted to these matters depended somewhat on each journal's periodicity. Weeklies such as *The New-York Mirror* and the *Literary World*, being greatly in need of filler items, contained larger reviews of exhibitions and more frequent news of artists than did a monthly such as *The Knickerbocker*. Much depended also on the backgrounds of the editors, for an editor whose friends were artists was sure to champion their cause and reflect their interests in his magazine.

Although indebted, of course, to Frank Luther Mott's excellent surveys, this chapter attempts a closer study by limiting its scope. After a brief treatment of *The New-York Review*, the three journals with the greatest number of characteristics later belonging to art magazines will be analyzed at length; then several other periodicals will be mentioned for their most striking connections with the visual arts.

The New-York Review

The story of journalistic interest in art during the second quarter of the nineteenth century begins in New York with *The New-York Review and Atheneum Magazine* (1825-26), a short-lived periodical edited by three members of The Sketch Club—Henry J. Anderson, William Cullen Bryant, and Robert Charles Sands.[1] Some anonymous letters from American artists studying abroad;[2] a rather skimpy news item devoted to engraving and archeological discoveries;[3] a full survey

1. Sands and Anderson had previously edited *The Atlantic Magazine* (1824-25), the direct predecessor of *The New-York Review and Atheneum Magazine*. The earlier journal had contained occasional pieces on the fine arts, for example, "To the Editors of the Atlantic Magazine," I (July, 1824), 214-15; "Original Busts and Portraits of Washington," I (Oct., 1824), 433-37.

2. "Extract of a Letter from an Artist in London, to His Friend in this City," *NYRAM*, I (Aug., 1825), 243-45; "Letter from an Artist in Italy," *NYRAM*, I (Oct., 1825), 396-98.

3. "Intelligence Respecting the Fine Arts, Antiquities, &c.," *NYRAM*, I (Oct., 1825), 409-10.

of painting, sculpture, and patronage in New York City;[4] a brief but sympathetic essay on the founding of the National Academy;[5] and two unsigned reviews of an exhibition held at the American Academy, written by William Dunlap,[6] comprised the total amount of art-material in this periodical's two volumes.[7] However modest these beginnings, they foreshadowed more successful treatments by magazines of greater distinction and endurance. The fine arts had at least become a noticeable department in *The New-York Review*.

The New-York Mirror

The most complete coverage of the American art scene before 1855 was accomplished by *The New-York Mirror* (1823-42).[8] Its able editors, especially George Pope Morris, not only gave this literary magazine a longevity surprising for its day but also greatly widened its scope without reducing the contents to mere superficiality. Thus, lovers of the fine arts could rely on the *Mirror* for accurate news items, entertaining feature articles, cogent editorials, and detailed reviews; they could further delight in its many original engravings.

Practically every number of the *Mirror* treated current happenings in the art world. If an artist died, moved, opened a new studio, received an appointment or a commission, was paid well for his work, or

4. "Fine Arts," *NYRAM*, II (April, 1826), 367-72.

5. "Fine Arts," *NYRAM*, II (Feb., 1826), 244.

6. "A Review of the Gallery of the American Academy of Fine Arts, as Now Opened for the Exhibition of Dunlap's Painting of 'Death on the Pale Horse,' " *NYRAM*, II (Dec., 1825), 71-78; *NYRAM*, II (Jan., 1826), 152-59. The first of these reviews was attributed to Dunlap by Bryant in a marked copy of this magazine in Berg Collection, NYPL. Since the second review was promised in the first and bears an identical title, it was probably also written by Dunlap. The reviewer's generous estimate of Dunlap's "Death on the Pale Horse" might therefore be self-praise: ". . . he [Dunlap] has produced an effect greater than we ever saw produced by painting" *NYRAM*, II [Jan., 1826], 155).

7. By merging with *The United States Review and Literary Gazette* in 1826, *NYRAM* became a bi-regional publication, Charles Folsom editing it in Boston, Bryant in New York. This new periodical contained one lengthy and notable review: "The Exhibition of the National Academy of Design, 1827 . . . ," *USRLG*, II (July, 1827), 241-63.

8. The study that follows is concentrated on the years before 1843, when the *Mirror* changed its name to *The New Mirror*. Unless otherwise noted, all the articles and engravings cited throughout this section appeared in *NYM*.

had on his easel a promising canvas for the next local exhibition, the reader was informed of it. These news items were generally confined to the American artist at home,[9] but some treated his activities abroad.[10]

Each volume contained approximately a dozen full-length articles on the fine arts, provided primarily by correspondents[11] or members of the staff, although occasionally reprinted from other sources.[12] Many of these essays embodied historical,[13] biographical, and anecdotal material.[14] Other articles were devoted to specific types of native art: painting, sculpture, engraving, and architecture.[15] Chief among these was an elaborate series on the buildings of New York, past and present. For seven years, from 1827 to 1834, the *Mirror* dedicated a column entitled "Public Buildings" to descriptions of churches, theaters, pub-

9. A sampling of these American news items includes "Gilbert Stuart," VI (July 26, 1828), 23; "Inman's Portrait of Van Buren," VII (March 20, 1830), 291; "Greenough's Chanting Cherubs," IX (Nov. 19, 1831), 155; "Teacher of Drawing at the Military Academy," XI (April 19, 1834), 334; "Ingham's Ariel," XI (July 13, 1833), 14; "Durand's Ariadne," XIII (Oct. 10, 1835), 119; "Mr. Cranch's Studio," XVI (July 18, 1838), 39; "Audubon, the Ornithologist," XVII (Sept. 21, 1839), 103; "American Portrait Gallery," XVIII (Sept. 26, 1840), 111.

10. See, for example, [William] C[ox]., "Americans in London," VIII (March 12, 1831), 284-85; "Newton, the Artist," XIII (Oct. 3, 1835), 111; "Statue of Washington," XVI (July 28, 1838), 39; "American Painters Abroad," XVI (Sept. 8, 1838), 87; "The Society of St. George and Thomas Sully," XVII (June 29, 1839), 7.

11. See "Arts and Artists," XVI (Nov. 3, 1838), 151, and a series descriptive of Florence, "Letters from an American Artist Abroad," which appeared throughout Vol. XIII.

12. These articles were taken from other American and European periodicals: "The Late Gilbert Stuart," VI (Aug. 2, 1828), 30; "Greenough's Statue of Washington," XIX (Sept. 4, 1841), 287. Some articles were excerpts from Dunlap's *Arts of Design*: "Anecdotes of American Artists," XI (Feb. 1, 1834), 248; "Excerpts from Dunlap's History of the Arts of Design," XIII (Dec. 19, 1835), 195; "John Wesley Jarvis," XVII (Jan. 25, 1840), 246.

13. See, for example, n—C., "The Fine Arts during the Reign of Charles V," IV (April 14, 1827), 297-98; "Paintings Discovered in the Excavation at Pompeii," VI (Aug. 2, 1828), 30-31.

14. See "William Dunlap," X (Feb. 23, 1833), 265-66; "Early Talent of Michael Angelo," XI (Dec. 14, 1833), 187; "Newton, the Painter," XIII (Jan. 9, 1836), 222; "Thomas Sully," XVI (Aug. 18, 1838), 63; "Anecdote of Hogarth," XVII (June 6, 1840), 398; "Stuart, the Painter," XX (Jan. 15, 1842), 19.

15. See "Our Landscape Painters," XVIII (July 18, 1840), 29-30; XVIII (July 25, 1840), 38; "Busts and Portraits," XX (Sept. 10, 1842), 293; "Engravings," X (Dec. 22, 1832), 198-99; "The City of Modern Ruins," XVII (June 13, 1840), 407; "Rustic Architecture," XX (May 21, 1842), 167; "A Short Chapter on Architecture," XX (Jan. 29, 1842), 38.

lic halls, jails, hotels, schools, and old Dutch houses in New York City. Only contemporary domestic architecture was ignored. Most of these illustrated articles were unsigned, but some were attributed to John Pintard, Theodore Fay, and Charles Fenno Hoffman. Like the accompanying engravings, the text sometimes varied in size, being in one issue copious and full of architectural statistics, in another reduced to a single paragraph of description or merely to a short lead-in for one of Paulding's tales with a New Amsterdam setting. But taken as a whole, this was the most important architectural survey to appear in a Knickerbocker magazine.[16]

Some articles in the *Mirror* were written primarily to entertain rather than to inform. Such were the essays commenting on the inability of painters to judge their own work, exposing the duplicity of picture dealers, and describing the proper manner of sitting for a portrait.[17] The whimsical essay soon gave rise to the fictional art tale, a story employing either real or imaginary painters and sculptors. Several minor authors wrote sketches of this type for the *Mirror*, but the best came from the pens of William Cox, Theodore Fay, and Nathaniel Parker Willis.[18]

The short editorial appeared more frequently than the full article, from which it differed not only in length but also in tone, its aim being persuasion rather than information or entertainment. An example quoted in its entirety, indicates the extreme economy of this form:

We understand that the approaching exhibition of the American Academy of Fine Arts at Clinton-Hall, is to be one of the most attractive ever offered in this city. Where there is so much genius for painting in our country, is it not deplorable that it has such a limited opportunity for complete development, through a deficiency of encouragement? We trust

16. See Chapter VII for an analysis of these articles.

17. See "Judging of Pictures," IV (Jan. 20, 1827), 202-203; "The Sale of Paintings," XVII (Nov. 9, 1839), 156; W., "Sitting for One's Picture," III (Feb. 18, 1826), 234.

18. See Miss M. S. C., "The Young Artist," XX (April 23, 1842), 132-33; William Cox, "Portrait Painting," XIV (Nov. 26, 1836), 173-74; Theodore Fay, "Rubens and His Scholars," XIII (Oct. 17, 1835), 125-26; T. S. Fay, "The Antique," XIII (Nov. 7, 1835), 147-48. Willis' short stories for the *Mirror* were collected and re-collected in *Romance of Travel, Dashes at Life with a Free Pencil, People I Have Met,* and *Fun-Jottings.*

that our princely merchants and retired millionaires will look in upon this exhibition of American paintings, and avail themselves of the chance of procuring some of the best productions of our artists.[19]

With such diminutive essays the editors were able to pass judgment, however briefly, on a multitude of matters, including art associations, benefits for ailing painters, the function of rural architecture, the quality of gift-book illustrations, bank-note engraving, the integrity of picture dealers, and the choice of artists for governmental commissions.[20] At the same time, the *Mirror* could retain ample space for feature articles and stories.

One of the *Mirror*'s most substantial contributions to American art was its reviews of local exhibitions, which ranged in content from a single painting, such as Samuel Morse's "Gallery of the Louvre," to the entire yearly output of the National Academy of Design. Some reviews of one-man or one-collector exhibitions were merely notices, but the majority contained enough evaluation and analysis to classify them as legitimate critical articles.[21] But these smaller reviews were overshadowed by the elaborate treatises occasioned by the annual exhibitions of the American Academy, the National Academy of Design, and the Apollo Association (later the American Art-Union). The *Mirror*'s concept of its own role as a vehicle of art criticism was

19. "Our Painters," XVI (April 27, 1839), 351.

20. Typical short editorials were "The Apollo Association for the Encouragement of the Fine Arts," XVI (March 30, 1839), 320; "William Dunlap, Esq.," XVI (Oct. 20, 1838), 134; "American Rural Architecture," XV (Aug. 26, 1837), 71; "Subjects for Engravings," XIV (Sept. 24, 1836), 103; "Bank-Note Engraving," XI (March 1, 1834), 275; "Caution to Picture-Fanciers," XIV (Sept. 17, 1836), 95; "National Paintings," XIV (July 16, 1836), 23.

21. For reviews of non-annual exhibitions, see F[ay?]., "Painting," VII (Jan. 16, 1830), 220, a review of Benjamin West's "Christ Rejected"; "The Paintings of Colonel Trumbull," VIII (April 30, 1831), 339; "Exhibition of Paintings, Collected in Spain by the Late Richard W. Meade, Esq.," IX (Sept. 17, 1831), 86-87; "Dunlap's Historical Paintings," IX (Feb. 11, 1832), 254; "Exhibition at Mr. Cole's Rooms," X (Jan. 12, 1833), 219; "The Paintings of Adam and Eve at the American Academy," X (March 30, 1833), 306-307; "Mr. Morse's Gallery of the Louvre," XI (Nov. 2, 1833), 142; "Exhibition at Clinton-Hall," XIII (Oct. 3, 1835), 110, concerning copies of Correggio's paintings; "Sanguinetti's Collection of Italian Paintings and Engravings," XVI (July 7, 1838), 15; "The Panorama of Thebes," XVII (June 29, 1839), 6, on a panorama by Frederick Catherwood; T. S. C., "Cole's Pictures of the Voyage of Life," XIX (Jan. 2, 1841), 3.

helpful and humble: "We have become a powerful, populous, and *rich* nation," a reviewer declared in 1826, "and it does not become us to go for ever plodding on in the beaten track of interest, without turning a kindly hand to drooping genius by the road-side." The drooping geniuses in this case were the members of the National Academy of Design, and the critic added: "Without entering into any thing like an arrangement, we offer our poor opinion upon a few of the pictures, [formed] during the hasty glance we have as yet been enabled to take of them."[22] But, as time went on, litotes were abandoned for more positive if not aggressive statements, and reviewers represented themselves as biased, natural men, possessed of common sense and intuitive ability to sense artistic values: "There is an advantage in having a critic who has no picture badly hung, and whose taste cannot be galled by rivalry. It is not necessary that one should be able to paint the 'Transfiguration,' to know cobalt from Spanish brown. A good picture pleases even the unlearned, and, as one of these, we speak."[23] No matter what tone reviewers for the *Mirror* adopted in their prefacing remarks, they soon fixed their eyes steadily on the pictures themselves and assessed them one by one. Their shortest comments might be deprecating: "No. 12.—E. Withers. A portrait. Very flat";[24] enigmatic: "No. 11. Portrait of a Lady.— William Swain. This venerable gentlewoman is stated to be ninety-three years of age, and appears yet in the enjoyment of health and strength";[25] or appreciative: "No. 315. Portrait of a lady. W. Page.— A bold attempt to produce an impossibility—to wit, rotundity without shade or shadow, and brilliancy without colour or atmosphere—yet executed in a manner that exhibits an investigating mind, and a skilful hand."[26] Because many paintings were given a full paragraph of discussion, these reviews are something more than annotated catalogues. Nearly every exhibition of the two academies and the Apollo Association was noticed. This regularity and the usual competence of the critics,

22. "The National Academy of the Arts of Design," III (June 10, 1826), 366.
23. "National Academy of Design," XIX (May 15, 1841), 159.
24. C[harles]. F[enno]. [Hoffman], "Exhibition of the National Academy of Design," XII (May 16, 1835), 366.
25. [William] D[unlap]., "National Academy of Design," X (May 18, 1833), 366.
26. "National Academy of Design," XVI (July 7, 1838), 15.

most of whom remain anonymous,[27] make the *Mirror*'s reviews a rich storehouse for the art historian, who in them may find not only nineteenth-century attitudes but also detailed descriptions of lost or hitherto unidentified paintings. For this reason a check list of reviews in the *Mirror* and other literary magazines has been compiled as Appendix II.

The number and quality of its engravings distinguished *The New-York Mirror* from the city's other journals. The first three volumes were not illustrated; but from 1827 through 1842 there appeared a total of seventy-six full-page steel and copperplate engravings (exclusive of title-page vignettes), an average of over four per year. Nineteen of these plates were representations of landscape; nineteen of genre; eighteen of architecture; fifteen of portraiture; and five of historical subjects such as Thomas Sully's "Washington, Crossing the Delaware." One hundred and seventeen woodcuts, usually figures rather than plates, were scattered throughout the twenty volumes issued from 1823 to 1842, an average of almost six illustrations a year. Approximately the same balance of subject matter among the steel plates was maintained in the woodcuts, so that in both cases every facet of American design was represented.[28] Throughout the years, "embellishment" became increasingly important to the editors. As a result, several plates in the nineteenth volume were given more dignity than adjacent literary pieces, which were humbly referred to as illustrations of the engravings.

Most of the pictures in the *Mirror* were exclusive: paid for by the editors, not pirated from other journals. Since the majority of nineteenth-century periodicals either were not illustrated or contained only "borrowed" plates, the *Mirror* deserved some credit for its integrity. By hiring the best available engravers and artists, the editors of this

27. William Dunlap's *Diary* (III, 679, 683, 687) reveals him as the author of two serial reviews for the *Mirror* in 1833. See Appendix II, below. John Durand (*A. B. Durand*, p. 63) considered Dunlap the *Mirror*'s regular "art critic"; but it should be remembered that Dunlap died in 1839, when the *Mirror* was still middle-aged.

28. Of these 117 woodcuts, 3 were engravings of landscape; 32 of genre; 31 of architecture; 15 of portraiture; 4 of historical subjects; 23 of fashion designs; and 9 of miscellaneous subjects.

magazine were able furthermore to guarantee quality, not merely originality.

From 1827 through 1842 the *Mirror* reproduced paintings by John Trumbull, Gilbert Stuart, Thomas Sully, Asher Durand, Chester Harding, Henry Inman, and William Sidney Mount, to name a few of the better artists. Drawings by Robert W. Weir, John G. Chapman, and Alexander J. Davis; wood engravings by Alexander Anderson, Abraham John Mason, Joseph Alexander Adams, and W. W. Hooper; and steel engravings by James Smillie and George Parker enjoyed such ubiquity that these artists might be called members of the *Mirror*'s artistic staff. In the 1840's the services of two very competent workers on steel, Joseph Napoleon Gimbrede and his uncle John Francis Eugene Prud'homme, were enlisted.

The high quality of the illustrations was due in large part to George Pope Morris, who as principal editor assumed much responsibility and worry. His ideals were lofty, as is indicated by his letter to Asher Durand concerning a proposed plate depicting the presidents of the United States. Durand was instructed to paint James Madison from real life—all expenses to be paid by Morris, who continued:

It will not answer to engrave from portraits already issued in engravings.—The likeness *must be undeniable*, as I said before, and the plate of *the first order of merit*. It wd. be better never to issue it, than to disappoint private and public expectation, by giving my readers an affair of questionable accuracy.—I should never be able to hold up my head afterwards, nor to promise any thing, in the way of pictorial embellishments, of a superior quality, again. This presidential cluster is a load of responsibility upon my mind, and you will not wonder, if I feel very anxious about it.[29]

It took almost two years to finish the plate and when it finally appeared, Morris could boast that "the amount of time, labour, and

29. MS letter, Morris to Durand, West Point, Sept. 11, 1833, Durand Papers, NYPL. Also see Durand to Casilear, Montpelier, Se[p]t. 24, 1833, Morris to Durand, Albany, July 12, 1833, Saratoga Springs, Aug. 8, 1833, Thos. W. Harman to Durand, Albany, Aug. 5, 1833, Durand Papers, NYPL; "The National Academy," *NYM*, XI (May 17, 1834), 367.

expense . . . devoted" to it was "without precedent . . . ."[30] The magazine's other engravings were executed with more rapidity, but the
illustrations on steel nevertheless required six months' work. Furthermore, when Morris promised approximately an engraving a month
(as he did in the 1840's), he found himself forced to cope with a
new problem, the scarcity of capable engravers, made even more
acute when Durand switched from burin to brush.[31] Morris solved
the matter by hiring new, talented engravers, such as Gimbrede and
Prud'homme, whom he apparently inspired with his own high ideals.

Several engravings stand out. Alexander J. Davis' drawings of
New York buildings, reproduced in wood and steel cuts, were not
only artistic[32] but highly functional; for by isolating each structure
they called the reader's attention to it and gave him the opportunity
to judge it on its architectural as well as scenic merits.[33] Equally
superb were Asher Durand's copperplate engravings which in 1832
and 1833 the *Mirror* reissued from *The American Landscape, No. I.*
Other works, such as H. R. Buss's "A Musical Bore," George W.
Twibill's "Geo. H. Hill, Comedian," and Thomas Kelah Wharton's
"New York from Brooklyn Heights," although by little-known artists,
were only slightly less outstanding.[34] The landscape by Wharton takes
on added interest because of the background which his unpublished
journal provides for it. We learn, for example, that James Smillie,
chief engraver for the *Mirror,* had been finding it difficult to work
from Robert Weir's oil colors, so Wharton sketched his own scene in
black and white. For future drawings he was to receive approximately $25 apiece, although his pictures were not to be used without

30. "The Presidents of the United States," XII (Aug. 9, 1834), 41. The plate was
highly praised by L. Gaylord Clark ("Editor's Table," *K*, IV [Sept., 1834], 247) and
by William Dunlap (*Arts of Design*, III, 278). The portrait of James Madison engraved for this cluster had been painted by Durand on commission from Morris.
Paulding's letter of introduction for Durand to present to Madison at the time of the
sittings is in Paulding, *Letters*, pp. 132-33.

31. See "Engravers," XIII (Nov. 28, 1835), 175.

32. See Talbot Hamlin, *Greek Revival Architecture in America*, p. 327.

33. See "Public Buildings," VII (Sept. 26, 1829), 89.

34. Respectively in *NYM*, XX (March 12, 1842), facing p. 81; XII (Nov. 22, 1834),
facing p. 160; XI (April 19, 1834), facing p. 329.

the permission of Weir, whom Morris had already contracted to furnish an annual landscape for the same purpose and price.[35]

Perhaps William Dunlap best explained the effect of the *Mirror's* illustrations on American culture: "By the engravings which ornament this popular work," he declared, "taste is propagated, and the study of the fine arts in all their branches encouraged. . . . The designs . . . have done honor to the country, and added reputation to those employed."[36] Furthermore, the *Mirror* could justly be proud of its editorials and reviews, its wide coverage, and its longevity. In all, the *Mirror* well deserves to head our list of literary magazines which helped American art to grow.

The Knickerbocker

The next most important journal of this type was *The Knickerbocker* (1833-65).[37] Edited principally by Lewis Gaylord Clark, it rivalled the *Mirror* in longevity and surpassed it in number of special, full-length articles devoted to the fine arts; but its news items and short editorials were infrequent and negligible,[38] and its illustrations—sixteen steel plates, eighteen woodcuts, and three etchings in all—were definitely inferior to those ordered by Morris.

A number of full-length articles were biographical sketches of such artists as Frederick S. Agate, Gilbert Stuart, Hiram Powers, and Horatio Greenough.[39] Other topics treated by various contributors,

35. Thomas Kelah Wharton, MS "Journal: 1830-1834," NYPL, entries for March 23 to July 13, 1834, pp. 248-74.

36. *Arts of Design*, III, 278.

37. The definitive study of this journal is Herman E. Spivey, "*The Knickerbocker Magazine*, 1833-1865."

Unless otherwise noted, all of the articles cited throughout this section appeared in *The Knickerbocker*.

38. For news items, see "Our Young Artists," XVI (Sept., 1840), 271; "Paintings, Etc.," XVI (Oct., 1840), 360. Typical short editorials on topics of the fine arts are "Henry Inman," IV (Nov., 1834), 410; "Landscape Gardening and Rural Taste," X (Oct., 1837), 366; "The Fine Arts," X (Nov., 1837), 452-53; "Editor's Table," XVI (Nov., 1840), 456.

39. F. W. E[dmonds]., "Frederick S. Agate," XXIV (Aug., 1844), 157-63; William Dunlap, "Biographical Sketch of the Late Gilbert Stuart," I (April, 1833), 195-202; Benjamin B. Thatcher, "Sketch of a Self-Made Sculptor," V (April, 1835), 270-76; J. N. B[ellows]., "Horatio Greenough," VII (April, 1836), 343-46.

including some artists, were ornamental gardening, old Dutch houses, the American Art-Union, the relation of size to sublimity,[40] and the progress of art in the United States.[41] Although far from plentiful, such essays were effective by accumulation and served to entice lovers of literature to other facets of the arts.

The Knickerbocker was always open to artists who wished to see themselves in print. Among these contributors were the Englishmen Thomas R. Hofland and George Harvey and the Americans Francis W. Edmonds, Henry Inman, Robert W. Weir, and Thomas Cole. Writer-artists of more recognized literary ability, such as William Dunlap and Thomas Bangs Thorpe, also wrote for The Knickerbocker.[42]

Cole sent no less than two prose articles and two poems to the magazine. One of these pieces, "A Letter to Critics on the Art of Painting," was published almost immediately after Clark received it,[43] appearing in September, 1840, over the signature of "Pictor."[44] The reason for the pseudonym is quite evident: Cole takes art critics to task, tells them to forsake their hackneyed vocabulary of praise, gleaned from the annuals, to use nature as their touchstone, and to judge a work according to its purpose, not its striking techniques. During the next year Cole sent two poems at Clark's request:[45]

40. W. A. B., "Ornamental Gardening," X (Oct., 1837), 311-16; T. B. Thorp[e], "Old Dutch Houses," XVIII (Aug., 1841), 150-55; Anon., "The American Art-Union," XXXII (Nov., 1848), 442-47; George Harvey, "The Fine Arts: A Few Hints on the Philosophy of Size in Its Relation to the Fine Arts," XXIII (Feb., 1844), 156-59.

41. See J. Houston Mifflin, "The Fine Arts in America," II (July, 1833), 30-35; "Liberty vs. Literature and the Fine Arts," IX (Jan., 1837), 1-11; Thomas R. Hofland, "The Fine Arts in the United States, with a Sketch of Their Present and Past History in Europe," XIV (July, 1839), 39-52.

42. See the three preceding notes and G. R. V. [George Harvey], "A Veritable Ghost Story," XXIII (April, 1844), 338-43; Henry Inman, "The Whooping Hollow," I (April, 1833), 238-45; R. W. Weir, "To My Old Clock," XXXIX (March, 1852), 262, a poem; and Anon., "Musings by the Hearth: By a Landscape Painter," XXXVI (Nov., 1850), 457-59; XXXVI (Dec., 1850), 546-49, familiar essays.

43. Clark acknowledged receipt, with thanks, of what must have been this article in MS letter, Clark to Cole, New York, August 1, 1840, Cole Papers, NYSL.

44. Clark called Cole by this pseudonym in MS letter, Clark to Cole, New York, March 19, 1841, Cole Papers, NYSL.

45. MS letter, Clark to Cole, New York, Nov. 20, 1840, Cole Papers, NYSL. Earlier in the year Clark had approached Cole through Francis W. Edmonds: MS letter, Edmonds to Cole, New York, May 26, 1840, Cole Papers, DIA.

"Winds," which appeared in May of 1841,[46] and "The Lament of the Forest," which was published in the June number.[47] But "The Lament" was not at first acceptable. Its rough metrics displeased Clark, so he recommended that it be shown to Bryant, whom he considered a master of prosody.[48] Cole apparently agreed, for Bryant made some revisions, and Clark expressed his satisfaction with the results.[49] A few years later Cole contributed a prose sketch called "Sicilian Scenery and Antiquities," which Clark published in two parts.[50] Cole may have never been paid for these pieces, even though *The Knickerbocker* was one of the few magazines which did compensate their writers. Instead, Clark had tried to coax a painting from Cole in trade for books that the painter might want,[51] but nothing indicates that Cole heeded the editor's odd request, even later when Clark asked only for a sketch.[52]

Every volume of *The Knickerbocker* contained poems inspired by art objects. Some were humorous verses, such as these anonymous "Lines on a Naked Statue of Apollo Crowning Merit":

> Merit, if thou art blest with riches,
> For God's sake, buy a pair of breeches!
> And give them to thy naked brother,
> For one good turn deserves another.[53]

Others were full of pious sentiments, written to accompany miniatures and portraits:

> WHAT I WAS, is passed by;
> What I AM, away doth fly;
> What I SHALL BE, none doth see,
> Yet in THAT my beauties be.[54]

46. XVII, 399, attributed to "Pictor" in the index.
47. XVII (June, 1841), 516-19.
48. MS letter, Clark to Cole, New York, March 19, 1841, Cole Papers, NYSL.
49. MS letter, Clark to Cole, 2 Park Place, June 1 [1841], Cole Papers, NYSL.
50. XXIII (Feb., 1844), 103-113; XXIII (March, 1844), 236-44.
51. MS letter, Clark to Cole, New York, Nov. 20, 1840, Cole Papers, NYSL.
52. MS letter, Clark to Cole, 2 Park Place, June 1 [1841], Cole Papers, NYSL.
53. XIII (June, 1839), 483.
54. "Lines Written under a Portrait," XXIV (Nov., 1844), 463.

Verse of this type reflected rather than stimulated popular interest in the fine arts.[55]

In the fields of painting and sculpture *The Knickerbocker* educated readers chiefly through its reviews. Special exhibitions were discussed in full,[56] but the annual shows of the National Academy were given even more extensive treatment, although *The Knickerbocker* seldom contained serial reviews or notices of virtually every painting in the exhibitions, as did *The New-York Mirror* and the *Literary World*. From 1834 through 1855, a period of twenty-two years, there were eighteen reviews of the National Academy exhibitions. There were no reviews for the exhibitions of 1838, 1845, 1848, and 1851.

Several of these reviews were not written by Clark, even though they appeared in "The Editor's Table." Clark definitely attributed one (1839) to John Kenrick Fisher, another (1852) to a "friend," and two others (1849 and 1855) to correspondents.[57] A fifth review (1841) was almost certainly worked up by the editor from an exhibition catalogue marked for him by Thomas Cole,[58] whose help was acknowledged with the utmost subtlety: "We have taken up our marked Catalogue," Clark told his readers, "but on looking over it, find that the gossiping comment running through it in pencil would, if written out, so impinge upon this department as to exclude much matter

55. See also G[eorge]. P[ope]. M[orris]., "Defence of Poesy," IV (Dec., 1834), 432-33; B. B. T., "The Seaman's Daughter: Suggested by Fisher's 'Portrait of a Girl,' at a Late Fair in Boston," V (Feb., 1835), 123; W[illis]. G[aylord]. C[lark]., "Guido's Cleopatra," V (March, 1835), 220; H. T. Tuckerman, "Vanderlyn's Ariadne," XX (Sept., 1842), 241.

56. See "The Group from Tam O'Shanter," II (July, 1833), 69-70; "F. A. Danby's Opening of the Sixth Seal," II (Nov., 1833), 399; "[Ball Hughes'] Uncle Toby and the Widow Wadman," III (May, 1834), 398-99; "Ancient and Modern Rome," IV (Aug., 1834), 161; "Raffaelle's Cartoons," IV (Aug., 1834), 161-62; "The Fine Arts [paintings by West and Daniel]," IV (Oct., 1834), 325-26; "Hyalocaustics," V (Jan., 1835), 88-89; "Departure of the Israelites from Egypt," V (Feb., 1835), 171-72; "Belshazzar's Feast," V (April, 1835), 359; "Gallery of Paintings,—Washington Divan," VI (July, 1835), 83; "The Fine Arts [West's 'Death on a Pale Horse']," VII (May, 1836), 550; J. Huntington, "The Allston Exhibition," XIV (Aug., 1839), 163-74; "A Picture by Murillo," XXIII (May, 1844), 503-505; Gen. A. H. S. Dearborn, "Allston's Feast of Belshazzar," XXIV (Sept., 1844), 205-217.

57. See Appendix II, below.

58. See MS letter, Clark to Cole, 2 Park Place, June 1 [1841], Cole Papers, NYSL.

already in type."[59] One wonders if Clark compiled most of his art reviews in this manner.[60] He once declared: "Fearing that we might at times be wrong in our judgment, we have freely sought the opinions of those whose knowledge and taste in the arts are well known to many of our readers."[61] Perhaps one of these advisers was Charles Loring Elliott, Clark's closest friend among the artists.

Reviewing policy, which seldom varied in *The Knickerbocker*,[62] combined candor, restraint, and nontechnical observations. Frank condemnations were not unknown: "Probably the worst painting in the room," snarled a critic especially annoyed with a portrait. "Perhaps we shall find one more utterly destitute of merit as we go on, but as yet it stands preeminent. Drawing and coloring, all as bad as can be."[63] And irony was employed at times: "Mr. FLAGG has five pictures, of which we may have more to say hereafter. We cannot express any great admiration of his style in general. His faces are not disfigured by any thing that can be called expression, exactly; yet he makes very large eyes and quite elaborate bosoms."[64] But such remarks were not the rule; greatly inferior works were usually passed by in silence,[65] and readers were frequently warned not to judge a picture at first sight.[66] Lastly, *The Knickerbocker* retained its amateur status by avoiding technical considerations.[67]

Over a period of twenty-two years *The Knickerbocker*'s menu

59. "National Academy of Design," XVIII (July, 1841), 86.

60. In 1845 Clark asked Cole for his marked catalogue, but *K* for that year contains no review of the exhibition. See MS letter, Clark to Cole, n.p., May 1, 1845, Cole Papers, NYSL.

61. "National Academy of Design," XIX (June, 1842), 588.

62. A notable exception to this homogeneity was John K. Fisher's cantankerous review in 1839. Among other things, the paintings of Sully and Ingham were attacked and the validity of the Indian as subject matter for pictures was denied. Fisher was an American artist who had studied in England. See J. K. F., "National Academy of Design," XIII (June, 1839), 545-49.

63. "National Academy of Design: Eleventh Annual Exhibition," VIII (July, 1836), 113.

64. "Editor's Table," XXVII (May, 1846), 465.

65. See "National Academy of Design," XIX (June, 1842), 588.

66. This policy of moderation was best articulated in "Exhibition of the National Academy of Design," XLII (July, 1853), 93-94.

67. "We are not sufficiently well versed in the terms of art to say technically what this picture requires, but it wants *something* very much" ("National Academy of Design: Second Notice," XXVII [June, 1846], 557).

never varied: literature was the main course; painting, sculpture, architecture, and engraving were served as side dishes. Readers therefore had ample time to cultivate a taste for the fine arts, and the magazine to make its influence important.

The Literary World

As the Knickerbocker period closed, the *Literary World* (1847-53) supplemented the pioneering work of earlier magazines; for this weekly journal, edited by Charles Fenno Hoffman and the Duyckinck brothers, also catered to the visual arts in news items, special articles, and copious reviews. Unlike these other magazines, however, the *Literary World* was short-lived, its thirteen volumes covering only a seven-year period.[68] But at this time the general public was being stirred to a greater interest in painting, sculpture, and architecture by Ruskin's books, Powers' "Greek Slave," and Paxton's sensational Crystal Palace, opened in 1851. The *Literary World* was therefore as much exploiting public taste as shaping it.

The activities of American artists, especially those working abroad, were frequently noticed. The *World's* sources of information were extensive and included a number of foreign publications. A sample news item, from which the longer entries have been deleted, is quite typical of the manner in which this periodical kept its readers informed, week after week:

LEUTZE, who was to have returned to America this summer, has postponed his visit until autumn. He has been somewhat interrupted in his pursuits by the political difficulties which for a year or two past have disturbed the community of Dusseldorf. He has just finished his picture of the "Attainder of Stafford" for the Art-Union, which is now on its way to this country.

CHAPMAN is still in Paris, from which city he has already sent hither several excellent copies of well-known masterpieces of the Dutch School.

68. Surveys of the *Literary World* may be found in Mott, pp. 766-68, and in George E. Mize, "The Contributions of Evert A. Duyckinck," pp. 108-79.

Unless noted otherwise, all of the articles cited throughout this section appeared in the *Literary World*.

THE troubles in Italy have driven many American artists from their residences in that country. It is believed, however, that BROWN, the landscape painter, and TERRY, still remain in Rome or its vicinity, although nothing has been heard from them of late.

HICKS is in Paris. . . .[69]

Abrupt, skimpy, ephemeral—these miscellanies still served their purpose.[70]

Special articles on the fine arts were abundant. Though a number of these were reprints, the majority were anonymous contributions by staff and correspondents, who found interesting topics in the work of Evert Duyckinck's friends Page and Mount, the structure and functions of the National Academy, and the choice of William Henry Powell to decorate the Rotunda in the Capitol.[71] A few essays ran serially[72] and readers could always count on regular discussion of the American Art-Union, because Evert Duyckinck was a member of its Committee of Management. In fact, the Art-Union's debt to Duyckinck and his magazine was acknowledged by Prosper Montgomery Wetmore, one of its presidents, in several letters.[73]

69. "Movements of Artists," V (Aug. 11, 1849), 113.

70. For items pertaining to the activities of American artists at home, see "The Fine Arts," I (Feb. 6, 1847), 16; "Fine Art Gossip," III (March 11, 1848), 106-7; "Fine Art Intelligence," IV (March 10, 1849), 228-29; "The Fine Arts," VI (Jan. 5, 1850), 16; "Fine Arts," VIII (Jan. 18, 1851), 51; "Movements of Artists, &c.," IX (Dec. 13, 1851), 471-72; "Horatio Greenough," XI (Dec. 25, 1852), 409; "Miscellany and Gossip," XII (March 5, 1853), 196. American artists working abroad are discussed in "Fine Art Gossip," II (Oct. 2, 1847), 205; "American Artists in Italy, &c.," IV (May 26, 1849), 458; "Miscellany and Gossip," XII (Feb. 19, 1853), 153-54, a reprint; "Miscellany and Gossip," XII (July 2, 1853), 534, a reprint.

71. See respectively "Page's Ruth," II (Oct. 9, 1847), 231; "Long Island Mount," VI (March 9, 1850), 227; "The National Academy of Design.—Some Account of Its History and Objects," VIII (April 26, 1851), 341; "The Fine Arts," I (March 20, 1847), 159. The following articles are typical in their diversity of subject matter. "A Pair of Landscapes. By Durand," I (Feb. 6, 1847), 15-16; "American Medals," I (April 10, 1847), 233-34; "Mr. Deas. (from a Correspondent)," I (April 24, 1847), 280; G. H. Calvert, "The Process of Sculpture," II (Sept. 18, 1847), 159-60; "How to Learn to Draw," III (Feb. 12, 1848), 29-30; "Church Architecture. Grace Church, Newark, N.J.," III (Oct. 14, 1848), 733-34; "The Clinton Monument," IV (Jan. 13, 1849), 34-35; L. L. Noble, "Cole's Dream of Arcadia," V (Sept. 19, 1849), 277-78; "Mr. Darley's Outlines of Sleepy Hollow," VI (Jan. 12, 1850), 39; "Opening of the Crystal Palace," XII (July 23, 1853), 571.

72. See Athenian's "Remarks on the Fine Arts" in Vol. II and "Architectonics, by an Architect" in Vols. III and IV.

73. See Mize, p. 280.

Reviews of paintings exhibited in New York City and elsewhere comprised the strongest department of the fine arts in the magazine. Noticing almost every picture in the catalogues of the National Academy of Design and the American Art-Union, reviewers for the *Literary World* stressed the technical aspects of a painting more than its sublimity or national sentiment. This was a difficult task for a literary magazine. As one reviewer noted, it is harder to judge painting than poetry, the former demanding a knowledge of its "peculiar science" that only special training can give.[74]

The tone of all reviews was usually frank and sometimes amusing. For example, "The Blacksmiths," a painting by J. W. Glass, drew forth this comment:

Mr. Glass, there was a screw loose somewhere in your noodle when you composed this picture. We lay a wager of a half pint of potatoes that you were never inside of a country Blacksmith's shop, or never had a horse of your own "shod" by a bona fide blacksmith. If you did, you never sat upon his back (meaning the horse) while he was undergoing the operation, particularly if you had to ride in through so low a doorway—did you now? besides you never saw a blacksmith's shop with so many, and such shaped windows. It is all wrong, from beginning to end. . . . When you paint another blacksmith's shop, study it in one, and not in your own studio.[75]

A combination of good-natured earnestness, competence, and common sense placed these reviews among the best of the period.[76]

74. "The Exhibition of the National Academy," I (May 8, 1847), 323.

75. "Exhibition at the National Academy," I (May 29, 1847), 397.

76. "The greatest possible favor one can do for a friend is to remind him, in a friendly manner, of his faults, with a view to their correction . . ." ("The Fine Arts," I [April 17, 1847], 256).

Reviews in the *Literary World* of annual exhibitions in New York are listed in Appendix II. Reviews of special exhibitions also appeared quite frequently: "The Fine Arts," I (June 12, 1847), 448, a review of an exhibition at the Philadelphia Academy; "The Fine Arts," II (Sept. 4, 1847), 112, on Powers' "Greek Slave"; "Exhibition of Paintings at the Brooklyn Institute," II (Nov. 27, 1847), 405-6; "The Cole Exhibition," III (April 8, 1848), 186-87; "The Cole Exhibition. Second Notice," III (April 15, 1848), 207-8; "Messrs. Goupil, Vibert & Co.'s Exhibition," III (June 10, 1848), 367; "Lyceum Gallery—Old Masters," IV (March 10, 1849), 227-28; "The Dusseldorf Pictures," IV (April 28, 1849), 376-77; "Exhibition of Powers' Works," V (Oct. 13, 1849), 318; "Messrs. Goupil, Vibert & Co.'s Exhibition," V (Nov. 10, 1849), 407; "The Huntington Gallery," VI (Feb. 16, 1850), 156-57; "Exhibition of the Royal

Two facts lessened the importance of the *Literary World*'s influence on the progress of American art. In the first place, this magazine was not long-lived enough to make an indelible impression. Secondly, it had no illustrations. For these reasons the *Literary World* was, in the light of this study, inferior to both the *Mirror* and *The Knickerbocker*. But by temporarily sustaining interest in the fine arts at the turn of the half-century, the *Literary World* made way for the appearance of *The Crayon* in 1855; therein lies its importance.

Other Magazines

Several other literary periodicals deserve mention for promoting the fine arts in America. Of these, only *The Columbian Lady's and Gentleman's Magazine* (1844-49), edited by John Inman, contained notable engravings. Henry J. Sadd executed many of the plates, a number of which were mezzotints. Artists included the Americans Daniel Huntington, John G. Chapman, and Henry Inman (the editor's brother), as well as British, Dutch, French, and Spanish painters. Tompkins H. Matteson contributed designs of scenes from the works of Irving and Cooper; there were some "borrowed" landscapes after Bartlett, and portraiture was well represented. Since the pages of *The Columbian* were not large, the subject matter of its illustrations was somewhat restricted; and unlike the *Mirror* it was never able successfully to publish plates based on multi-figured paintings such as "The Battle of Bunker's Hill" by Trumbull. In spite of this limitation its engravings covered a wide range of genres for the period.

Excellent reviews characterized *The American Monthly Magazine* (1833-38) and *The Corsair* (1839-40), although both of these periodicals contained other material on the fine arts.[77] Two of *The American*

Academy," VI (June 15, 1850), 593-95; VI (June 22, 1850), 617-18, a reprint; "Panorama of Pilgrim's Progress," VII (Dec. 7, 1850), 460; "Professor Sattler's Cosmoramas," VIII (Jan. 11, 1850), 31; "Mr. Healey's Webster and the Senate Chamber," IX (Oct. 11, 1851), 290; "Leutze's Washington Crossing the Delaware," IX (Oct. 18, 1851), 311; "The Washington Exhibition," XII (March 12, 1853), 212-13.

77. See, for example, in *The* (New York) *American Monthly Magazine*: [Charles Fraser], "An Essay on the Condition of the Art of Painting in the United States of America," VI (Nov., 1835), 213-20; VI (Dec., 1835), 241-47; F., "The Sister Arts; or, Poetry, Painting, and Sculpture," VIII (Oct., 1836), 357-67. Examples of art-material

Monthly's four editors were associated with artists, and these connections are reflected on its pages. The first of these editors was Henry William Herbert, better known to his readers as "Frank Forester," an Englishman by birth, a Knickerbocker by adoption. Herbert was a close friend of the painter Henry Inman; both were members of "a famous piscatorial club," and at one time Herbert purportedly "entertained a tender passion" for Inman's daughter.[78] Herbert probably wrote all the art reviews in the magazine's first four volumes;[79] when he left the periodical in 1835, the task was apparently taken over by Charles Fenno Hoffman, the associate editor.[80] A member of The Sketch Club and a friend of the painter Christopher P. Cranch, Hoffman was well equipped to judge the merits of contemporary art. His characterization of Thomas Doughty's method as the "tea-tray style" is still remembered.[81] Whether written by Herbert or Hoffman, reviews in *The American Monthly Magazine* were both judicious and detailed. For this reason they have been listed in Appendix II.

The Corsair, edited by N. P. Willis and Dr. T. O. Porter, lasted only one year, but during that time it contained some of the best art reviews of the period. While in England, Willis had hired William Makepeace Thackeray to write epistolary sketches of France for this journal at a guinea a column.[82] Two of Thackeray's eight letters were reviews of collections in the Louvre, the Luxembourg, and the Ecole des Beaux Arts, in which Thackeray not only humorously

---

in *The Corsair* were "The Studio of Thorwaldsen," I (May 16, 1839), 6; "The Pencil of Nature," I (April 13, 1839), 70-72; "Mr. Sully's Portrait of the Queen," I (June 15, 1839), 219; "American Rural Architecture," I (June 29, 1839), 249; "Fine Arts," I (July 6, 1839), 270; "Recollections of a Portrait Painter," I (Nov. 23, 1839), 581-83; "Pictures by the Daguerrotype," I (Feb. 22, 1840), 794; "Salvator Rosa; or the Two Portraits," I (Feb. 29, 1840), 801-3.

78. See David W. Judd (ed.), *Life and Writings of Frank Forester (Henry William Herbert)*, I, 68-69, 70.

79. These reviews appeared under a column entitled "Miscellaneous Notices," the authorship of which has been attributed to Herbert for all numbers in volumes I to IV (1833-February, 1835) inclusive. See William M. Van Winkle and David A. Randall (compilers), *Henry William Herbert [Frank Forester]: A Bibliography of His Writings: 1832-1858*, pp. 126-34.

80. *Ibid.*, p. 134.

81. See, for instance, Oliver Larkin, *Art and Life in America*, p. 201.

82. Beers, pp. 253-54.

satirized such fictional characters as the Duchess of Dash and the Rev. James Asterisk but also seriously praised such real people as the artists Delacroix, Delaroche, Vernet, and Poussin. With his characteristic gift for exaggeration, Thackeray exploded the "humbugs" of neoclassic and neo-Christian paintings, complimented the French people for giving their artists higher social status than that enjoyed by English painters, and denied that violent subject matter necessarily produced sublimity in works of art.[83] In all, his lively and outspoken approach to his topic furnished American readers with a useful introduction to French paintings.

Willis' own art reviews in *The Corsair* were unique, because they rejected the serious style of many Knickerbocker reviews for the familiar approach of the personal essay. After the fashion of *Noctes Ambrosianae* Willis cast one review[84] into dialogue form, consisting of witty conversation between himself and his fellow editor T. O. Porter, whom Willis addressed as "dear Doctor":

> Do you see any picture that strikes your eye particularly, dear Doctor?
> "I was thinking of buying Weir's picture of the Indian Captives, and cutting it in two. I think the savage and his fellow prisoner, taken separately, a perfect and beautiful poem—but there are some staggering anachronisms in the rest of the picture which I cannot get over."
> Yes . . . Mr. Weir should have consulted the Professor of History at West Point for his proprieties of time—but how beautifully it is painted! —that fault aside![85]

But a comparison of this review to one published a few weeks earlier reveals that Willis wrote much better without a frame of dialogue.

83. T. T. [William Makepeace Thackeray], "A Ramble in the Picture-Galleries. By the Author of 'The Yellowplush Correspondence,' the 'Memoirs of Major Gahagan, &c.,'" *The Corsair*, I (Dec. 28, 1839), 665-67; M. A. T. [William Makepeace Thackeray], "A Ramble in the Picture Galleries. By the Author of the Yellowplush Correspondence, &c. &c.," *The Corsair*, I (Jan. 18, 1840), 716-17.

84. [Nathaniel Parker Willis], "The Gallery," *The Corsair*, I (May 18, 1839), 152-53. Internal evidence consisting of an allusion to his friendship with Francis Alexander makes it possible to attribute this review to Willis: "I will ask *Alexander*, who has made this most artist-like and skilful picture of his wife, to give us with as much art, the face with which he and I travelled to Venice in company. (Remind me to tell you about her, dear Doctor!)" (*idem*, I, 153).

85. *Ibid.*, p. 153.

By substituting apostrophe for this device, rigorously selecting his materials, and infusing all with whimsicality and humor, Willis achieved something new in the technique of picture-reviewing. Like any true informal essayist, he was extremely subjective. His readers, entering into the spirit of the piece as they strolled vicariously through the galleries of the National Academy, could see his personality unfold as he exclaimed:

Very well, indeed, Mr. Inman! Bishop Croswell to the life, and a good picture.

Signor Gamba[r]della, "Caius Gracchus" should be obliged to you. You have lent him a good face, (which you had a right to do, as it was your own) and the flesh is as warm as my hand. . . . I should like to be acquainted with "number 206!" A capital piece of coloring, and only one defect in the picture:—Pray, *Signor mio*, why should this fair creature's right arm be Siamesed to her left hand?

Oh stately and most admirable No. 195! Spirit, energy, and *maintien* personified. A painter after my own heart is Mr. Page, and here stands a theme fit for Titian, done in a manner most Titianesque and masterly. . . .

"Portia," "swallowed fire," and Signor Gamba[r]della probably wished her well over it, for No. 238, done for Portia, looks as if she were holding ice in her mouth. Otherwise a fair dame, fairly tinted.

What could be His Excellency Gov. Mason's fancy, for being *done* in his flannel shirt? "God bless my soul? [*sic*]" as old Matthias used to say, that one of the most gentlemanly-looking of men in real life, should in his picture remind one of a butcher stripp'd for slaughter. I would not willingly be *done* by "A. Smith!"

Pray, No. 11, what may be the *superfluous* length of your left leg? That large wen on your calf, it strikes me, should produce some contraction, yet clearly you have a *foot* to spare.

"Mine host" done to the life, in Hite's miniature, and three sweet children, done to the life too. . . .

My dear Powell, that picture of our friend Alban Smith, I see by the catalogue belongs to yourself. Keep it, at least, till you are quite sure you have done something better. If I had achieved a thing as good as that, I would not lose sight of it for a gold pallette.

Col. Stone looks as if he were pleased at sitting down on something warm. There is an animal extacy [*sic*] in the upturned roll of the eyes, as if he were looking round to thank some fat old lady for having taken off the chill from his chair. Is it so, Col, or is there a litter of puppies under you? I will never believe Page painted that picture!

Thanks, Doughty, for another leaf out of Paradise. "Returning from School" is your best work, hitherto, to my liking.

Here is a good thing! How complete is that boy's attention to his book. "Portraits of Brothers by Freeman." I shall look out next year for Mr. Freeman's work.

. . . Cut off 180's head, set it in a deep round frame, and you would scarce find a more adorable image of delicacy of skin and beauty of contour. What a pity the bust spoils it.

I presume the gentleman done in the scarlet cravat either cut his throat or designs to. There should be some meaning in such a monstrosity. . . .

Pictures enough for one day. I'll see the remainder tomorrow.[86]

Is this impressionism? Certainly, but also a useful method of exposing the faults, emphasizing the merits, and predicting the possibilities of paintings without angering the artists, boring the public, and damn-

86. [Nathaniel Parker Willis], "Pencil Notes on a First Visit to the Gallery," *The Corsair*, I (May 4, 1839), 121-22. The correct titles of the paintings and the full names of their artists, determined through *NADER*, are given here in the order followed by Willis: Henry Inman, "Portrait of the Rev. H. Croswell"; Spiridione Gambardella, "Caius Gracchus"; Spiridione Gambardella, "A Young Lady" (No. 206); William Page, "Portrait of a Lady" (No. 195); Spiridione Gambardella, "Portia" (No. 238); Allan Smith, Jr., "Sketch, His Excellency Stevens T. Mason"; C. Dorratt, "Portrait of Col. C. Ming"; George H. Hite, "Frame of Miniature Por[trai]ts"; William H. Powell, "Portrait of Professor Alban G. Smith"; William Page, "Portrait of Col. Stone"; Thomas Doughty, "Landscape, Returning from School"; James E. Freeman, "Portraits of Brothers"; Charles C. Ingham, "Portrait of a Lady" (No. 180). The portrait of "the gentleman . . . in the scarlet cravat" is not identifiable.

The antecedents of this light manner appear in Willis' earlier reviews for *The* (Boston) *American Monthly Magazine*, of which he was sole editor: "We meant to have given a sketchy glance at the Gallery of Pictures just opened at the Athenaeum, but we are at the end of our tether. . . . To look at the Pictures, after a day or two, is the least object of visiting the Gallery. It is a kind of fashionable Exchange, where, in the Spring dearth of parties, gentlemen and ladies come to refresh their memories with each other's faces. The light is very becoming there, and the gray floor cloth is a dainty relief for the foot. . . . Oh, there's nothing like it! The 'premature white hat' of the beau, and the light straw of the belle, are sported first at the Gallery. Misses in teens hang a glass at their belts, and take there the first lesson in near-sightedness. Idle men come there to lounge, impudent men to stare, Editors to refresh their bleared een and get matter for articles . . . ([Nathaniel Parker Willis], "The Editor's Table," pp. 147-48).

Thomas Doughty
IN NATURE'S WONDERLAND
(*The Detroit Institute of Arts*)

Thomas Kelah Wharton

NEW YORK FROM BROOKLYN HEIGHTS
(*The New-York Mirror*, 1834)

Asher B. Durand

DELAWARE WATER-GAP
(*The New-York Mirror*, 1834)

ing the nation. In the hands of a craftsman like Willis this blending of familiarity and perception could have been a means of educating Americans or, better yet, of enticing them to exhibitions, where they could judge for themselves. Here was constructive romanticism at its best: subjectivity with a purpose. Unfortunately *The Corsair* sank after a year's voyage, and the familiar review went down with it.

The Close of the Period

In the 1850's two more literary journals—*Putnam's Monthly Magazine* (1853-57)[87] and *Harper's New Monthly Magazine* (1850-current)—[88] arose to bring art to the public; but their influence was overshadowed in this decade by *The Crayon* (1855-61), America's first real art magazine.[89] Edited by John Durand and William J. Stillman, *The Crayon* contained all the departments of art intelligence that had been pioneered by literary magazines, although it had no illustra-

87. Following are the leading articles on the fine arts that appeared in *Putnam's Monthly Magazine* before 1856: "Our Crystal Palace," II (Aug., 1853), 121-29; "On the Gothic Style in the Fine Arts," II (Aug., 1853), 191-94; "The Great Exhibition and Its Visitors," II (Dec., 1853), 577-93; "John Vanderlyn," III (June, 1854), 593-95; "Fine Arts," IV (Aug., 1854), 231-32; "Fine Arts," IV (Nov., 1854), 568; "Original Portraits of Washington," VI (Oct., 1855), 337-49. Excellent illustrations accompanied essays on the architecture of New York City: "Educational Institutions of New York," II (July, 1853), 1-16; "New-York Church Architecture," II (Sept., 1853), 233-48; "Public Buildings of New-York," III (Jan., 1854), 10-15; "Places of Public Amusement: Theatres and Concert Rooms," III (Feb., 1854), 141-52; "New-York Daguerreotyped: Private Residences," III (March, 1854), 233-48. In addition to those reviews listed below in Appendix II, there was a review of an exhibition in Boston: "The Athenaeum Exhibition at Boston," VI (Sept. 1855), 331-33.

88. Although it began three years earlier than *Putnam's, Harper's New Monthly Magazine* had published fewer articles on the fine arts by the end of 1855: "Story of Rembrandt," IV (March, 1852), 516-19; Benjamin J. Lossing, "Monticello," VII (July, 1853), 145-61; "A Visit to Overbeck's Studio in the Cenci Palace," VIII (Dec., 1853), 87-92. Departments entitled "Literary Notices," "Monthly Record of Current Events," "Editor's Drawer," and "Editor's Easy Chair" contained occasional remarks on art and artists. See especially I (Sept., 1850), 573-74; II (Feb., 1851), 417; III (Nov., 1851), 850; VII (Sept., 1853), 556; VII (Nov., 1853), 843-44; IX (July, 1854), 260-61; IX (Nov., 1854), 850-51. Some essays on native scenery were accompanied by woodcuts: "Niagara," VII (Aug., 1853), 289-305, and the following series written and illustrated by T. Addison Richards: "The Landscape of the South," VI (May, 1853), 721-33; "Lake George," VII (July, 1853), 161-70; "The Susquehanna," VII (Oct., 1853), 613-23; "The Catskills," IX (July, 1854), 145-58.

89. A sketch of *The Crayon* is in David H. Dickason, *The Daring Young Men: The Story of the American Pre-Raphaelites*, pp. 47-64.

tions. In spite of this one shortcoming and the fact that the magazine was, to quote young Durand, "a Quixotic undertaking"[90] and a financial failure, it filled a great need. "We shall speak of the pictures as we get leisure to see them," *The Home Journal* told its readers when faced with the task of reviewing the National Academy's annual show. "But we are glad that the Arts have now a professed organ of their own. THE CRAYON will tell us what they themselves have to say of the Exhibition. We shall look to that for a critical estimate of what is there."[91] *The Crayon* disseminated the gospel of art with greater effect than any single literary journal could have claimed. Yet *The Crayon* itself was in part a literary magazine: it not only printed miscellaneous selections from Willis, Irving, Cox, and other writers but also ran a series of articles on such landscape poets as Bryant and Street.[92] Before, literary magazines had dabbled in the fine arts; now an art magazine was dabbling in literature—proving simply that literature and art were as inseparable in journalism as they were in other phases of Knickerbocker life.

90. Durand, *A. B. Durand*, p. 189.
91. "National Academy of Design," *The Home Journal*, March 24, 1855.
92. G. M. James, "The Landscape Element in American Poetry," *The Crayon*, I (Jan. 3, 1855), 3-4; I (Jan. 17, 1855), 39-40; I (March 24, 1855), 179-80.

CHAPTER IV

PIONEERING

FOR THE LANDSCAPE PAINTER

The advent of the Hudson River School, America's first group of landscape painters, cannot be fixed any earlier than 1825, the year of Thomas Cole's arrival in New York.[1] By 1835 Cole had earned his reputation, but reviewers were also praising the landscapes of Weir, Harvey, Bennett, Hill, and Chapman, and would soon be congratulating Durand for switching to this branch of art. By 1845 landscape painting was decidedly popular. Examining the list of pictures hung in the exhibition of the National Academy for that year, we find scenes painted by Church, Kensett, Cropsey, and Inness, as well as many lesser artists. The Hudson River School had grown noticeably in membership and fame since its birth in 1825.

But the Knickerbockers, although themselves by no means the first American writers to utilize landscape in their works, had antici-

1. Frederick A. Sweet, *The Hudson River School and the Early American Landscape Tradition*, pp. 12, 56.

pated these painters by almost a quarter of a century. *Salmagundi* (1807) and *A History of New York* (1809) contained rhapsodies to nature which were especially apparent against the general pattern of satire in these books. In *The Backwoodsman* (1818) Paulding used panoramic settings for dramatic effects, and by so doing paid tribute to the vastness of American scenery. Drake, Halleck, Woodworth, and Sands also wrote about nature at this time, but the most consistent celebrators of landscape before 1825 were, of course, Bryant and Cooper. Although nature would find even more devotees among the writers in the second quarter of the century, it is clear that she already had many literary admirers.

In their anticipation of the Hudson River School, the Knickerbockers were actually cultural explorers who, by announcing their own discoveries of the American landscape in glowing terms, prepared the way for future settlements by native painters and urged the public to accept these enterprises. The writers effected this result by (1) explaining that the study and portrayal of nature has religious, therapeutic, and didactic values, (2) pointing out the merits of American scenery and finding remedies for its defects, and (3)—a more direct method than the first two—praising the landscape painters in magazines, books, orations, and letters. Much of the acclaim won by the Hudson River School should be attributed to these efforts.

The Power of Nature

Of course, the Knickerbockers were not the first to proclaim the discovery of nature's values. This had already been a pronounced feature of English and continental romanticism. In France Rousseau had exalted nature as the very essence of his primitivistic philosophy. In England as early as the first quarter of the eighteenth century, such poets as John Philips, Lady Winchilsea, Thomas Parnell, and William Pattison occasionally described nature as a powerful teacher and healer and, to a lesser extent, as a spiritual force. These metrical whispers culminated in James Thomson's *The Seasons* (1726-30), the first effective expression of nature's power in English literature. The poets who followed Thomson—John Dyer, Mark Akenside, James Beattie, and William Cowper, to name a few—repeated and amplified this message in many ways, but none so well as William Wordsworth, in whom nature found her most articulate champion.

Obviously influenced by this tradition as well as by their own environment, the Knickerbockers transmitted a similar message and therefore deserve a goodly share of the credit for popularizing nature in America. Perhaps they made their most extravagant claim for the study of nature by equating it with religious exercise. They denied that worship is appropriately conducted only in churches, for they agreed with Archibald Alison's *Essay on . . . Taste* (1790) that nature is "the temple of the LIVING GOD, in which praise is due, and where service is to be performed."[2] If they had a chief druid, it was Bryant. "The groves were God's first temples," he wrote in "A Forest Hymn." He saw no reason why they should not continue as such for the people of his own century: "As now they stand, massy, and tall, and dark, / Fit shrine for humble worshipper to hold Communion with his Maker."[3] Nor did Bryant limit his outlook to trees, groves, and forests: "The Prairies" and "A Hymn of the Sea" prove that he considered almost all of nature to be spiritually adaptable.[4] Second only to Bryant in consistently spiritualizing nature was Cooper, who found it impossible to look at certain scenes without deep reverence[5] and a firm conviction that the finest "stimulant for religious meditation" was a panoramic view of God's earth.[6] For here was "the immediate presence of the majesty of the Creator."[7] Thus, a Sunday of strolling among Italian ruins became for Cooper a "Sabbath of nature,"[8] and engaging in *"low-country pursuits"* at such a time smacked

2. P. 461.

3. *Poetical Works*, I, 130-31.

4. For his prose statements of these ideas, see William Cullen Bryant, "Lake George," NYM, I (Dec. 20, 1823), 164-65, and *Letters of a Traveller*, p. 97.

5. James Fenimore Cooper, *Excursions in Switzerland*, p. 41.

6. Cooper, *Gleanings in Europe: Italy*, I, 231.

7. James Fenimore Cooper, *The Headsman*, I, viii. Also see James Fenimore Cooper, "Preface to the Leather-Stocking Tales," *James Fenimore Cooper: Representative Selections*, pp. 307-8.

8. Cooper, *Gleanings in Europe: Italy*, I, 233.

of sacrilege.[9] Willis, another druid, entertained similar motives for observing a Sabbath in nature's "vast cathedral": "The Hudson a broad aisle, the Highlands a thunder-choir and gallery, Black Rock a pulpit, and a blue dome over all—and lo! Nature, in her surplice of summer, ready to preach the sermon! Why not do my worshipping out of doors?"[10] If Irving Babbitt had read these words and found in them a vile romantic attempt to replace religion,[11] he would have been wrong; for generally the Knickerbockers used nature to supplement rather than supplant formal religion in their lives.

While all of nature was a grand cathedral to these men, no spot was more appropriate for religious ecstasy than Niagara Falls. The earliest visitors to the falls, those who had gone there in the seventeenth and eighteenth centuries, had sometimes let feelings of intense discomfort smother their spiritual impulses,[12] but nineteenth-century visitors often translated the horrible din of this chaotic scene into the voice of their Creator. Willis Gaylord Clark's retelling of the experience was typical of the new attitude: "You stand beneath the rushing tributes from a hundred lakes; you seem to hear the wailings of imprisoned spirits, until, fraught and filled with the spirit of the scene, you exclaim—THERE IS A GOD!—and this vast cataract, awful, overpowering as it is, is but a play-thing in his hand!"[13] To discover literary manifestations of druidism, the curious reader should limit himself neither to "writers from the falls" nor to such major figures as Bryant and Cooper, however, for the idea permeated the works of almost every member of the New York group.[14] It was

9. Cooper, *Excursions in Switzerland*, p. 143.

10. Willis, *Out-Doors at Idlewild*, p. 28.

11. See his *Rousseau and Romanticism*, p. 304.

12. For a general survey of native reactions to Niagara Falls, see Paul H. Shepard, Jr., "American Attitudes toward the Landscape in New England and the West, 1830-1870," pp. 14, 36-41.

13. [Willis Gaylord Clark], "Ollapodiana," *K*, VIII (Oct., 1836), 469. Other effusions of this type were "Niagara," *NYM*, I (June 19, 1824), 376; Horace Dresser, "To Niagara," *K*, XXIX (May, 1847), 412; and M'Donald Clarke, "Niagara," *Poems of M'Donald Clarke*, pp. 198-99.

14. Druidism appears in Washington Irving, "A Tour on the Prairies," in *The Crayon Miscellany*, pp. 42-43. For Paulding, see Amos Herold, *James Kirke Paulding, Versatile American*, pp. 123-26; W. I. Paulding, *Literary Life of James K. Paulding*, pp. 31-33. For Alfred B. Street, see *The Home Book of the Picturesque*, p. 163. Further

reinforced, moreover, by a corollary which emphasized nature's roles as healer and teacher.

The Knickerbockers also pointed out the value of nature's therapeutic and didactic powers, an idea based primarily on the benefits of romantic escape from the stifling world of mammonism and clearly if not eloquently expressed in stanzas written by Alfred Billings Street:

> Nature is Man's best teacher. She unfolds
> Her treasures to his search, unseals his eye,
> Illumes his mind, and purifies his heart.
>
> . . . .
>
> Rest yields she to the "weary" of the earth—
> Its "heavy-laden" she endows with strength.
>
> . . . .
>
> And Nature teaches us Philosophy;
> In the quick shading of her brilliant morn
> By the dark storm-cloud; in the canker-spot
> That lurks within her blushing fragrant rose,
>
> . . . .
>
> She warns how full of direct change is life,
> How perishing our sweetest, brightest joys,
> How oft death lays our dearest feelings waste
> And makes existence cold and desolate.
> But oh! she teaches also blessed Hope;
>
> . . . .
>
> In the light seed that cradles the green plant—
> In the bright sun succeeding the dark night—
> In blue-eyed Spring, that plants her violets
> Within departing Winter's melting snows.
>
> And—holier theme—she teaches us of God,
>
> . . . .

---

expressions of the druidical urge were Mrs. Mary E. Hewitt, "Lines Written in the Notch of the White Mountains," *Arcturus*, III (Feb., 1842), 223-25; F, "The Forest Temple," *The* (New York) *American Monthly Magazine*, II (Dec., 1833), 244; F., "View of New-York from Wehawk Heights," *NYM*, I (Sept. 27, 1823), 68-69; Anon., "American Scenery," *NYM*, I (June 26, 1824), 378; and H., "Nature's Temple," *K*, VII (Jan., 1836), 70.

She shows His awful power, yet tender care.
In the free sunlight—in the drooping clouds,
And changes of the seasons, she proclaims
His boundless goodness and exhaustless love.[15]

Nature as an outdoor clinic and schoolroom had appeared in the works of several other Knickerbocker writers[16] but was treated most extensively in verses by Bryant, the foremost American spokesman for this idea, who, more than any other literary figure in the United States, taught men to go to nature for physical, mental, and spiritual health. This was the message not only of "Thanatopsis," "Green River," "A Forest Hymn," and "Inscription for the Entrance to a Wood," but also of such lesser-known pieces as "The Early Anemone," "The Old Man's Counsel," "The Gladness of Nature," "Autumn Woods," "A Summer Ramble," and "Lines on Revisiting the Country."

Literature lent itself more readily to the task of explaining nature's values than did the fine arts. If the pen is not mightier than the brush, it does at least teach more directly. The essential difference between these mediums is clearly seen in a comparison of Bryant's "To a Waterfowl" and Thomas Doughty's "In Nature's Wonderland." As Edgar Richardson has pointed out, the works resemble each other in several ways.[17] In both painting and poem the civilized world is practically absent; nothing remains but all-important nature. With its "boundless sky" and "abyss of heaven" it fascinates and overwhelms the human intruder, who in Doughty's picture stands with gun in hand, reminding us of the "fowler" introduced by Bryant in his second stanza. Above all, the merit of each work is based chiefly on the effective communication of a solitary mood. Both artists also

15. "Nature," *The Poems of Alfred B. Street*, pp. 23-25.

16. See Irving, *Crayon Miscellany*, pp. 89-222; *Bracebridge Hall*, p. 107; William Irving *et al.*, *Salmagundi*, p. 323; Joseph R. Drake, "Bronx," in Taft, *Minor Knickerbockers*, p. 223; Willis, *Rural Letters*, pp. 244-46; Anon., "American Scenery," *NYM*, I (June 26, 1824), 378; Jonathan, "The Wilderness," *NYM*, II (Aug. 28, 1824), 40; Anon., "Nature's Teachings," *K*, XIX (April, 1842), 322-23; Park Benjamin, "Spring's Advent," *Poems of Park Benjamin*, pp. 108-9.

17. Richardson, *Painting in America*, p. 157.

employ dramatic figures, Doughty's woodsman placed solidly in the center of the middle distance and bathed in a strong light, Bryant himself stepping into his poem's last stanza to reveal that, like the waterfowl, he will rely on God's guidance "in the long way" that he "must tread alone." Yet in this very similarity lies the difference between not only these two works but also most paintings and poems. Doughty's dramatic figure is a figure only. He is inarticulate. Bryant's figure, on the other hand, is a dramatic speaker who can produce abstract ideas for immediate and direct conveyance to the reader. He says that he sees God in nature, and his audience quickly understands him, for his message is instantaneous. But Doughty's moralizing is restricted to impressions of solitude and awe in the face of nature's wonders—some part of even these ideas being conveyed by the engraved title on the frame rather than by the picture itself. If Doughty had wished to broaden his didacticism into lessons of divine presence, power, and guidance, he could have done so only indirectly through the imagination of his audience, which, if stimulated, might then have formulated these ideas.

Aware of the limitations of their medium but driven by the urge to celebrate nature's power, the painters either experimented with "before and after" canvases such as Cole's "Course of Empire" series, which will be discussed later, or temporarily abandoned the studio for the study or lecture hall. Washington Allston wrote among other things a long nature poem entitled "The Sylphs of the Seasons."[18] Thomas Cole, convinced like his friend Bryant of nature's religious, therapeutic, and didactic values,[19] gave vent to his literary impulses in lectures on American scenery and in poems such as "The Wild," which contains his wish

> To kneel in nature's everlasting dome,
> Where not the voice of feeble man does teach,
> But His, who in the rolling thunder speaks . . . .[20]

18. See especially Washington Allston, *Lectures on Art and Poems*, p. 205.
19. See LaBudde, pp. 60-64, 71-75.
20. Quoted in Noble, p. 64. Also see Thomas Cole, "Proceedings of the American Lyceum. Essay on American Scenery," *The* (New York) *American Monthly Magazine*, VII (Jan., 1836), 1-12.

William Dunlap, John Kenrick Fisher, and Charles Lanman also achieved a measure of success with their essays, poems, plays, and stories.[21]

But the professional writer was still needed to help condition the public to accepting nature and its painters. The artists could not rely solely on their own activities to propagate the gospel of spiritualized landscape, and their shifting from paint to print indicates that they knew where help could be found. The Knickerbockers responded by developing in their readers the habit of equating spiritual health and moral lessons with nature. When these readers took to strolling galleries, they easily detected on canvas the same God they had found on the page.

Dignifying the American Landscape

Pointing out the assets of American scenery and discovering remedies for its defects comprised the second method by which the Knickerbockers pioneered for the landscape artist. But before analyzing this contribution we must look briefly at the associational psychology popular at that time.

THE BACKGROUND OF AESTHETICS. Influenced by Scottish and English doctrines of taste as found in the imported works of Kames, Blair, Price, and Alison,[22] nineteenth-century Americans distinguished be-

21. See Charles L. Sanford, "The Concept of the Sublime in the Works of Thomas Cole and William Cullen Bryant," p. 436.

22. For the American influence of Lord Kames's (Henry Home's) *Elements of Criticism* (1762), Hugh Blair's *Lectures on Rhetoric and Belles Lettres* (1783), and Archibald Alison's *Essay on the Nature and Principles of Taste* (1790), see William Charvat, *The Origins of American Critical Thought*, pp. 27-58 and *passim*. For Bryant's acceptance of their theories, see Callow, "William Cullen Bryant." The influence of Alison on Bryant and Cole is discussed in Donald A. Ringe, "Kindred Spirits: Bryant and Cole," pp. 235-37, and Ralph N. Miller, "Thomas Cole and Alison's Essays on Taste," pp. 281-99. More sources for their ideas are given in Sanford, pp. 434-38. The American vogue of Uvedale Price, author of *Essay on the Picturesque* (1794, enlarged in 1796, reprinted in 1842), has not been thoroughly treated; but Price is mentioned along with other aestheticians by Agnes Addison, "Early American Gothic," in *Romanticism in America*, p. 120, and Shepard, pp. 18-20, 141-42, 151-52. Americans learned something about Price through Sir Walter Scott's praise of him in the *Quarterly Review*, easily accessible in the U.S. See Walter Scott, "On Ornamental Plantations and Landscape Gardening," pp. 302-44. American knowl-

tween the beautiful and the picturesque. Theological subtleties under-lay both categories. Beauty was earthly evidence of the harmony and order in the nature of God; picturesqueness was the manifestation of His tremendous power and creativeness.[23] Visual differences were also stressed: the beautiful embodies "simple and flowing forms," in architecture the Grecian temple; in landscape the placid, translucent lake, the smooth beech tree, grazing cattle, birds with unruffled plum-age, the shepherd or the city-dweller on an outing. The picturesque embraces "striking, irregular, spirited forms,"[24] in architecture the Gothic chapel; in landscape the waterfall and churning torrent, the gnarled and moss-covered oak, shaggy mountain goats, eagles, rob-bers, gypsies, or beggars.[25] Above all, the beautiful appealed primarily to man's intellect and was therefore classical; the picturesque directed itself chiefly to man's emotions and was therefore romantic.

A fashionable body of aesthetics commonly known as associational psychology supplemented these distinctions. Its principles were rather simple, resting at least with Archibald Alison, one of its popularizers, on a belief that aesthetic pleasure is a product of the mind. An object was beautiful or picturesque if mental connections with harmony and symmetry (in the first case) or with power and variety (in the second) made it so. One need only turn the pages of American and European novels, letters, journals, essays, and travel writings to discover the ubiquity of the word *association*, which, after all, was almost beauty in itself. One finds, however, this important difference: in the Old World, associations were frequently made with the past, especially with Hebraic, Grecian, and Roman cultures; in the New World, his-torical associations were just as popular but were supplemented with visions of the future. To the American an object was pleasing enough if it reminded him of ancient history, but was even more delight-ful if it hinted of his country's progress and coming-of-age.

edge of the Earl of Shaftesbury, and of Edmund Burke, William Gilpin, and William Combe (who created Dr. Syntax) is discussed in Hans Huth, *Nature and the Ameri-can*, pp. 10-13.

23. See C. E. Moore, *Backgrounds of English Literature, 1700-1760*, pp. 53-103.

24. A[ndrew]. J. Downing, *A Treatise on the Theory and Practice of Landscape Gardening*, p. 63.

25. See Uvedale Price, *Sir Uvedale Price on the Picturesque*, pp. 82-87.

Two other terms, the synonyms *grandeur* and *sublimity*, were commonly based on associations of size and terror. Actually they denoted superlative degrees of beauty and picturesqueness. If scenes, whether beautiful or picturesque, were monumental in their dimensions or infused one's mind with a sense of danger or awe, they were grand or sublime.[26] There was some diversity of opinion over the snowballing connotations of these terms, particularly over Edmund Burke's equation of terror and the sublime,[27] but the Knickerbockers usually subscribed to the definitions given here.

This body of aesthetics was especially suited to the environment of the United States. Had the word *picturesque* not been available for importation, Americans would have probably invented a similar term to express a new type of pleasure derived from the irregular and tangled mass, the kind of scenery America had in abundance. A new landscape aesthetics, not limited to the classical ideals of balance and finish, was needed to match it. Furthermore, the scenery of the United States, now that Americans had comparative leisure to appreciate it, was discovered to be of gigantic proportions, especially in the case of Niagara Falls. It also was capable of producing terror in some instances and was therefore sublime and grand. Moreover, it held interesting possible associations with past Indian civilizations and with future democratic triumphs. In short, European aesthetic doctrines were easily adapted to American scenery. A discussion of the Knickerbocker estimate of native landscape may be more profitably examined with this fact in mind.

DEFECTS AND MERITS OF THE AMERICAN LANDSCAPE. The writers of New York, especially Cooper, readily admitted that, compared with the scenery in Europe, native landscape had its shortcomings. The American spring was thought inferior to the same season abroad. American mountains lacked both grandeur and sublimity. Railroads, following the paths of convenience and utility, were likely to deprive the traveler

26. See Alison, pp. 192-94; Hugh Blair, *Lectures on Rhetoric and Belles Lettres*, p. 34; Edmund Burke, *A Philosophical Enquiry into the Origin of Our Ideas of the Sublime and Beautiful*, p. 124; Price, pp. 96-97.

27. See A. G. I., "Examination of Burke's Theory of the Sublime," *K*, II (Aug., 1833), 113-19.

of picturesque views. And the ubiquitous American fence was deemed a national eyesore, a waste of wood which should give way to the European hedge.[28] Furthermore, on this new continent, asked Cooper, where could one find a sky line of "gray, castellated outlines, and . . . walls of the middle ages . . . clustered around the high, pointed roofs and solemn towers of the church?" The American was more apt to detect "ill-shaped, and yet pretending cupolas, and other ambitious objects, half the time in painted wood, just peer[ing] above the village, . . . the most aspiring roof . . . almost invariably that of the tavern." To Cooper, this was "one of the hundred instances in which the thoughtful man finds reason to regret that the church, as it exists among us, is not really more Catholic."[29] Another defect noted by the Knickerbockers was the absence of picturesqueness in American waters and their banks.[30] But, more than anything else, native scenery lacked three very desirable assets—finish, associations, and ruins. It was, in the first place, raw and full of blemishes which naturally belong to a new country; time had not as yet eradicated its "girdled trees, . . . drowned woods, burnt or fallen stumps, rough enclosures, and stony land."[31] The seriousness of this charge is apparent in the fact that before George Inness' "Lackawanna Valley" (1855) almost no American painting depicted stump-filled scenes; even ploughed ground was not considered picturesque.[32] Secondly, there were no

28. Cooper, in *Home Book of the Picturesque*, pp. 61, 65-66, 53, *Home as Found*, I, 23, 126, *Wyandotte*, I, 9-10, *Notions of the Americans Picked up by a Travelling Bachelor*, I, 255-56; Anon., "Random Passages from Rough Notes . . . ," *K*, X (Nov., 1837), 395.

29. Cooper, in *Home Book of the Picturesque*, p. 69.

30. Cooper found American lakes inferior to those of Italy and Switzerland. He complained, too, of the unfinished character of American shores (*ibid.*, pp. 55, 57, 61-2). Willis observed that "the great defect in American Lakes, generally, is the vast, unrelieved expanse of water, without islands and promontories, producing a fatigue on the eye similar to that of the sea" (N. P. Willis, *American Scenery*, I, 136).

31. Willis, *American Scenery*, II, 26. Also see Willis, *Hurry-Graphs*, pp. 73-74, *Famous Persons and Places*, p. 136; James Fenimore Cooper, *Gleanings in Europe: Volume Two: England*, pp. 212-13, *Notions*, I, 254-55, *Chainbearer*, I, 89, "American and European Scenery Compared," in *Home Book of the Picturesque*, pp. 52, 54, 56.

32. See Shepard, p. 139; LaBudde, p. 141. Among the infrequent early attempts to represent such subjects are Thomas Cole's "The Notch of the White Mountains" (1839) and "Oxbow" (1836), and James Hope's "Bird Mountain, Castleton, Vermont" (1855).

associations to cover up these blemishes. Burns and Scott had transformed a treelessly desolate Scottish landscape into a picturesque region.[33] America needed just such champions for, as Willis remarked, a scene without associations is merely "enjoyable without being suggestive" and stimulates only the most ephemeral pleasures, leaving "the milk of thought too much agitated for the cream to rise."[34] Thirdly, the Knickerbockers noted that their country was sadly lacking in the ruins necessary to make it picturesque. Irving put it neatly when he excused an American (in this case, himself) for "being a little curious about antiquities, whose native land, unfortunately, cannot boast of a single ruin."[35] These were the limitations of American scenery.

But the Knickerbockers found merits to counterbalance nearly every blemish. The inferior American spring was compensated for by the superior American autumn, reputed to give "a gorgeousness to our scenery, which, in other countries, is but imagined in their visions of a fairy-land."[36] Bryant's praise of native mountains offset Cooper's lack of appreciation.[37] And railroads, once denounced as obstacles to the enjoyment of the picturesque, finally proved to be the very vehicles of it. This was especially true when in June of 1858 fifty artists and writers—including Durand, Willis, and Kensett—embarked on a five-day mass search for the picturesque at the invitation of the Baltimore and Ohio Railroad. The train for this excursion was lavishly fitted up with sofas, a piano, tables and desks, and even a special car for the photographers. The trip itself—from Baltimore to Wheeling and back—was deliberately slow-paced; the train often stopped so scenes could be sketched and photographed, and there was a side trip on a

33. Irving, *Crayon Miscellany*, p. 257.

34. Willis, *Rural Letters*, p. 348. Also see Willis, *Pencillings*, pp. 206-7, and *American Scenery*, II, 106; Grenville Mellen, "English Scenery," *The* (New York) *American Monthly Magazine*, X (Oct., 1837), 335-36; LaBudde, pp. 98-100; William M'Leod, "The Summer Tourist.—Scenery of the Franconia Mountains, N. H.," *Harper's New Monthly Magazine*, V (June, 1852), 11.

35. Irving, *Bracebridge Hall*, p. 15. Also see Shepard, pp. 71-82.

36. J. Houston Mifflin, "The Fine Arts in America, and Its Peculiar Incentives to Their Cultivation," *K*, II (July, 1833), 32. Also see "Fine Arts in America, *The* (New York) *American Monthly Magazine*, V (June, 1835), 318.

37. Bryant, *Letters of a Traveller*, p. 333, and *Orations*, p. 12.

steamboat. When the train climbed a steep mountain grade, the passengers rode on the cow-catcher in order to project themselves into the most thrilling views.[38] On the whole, this excursion was a clever bit of propaganda, but it was not the first time the railroad had been praised for giving new dimensions to landscape;[39] and the Knickerbockers had already included views of railroad bridges and trains in such works as *American Scenery* and *The Home Book of the Picturesque*.

Other indigenous assets were uncovered: American skies were pronounced more interesting than those of Italy,[40] American rivers worthy of notice from poet and painter,[41] and American scenery generally picturesque in its diversity,[42] grand in its immensity,[43] Niagara Falls being "unquestionably the sublimest thing in nature."[44] The highest praise came from Irving: "No, never need an American look beyond his own country for the sublime and beautiful of natural scenery."[45]

REMEDIES FOR THREE MAJOR DEFECTS. Three deficiencies in American scenery, however, were not so easily counterbalanced, and it became necessary for the writers to find remedies for a natural lack of polish, associations, and ruins. With the first problem they failed—the rawness of American topography could be overcome only by "time, numbers, and labor."[46] The painter and the poet as well as the public must be content to wait although at the same time envying the "re-

38. "Artists' Excursion over the Baltimore and Ohio Railroad," *Harper's New Monthly Magazine*, XIX (June, 1859), 1-19.

39. See "Scenery on the Erie Railroad," *Harper's New Monthly Magazine*, I (July, 1850), 213-15.

40. Bryant, *Letters of a Traveller*, p. 24; Willis, *Pencillings*, p. 66.

41. Cooper, in *Home Book of the Picturesque*, pp. 61-62; Willis, *Pencillings*, p. 36. See also "Random Passages from Rough Notes . . . ," *K*, X (Nov., 1837), 395.

42. Irving, in *Home Book of the Picturesque*, p. 74, and *The Sketch-Book*, pp. 16-17; "The Early Experiences of Ralph Ringwood," *Wolfert's Roost and Other Papers*, p. 295; Bryant, *Picturesque America*, I, iii, and *Orations*, p. 7; Mifflin, *K*, II, 32; Willis, *American Scenery*, I, 2.

43. Irving, *The Sketch-Book*, pp. 16-17, and *Crayon Miscellany*, p. 115.

44. Willis, *American Scenery*, I, 33, 4; Cooper, in *Home Book of the Picturesque*, p. 56.

45. Irving, *The Sketch-Book*, p. 17.

46. Cooper, in *Home Book of the Picturesque*, pp. 55-56.

fined ruralities" of England.[47] On the other hand, Bryant noted that the "tamings and softenings of cultivation" tended to "break up the unity" of nature and were little compensation for "a far-spread wildness, a look as if the new world was fresher from the hand of him who made it, the rocks and the very hillocks wearing the shapes in which he fashioned them, the waters flowing where he marked their channels, the forests, enriched with a new creation of trees, standing where he planted them; in short, . . . something which, more than any scenery . . . suggested the idea of unity and immensity, and abstracting the mind from the associations of human agency, carried it up to the idea of a mightier power. . . ."[48] Perhaps native scenery was more desirable, after all, in its pristine state. Of course, this kind of thinking could easily lead to conservationism, and perhaps it was what had lured Cooper into becoming one of the earliest Americans to reach that position. Yet Cooper knew as well as Bryant that this approach had to be modified, for nature was created to be used. Nevertheless this emphasis on the value of the pristine must have had a beneficial effect on American artists by inspiring them with a sense of urgency. "Yankee enterprise has little sympathy with the picturesque," warned the *Literary World*, "and it behooves our artists to rescue from its grasp the little that is left, before it is for ever too late."[49] Curiously enough, this same motive has inspired many a local colorist and folklorist in the nineteenth and twentieth centuries.

The second defect, a lack of associations, was cured more quickly than the first. The Knickerbockers themselves gilded the American landscape with quaint characters, supernatural lore, legend, and history. What reader of Irving, for instance, could think of the Catskills without remembering Rip Van Winkle, Ichabod Crane, Hendrik Hudson, and Dolph Heyliger?

Irving's magic wand indeed turned the Catskills . . . into fairy mountains. After Irving . . . there never again could be any thought of "uncouth"

47. Willis, *Famous Persons and Places*, p. 136.
48. William Cullen Bryant, "Preface" to [W. C. Bryant and A. B. Durand], *The American Landscape, No.. I*, p. 6. Also see Willis, *American Scenery*, I, 1; James Fenimore Cooper, *The Redskins*, I, 205, II, 169.
49. "Exhibition of the National Academy," *LW*, I (May 15, 1847), 348.

mountains, and the "howling wilderness" of the seventeenth century was discarded forever. Irving had made an enormous advance toward bridging the gap which still existed between man and nature, though it was growing narrower from generation to generation. These were entirely new vistas Irving had opened up, and, as if responding to his call, artists began to people the amphitheater of the Catskills and the banks of the Hudson.[50]

And so did Irving's fellow authors. Joseph Rodman Drake filled Crow Nest with fairies in "The Culprit Fay"; Bryant contributed a lover's leap in "Monument Mountain"; Paulding invested Buttermilk Hill with the marvelous tale of Cobus Yerks and the hitchhiking dogghost; and N. P. Willis fashioned *American Scenery* and its companion gift book *Canadian Scenery* into vast literary storehouses of new associations for the American continent—items "which history . . . [had] not yet found leisure to put into form, and which romance and poetry . . . [had] not yet appropriated."[51]

Even while this exploitation of the past was being carried out, the Knickerbockers turned to a different kind of association, a mental connection with the future. At its most materialistic level this way of thinking was no more than the sort of real-estate speculation expected to arise in a new world, and it was already a part of American literature, stretching back as far as Captain John Smith and Thomas Morton. Perhaps it was best described by Willis, who observed that the American often looks at a scene without inquiring into its antiquity. "Instead . . . he sits over the fire with his paper and pencil, and calculates what the population will be in ten years, how far they will spread, what the value of the neighbouring land will become, and whether the stock of some canal or railroad . . . will, in consequence, be a good investment. He looks upon all external objects as exponents of the future. In Europe they are only exponents of the

50. Huth, p. 38. Cf. Paulding, *Letters*, pp. 124-25.

51. Willis, *American Scenery*, I, iv. Charles Fenno Hoffman also deserves credit for association-gathering in his "Primeval Woods," "The Laurel," and "Moonlight upon the Hudson," collected in *The Poems of Charles Fenno Hoffman*, pp. 28-29, 35-37, 58-62.

past."[52] As Cooper described it, this attitude seemed less selfish, more patriotic:

The speculator on moral things can enjoy a satisfaction [in America] . . . that he who wanders over the plains of Greece will seek in vain. The pleasure of the latter, if he be wise and good, is unavoidably tinged with melancholy regrets; while here all that reason allows may be hoped for in behalf of man [and] . . . depend on it, there is no pleasure . . . that is commensurate with that we enjoy, who have seen the birth, infancy, and youth, and who are now about to become spectators of the maturity, of a whole country.[53]

Cooper's friend William Dunlap said simply: "Better the prospect of a glorious futurity, than the remains of past greatness."[54] This idea of progress has been considered America's panacea for social, educational, and political ills; by adapting it to landscape the Knickerbockers provided an effective remedy for a national dearth of historical associations.

The third major shortcoming, the lack of picturesque ruins, was eradicated by finding architectural, vegetable, and human substitutes for the moldering castles of Europe. The first type was supplied by Cooper, who used the now-famous Newport ruin as the setting for some of *The Red Rover*, and by N. P. Willis and the artist Bartlett, who in their *American Scenery* pictured Ticonderoga, Fort Putnam, and the Willey House (White Mountains) as native antiquities.[55] In another work Willis lavished high praise on an abandoned saw-mill and iron-works at the outlet of Tuxeto Lake.[56] The most popular and plentiful New-World ruins were not crumbling buildings, however, but trees and men. As Cooper observed, the first things sought

52. Willis, *American Scenery*, I, 2.
53. Cooper, *Notions*, I, 251-52.
54. William Dunlap, *A Trip to Niagara*, p. 7.
55. Also see Nemo, "A Day in the White Mountains," *K*, IX (May, 1837), 473-77.
56. See Willis, *American Scenery*, I, 38, 40, 76-77; Willis, *Hurry-Graphs*, p. 127, and, for a treatment of Trenton as a ruin, *Rural Letters*, p. 354. Also see G. P. T., "The Ruins of Burnside," *K*, XXIII (Feb., 1844), 137-38; W. I. Paulding, *Literary Life of James K. Paulding*, pp. 69-70; James K. Paulding, *The Backwoodsman*, p. 31; and Bryant and Durand, p. 11.

out by European travelers were the huge wooded areas of the United States;[57] and Walter Scott once told Irving that America's " 'vast aboriginal trees' " were its real " 'monuments and antiquities.' "[58] Possibly with this in mind, Irving in 1822 began to rhapsodize over the trees of America and England and, unconsciously at least, gave them an aura of sublimity by adding the necessary Burkean touch of terror:

I have paused more than once in the wilderness of America to con- template the traces of some blast of wind, which seemed to have rushed down from the clouds, and ripped its way through the bosom of the woodlands, rooting up, shivering and splintering the stoutest trees, and leaving a long track of desolation. There was something awful in the vast havoc made among these gigantic plants; . . . I recollect, also, hearing a traveller of poetical temperament expressing the kind of horror which he felt on beholding . . . an oak of prodigious size, which had been, in a manner, overpowered by an enormous wild grapevine. . . . It seemed like Laocoon struggling ineffectually in the hideous coils of the monster Python. It was the lion of trees perishing in the embrace of a vegetable boa.[59]

Cooper was even more specific in the use of associational terminology to depict these indigenous ruins. In *Home as Found* he described a towering pine:

It now stood in solitary glory, a memorial of what the mountains which were yet so rich in vegetation had really been in their days of nature and pride. . . . The tall column-like tree . . . now so far overhung the lake that its summit may have been some ten or fifteen feet without the base. A gentle, graceful curve added to the effect . . . and infused enough of the fearful into the grand to render the picture sublime.

As Eve Effingham gazes in awe at this picturesque sight, she exclaims: "When the Conqueror first landed in England this tree stood on the

57. *Gleanings in Europe: France*, p. 57.
58. Scott, quoted in Irving, *Crayon Miscellany*, p. 262. Cf. E. E., "Letters Descrip- tive of New-York, Written by an Irish Gentleman, a Resident of This City, to a Literary Friend in Dublin," *NYM*, IV (Dec. 30, 1826), 183.
59. Irving, *Bracebridge Hall*, pp. 105-6.

spot where it now stands. Here, then, is at last an American antiquity."[60]

An even greater substitute for European castles was at hand—the fast-vanishing Indian, a true child of nature and a living monument of the past, a theme worthy of the country's ablest painters and writers. The desire to connect these human ruins with the antique world prompted a reviewer in *The Knickerbocker* to claim that, if Indians "had lived in the golden days of Greece or Rome, their names would have been immortalized, in sculpture or in song, and their daring valor adored as super-human." But these national monuments were crumbling: "The progress of civilization has swept away their wigwams, extinguished their council fires, and stilled their war whoop, while their last sad remnants, still wander among us like Ossian's ghosts, the spectres of their former glory. . . ."[61] One by one the Knickerbockers joined a sort of national society for the literary preservation of America's living antiquities.[62] Out of this ferment, which especially dominated the third and fifth decades of the nineteenth century, came not only *The Last of the Mohicans* (1826) but also *The Redskins* (1846), a less memorable but equally important contribution to the Indians-as-ruins theme. In this latter novel, the third of Cooper's anti-rent series, there are two human ruins, the Negro Jaap and the Indian Susquesus (Trackless). Both have played roles in *Satanstoe* and *The Chainbearer*, the preceding books of the series, so that in *The Redskins* they are approximately a century old. Although Cooper gives equal stress to the antiquity of these two men, he makes Susquesus into a more complex figure by using metaphors which associate him with the venerable trees of the forest. *The Redskins* is in general a drab book, but this juxtaposition of human and natural ruins, carefully foreshadowed earlier in the series, makes it extremely readable in parts.[63]

60. Cooper, *Home as Found*, I, 224-25. For other praise of American trees, see Mifflin, *K*, II, 32. A survey of American attitudes is in Shepard, pp. 70-78.

61. Review of *Indian Biography*, by Benjamin B. Thatcher, *K*, II (Aug., 1833), 139, 140.

62. This subject, as it bears on American literature and criticism, is covered in G. Harrison Orians, "The Cult of the Vanishing American," pp. 3-15.

63. See Cooper, *The Redskins*, I, 122, 128, 134, II, 70, 76, 206. His method is anticipated in Paulding, *The Backwoodsman*, p. 89.

With novels such as these Cooper earned a place at the head of his fellow Knickerbockers in the use of Indian materials, but collectively these writers surpassed him by dealing with the Indian in a greater number of literary forms, extending in prose from such critical essays as Irving's "Traits of Indian Character" through such short stories as Bryant's "Cascade of Melsingah" to such novels as Hoffman's *Greyslaer* and Paulding's *Koningsmarke*, in poetry from such lyrics as M'Donald Clarke's "The Last Indian" and Halleck's "Red Jacket" through such short narratives as Wetmore's "Mononeco" to such full-blown metrical romances as Street's *Frontenac* and Sands and Eastburn's *Yamoyden*.[64] Willis filled his bulky travel books *American Scenery* and *Canadian Scenery* with Indian legends, myths, and superstitions and, whenever possible, gave the aboriginal names of the localities he described. Bryant and Cornelius Mathews even attempted treatments of the Mound Builders, the former in "The Prairies," a kind of poetic dream-vision, and the latter in a novel called *Behemoth*. As a result of all this literary activity, the reading public was constantly being introduced and re-introduced to the American Indian, and the American artist could therefore feel a bit more confident that his own Indian work would find eager buyers.[65]

It is now apparent that the process of dignifying the American landscape was more involved than simply enumerating its merits. The writers also had to acknowledge its defects with all honesty but with an equal amount of zeal try to offset them with native associations of the past, present, and future, and with new discoveries in cisatlantic ruins. Their final optimistic assessment was motivated by a healthy patriotism and itself produced nationalistic effects since it stimulated the landscape artists to depict their own countryside, and the public to accept the resultant paintings.

Publicly Praising the Landscape Painter

The Knickerbocker writers not only popularized native scenery but also acquainted their readers with the merits of its painters. This

64. For John H. Payne's interest in Indians, see Grace Overmyer, *America's First Hamlet*, pp. 297-330.

65. Use of Indian materials by American painters is discussed in Shepard, pp. 72-78.

135

educational process, lasting approximately from 1825 to 1855, was carried on in letters, books, orations, and magazines and was one of the most direct methods by which Knickerbocker literature furthered American art.

As critics, the writers of New York maintained a certain integrity by seldom hesitating to call a painting absurd, slovenly, or miserable if they thought it deserved such scornful language. But optimism dictated their frankness and they criticized to improve, not destroy, hoping always that the artist whose faults were brought before the public would in the future paint better pictures. Taken as a whole, however, their comments show a preponderance of praise rather than censure. By preserving this ratio, the Knickerbockers were probably more effective pioneers than they would have been otherwise. Wholesale enthusiasm or criticism could have demolished the hope of progress. American landscape painting was as yet an infant growth, and the Knickerbockers helped it to bloom by shielding it from excessive rain and sunshine.

Their appraisal of the Hudson River School is rather fully documented in Appendix III, but we may evaluate it here by selecting their comments on four men, Thomas Doughty, Thomas Cole, Asher Durand, and George Inness. Each of these artists represented a different aspect of American landscape painting—Doughty, its beginnings; Cole, its imaginative strain; Durand, its softer side; and Inness, its transformation into newer modes of expression.

The Knickerbockers received Thomas Doughty, a founder of the Hudson River School, with warmth which cooled somewhat as they perceived his style degenerating into mannerism. Composed of "the lonely forest-brook, the misty wood-lake, the still river, the heart of the quiet wilderness,"[66] Doughty's pictures made a lasting impression on N. P. Willis, and in Willis' magazine *The Corsair* we find Doughty called "one of the first painters in the world."[67] Reviewers in other Knickerbocker magazines were at times just as enthusiastic but occasionally noted "glaring faults" such as his lack of variety, character-

66. Willis, *American Scenery*, II, 37. Also see Willis, *Pencillings*, p. 37.
67. "The Pencil," *The Corsair*, I (April 13, 1839), 74.

less trees, muddy water,[68] chalky finish, and feminine or " 'tea tray' " style.[69] The most enumerative criticism appeared in *The New-York Mirror*: "His foregrounds are always beautiful and good, and for this reason are too apt to attract all the attention of the spectator. He makes use too frequently of painters' tricks; sacrificing truth to effect. As, for example, you may discern in three-fourths of his pictures, a sailboat or vessel under the shadow of some hill, *with the sails painted white*. But in his skies Doughty excels. . . . He does not paint good figures and therefore attempts nothing beyond a simple view."[70] But this was in 1840—Doughty had been popular for almost two decades and it was inevitable that at least a few reviewers would tiptoe away from the adoring crowd to their studies, where they could loudly accuse this artist of sinking into bad habits. "Landscape painters are judged by much severer tests than they were when Mr. Doughty earned his reputation," wrote one critic who condemned him for not being true to nature.[71] But the majority of the Knickerbockers refused to detect this cardinal sin in pictures they had learned to love.

Among all the landscape painters treated by the Knickerbocker writers, the most popular figure was Thomas Cole. He was frequently discussed in magazines edited by the literary men of New York; after he died, Bryant and Cooper paid lengthy tributes to his memory.[72] The writers were also concerned with his place in history and persisted in comparing him with Claude Lorrain and Salvator Rosa even when at the same time they denied that such comparisons were valid.[73] Cooper, in fact, considered him superior to Claude in "high poetic feeling."[74] Despite some diversity of opinion about Cole's international stature, the writers readily acknowledged his preeminence in

68. "Our Landscape Painters," *NYM*, XVIII (July 18, 1840), 30.

69. "The Art-Union Pictures," *LW*, II (May 6, 1847), 330.

70. "Our Landscape Painters," *NYM*, XVIII (July 18, 1840), 30. Also see "National Academy of Design," *K*, XIX (June, 1842), 592; "Exhibition of the National Academy of Design . . . ," *USRLG*, II (July, 1827), 256.

71. "The Art-Union Pictures," *LW*, II (Nov. 6, 1847), 330. Cf. Clara Sears, *Highlights Among the Hudson River Artists*, p. 20.

72. Bryant, *Orations*, pp. 1-41; Cooper, in Noble, pp. 224-35.

73. See "National Academy of Design," *NYM*, XV (June 2, 1838), 390; "Exhibition of the National Academy of Design . . . ," *USRLG*, II (July, 1827), 249-50.

74. Cooper, in Noble, p. 225.

America, a typical judgment coming from the reviewer in *The Knick-erbocker* who pronounced him "a master, without rival among his own countrymen."[75]

Cole's pictures of American scenery were judged usually by one standard, faithfulness to the indigenous aspects of native landscape. In such cases, that ubiquitous critical phrase, "true to nature," took on new, patriotic connotations and meant actually "true to nature as it is found in America." This did not mean that the writers expected the painter to be a photographic realist: Cooper equated Cole's good taste with an ability "to reject what is disagreeable, and to arrange the attractive parts of his pictures."[76] But it did mean that the greatest merit of Cole's paintings was thought to be their resemblance to "the scenery from which he drew."[77] This nationalistic norm was the basis of *The Knickerbocker* magazine's estimate of "View in the White Mountains": "This is truly an American picture. The boldness of the scenery itself, the autumnal tints which are spread over the forest, and the wild appearance of the heavens, give it a character and stamp that we never see in the works of foreign schools. . . ."[78] Bryant expressed a similar motive for relishing this facet of Cole's art, "which carried the eye over scenes of wild grandeur peculiar to our country," forest-topped mountains, uncultivated banks of streams, and skies unique in their coloring.[79] In all, the Knickerbockers generally admired Cole's earlier landscapes because such paintings rewarded their search for a truly national art.[80]

Cole's foreign scenes were also valued for their nationalistic connotations. During the nineteenth century, American criticism was split into two factions. The first group, the cultural isolationists, believed that the native artist must ignore all civilizations but his own. The second group, the universalists, contended that working in such a

75. "National Academy of Design," *K,* XVI (July, 1840), 81.
76. Cooper, *Notions,* II, 19.
77. *Ibid.*
78. "National Academy of Design," *K,* XVI (July, 1840), 81.
79. Bryant, *Orations,* pp. 12-13.
80. For additional praise of Cole's American landscapes, see Appendix III. An early analysis of Cole's American paintings was notable for its inclusion of criteria based on principles not connected with nationalism: "The Exhibition of the National Academy of Design . . . ," *USRLG,* II (July, 1827), 250, 255.

vacuum amounted actually to wasting the accumulated wisdom of the past. It would be far better for the American artist, they thought, to make use of the universal storehouse of wisdom but to supplement it with original, native contributions.[81] In their discussions of Cole, who made two European trips, the Knickerbockers indicated that, without losing their patriotic fervor, they took the side of the universalists. There were dissenters, of course, like the reviewer who claimed that American painters who studied abroad had forsaken "GOD'S" landscape for "man's."[82] But William Dunlap gave the majority opinion: "We sometimes feel, when looking at the productions of native, untravelled artists, as if a visit to Italy was not necessary to their perfection; but viewing the paintings of Cole, Morse, and Weir in the present exhibition, the doubt vanishes."[83] Cooper distinguished between Cole's innate poetic genius, which no amount of travel could produce, and his artistic ability, which was "improved vastly by his visit to Italy."[84] Bryant claimed that Cole profited more from a study of Europe's scenery than from contact with its artists and traced three of Cole's best pictures to a bolder manner acquired abroad.[85] In all, the Knickerbockers were delighted with Cole's foreign paintings,[86] Willis even going so far as to proclaim "View of the Roman Campagna" "one of the finest landscapes ever painted."[87] These paintings proved to the writers that cultural universalism was a sound philosophy.

On the other hand, wholehearted approval was not given to this painter's fanciful and allegorical pictures. Since with such canvases as "The Course of Empire" and "The Voyage of Life" Cole was trying something new in the history of American landscape painting, he was bound to encounter some dissatisfaction on the part of critics. Public

81. See Callow, pp. 142-49; Harry H. Clark, "Literary Criticism in the *North American Review*," pp. 299-350.

82. "Exhibition at the National Academy," *LW*, I (May 15, 1847), 348.

83. [William] D[unlap]., "National Academy of Design," *NYM*, X (May 18, 1833), 366. Also see *idem*, X (June 29, 1833), 410.

84. Quoted in Noble, p. 224.

85. Bryant, *Orations*, pp. 20-22.

86. See "National Academy of Design," *K*, III (May, 1834), 400; *idem*, IX (June, 1837), 619.

87. Willis, *Pencillings*, p. 82.

taste had been developed with rather literal transcriptions of scenery, and the observation naturally arose that his fanciful paintings lacked the "truth-telling force" of his other landscapes.[88] Sometimes criticisms were based on technical grounds: "Dream of Arcadia" was condemned for its "broken lights and shadows";[89] "The Expulsion from Paradise" was declared too "pie-bald" in appearance.[90] Sometimes the subject matter itself was criticized, but the reviewers did not always agree on such points, as was the case with "The Architect's Dream."[91] Objections could be considerably modified. A writer in *Arcturus*, for example, was displeased only with the angel in "The Voyage of Life": "If the artist had . . . left these different scenes . . . in their mute grandeur . . . he would have relied more justly upon the imagination. As it is, . . . the presence of an angel . . . withdraws the subject from the imagination and substitutes a literal commonplace."[92] Nevertheless it was agreed that Cole had genius even in the imaginative branch of landscape painting. His occasional technical misdemeanors were outweighed by the loftiness of his poetic sentiment, especially in "The Course of Empire," pronounced by Cooper "a great epic poem, in which the idea far surpasses the execution, though the last is generally fine."[93]

The Knickerbockers' evaluation of Cole was in a sense prophetic. They cherished his native work, and modern criticism has echoed their opinion. They hesitated somewhat in praising his fanciful paintings; their concern with the technical faults of such pictures—a concern which they allowed to be subordinated to their love of didacticism—has now become the primary yardstick by which critics measure,

88. "National Academy of Design," *NYM*, XV (June 2, 1838), 390.

89. "National Academy of Design," *NYM*, XV (June 2, 1838), 390.

90. "American Academy of the Fine Arts," *The* (New York) *American Monthly Magazine*, I (Aug., 1833), 402.

91. See "National Academy of Design," *K*, XVI (July, 1840), 81. Cf. "Our Landscape Painters," *NYM*, XVIII (July 18, 1840), 29. Bryant (*Orations*, pp. 26-27) declined to pass judgment on this painting and merely described it, indicating, perhaps, his dissatisfaction with it. At the same time (p. 28) he ambiguously declared that Cole's "Garden of Eden" was "almost beyond the power of the pencil."

92. "Cole's Pictures of the Voyage of Life," *Arcturus*, I (Jan., 1841), 123.

93. Quoted in Noble, p. 224. See Appendix III for further references to Cole's allegorical paintings.

and condemn, these imaginative works. Cole's reputation will continue to suffer as long as emphasis is on the technique rather than the poetic sentiment of a painting.

"Second only to Cole"[94] was Asher Durand. Like his fellow painter, Durand was compared to Claude Lorrain and Salvator Rosa[95] but was occasionally the victim of some rather biting criticism. "Durand does not paint a good middle distance," remarked one critic, "because his foregrounds are too *light* and highly finished. In themselves they are perfect."[96] Another reviewer found some of his pictures too full of yellow hues.[97] A third critic was quite harsh but came close to the truth in his contention that Durand "has never approached . . . [nature] in her majestic sublimity, and . . . excited in us those noble feelings and emotions of greatness, that rise almost into the heroic. His pictures produce in us a calmness and complacency. . . . But in avoiding the rude and savage aspect of Nature, . . . he too often degenerates into the merely elegant and beautiful. . . ."[98] This reviewer hit upon what was both the strength and weakness of Durand, in his minor pictures a lack of boldness, but in his major efforts a twofold ability to "fill the heart with peace"[99] and to re-create nature as a living presence. "What BRYANT does with the pen, he effects with his pencil," commented another critic. "Nature rises, as if from miraculous invocation, before you. . . . Then remember that all this is of the most every-day character. There is no attempt at grand composition, no rude figures of eight feet in height, . . . no wonderful light and shade, and no brilliant coloring. Yet 'there lies the scene,' as SHAKESPEARE says . . . ."[100] In all, the Knickerbockers found much more to praise than to condemn in Durand's art, but they seldom approached the great enthusiasm of Bryant, who confessed: "If I were to be asked what other [landscape] painter . . . I would prefer to Durand, I should say—*no one.* There

94. "The Fine Arts," NYM, XV (Jan. 6, 1838), 224.
95. "A Pair of Landscapes. By Durand," LW, I (Feb. 6, 1847), 16.
96. "Our Landscape Painters," NYM, XVIII (July 18, 1840), 30.
97. "National Academy of Design," K, XXXIII (May, 1849), 469.
98. "National Academy Exhibition," LW, III (May 13, 1848), 287.
99. "A Pair of Landscapes. By Durand," LW, I (Feb. 6, 1847), 16.
100. "National Academy of Design," K, XXVII (May, 1846), 464.

are no landscapes produced in any part of the world which I should more willingly possess than his."[101]

Although the major literary magazines of the period welcomed new talent in their columns, they usually acclaimed it only when it approached in kind the familiar landscapes of Cole, Doughty, or Durand. The case of George Inness indicates that painters aspiring to escape from the stereotyped methods of the Hudson River School were not aided by the Knickerbockers. Inness began his career by employing the fashionable, literal, and delineatory techniques of the day but gradually achieved a looser, lyrical shorthand method of his own. In the late 1840's and during the 1850's he oscillated between these two styles and at this time, while he exhibited at the National Academy, his paintings were reviewed in the magazines of New York. The writers were not always severe—*The Knickerbocker* called his "Land-Storm" one of the "best pictures in the exhibition" of 1853—[102] but they frequently criticized him in rather blunt language. For example:

A most lamentable display is shown in NUMBERS 56 ["Banks of Tin Brook"] and 222 ["Nick Cruger's Saw Mill"], by GEORGE INNES [*sic*]. It is scarcely credible that an artist who is possessed of undoubted talents, and who has produced fine works, should so prostitute his abilities as to paint like this. One of these pictures is a mass of green cheese, dotted with sheep, (most persons imagine these sheep to be cows;) in the other, Mr. INNES[S] has striven to give the effect immediately after a summer thunder-storm. He has made a conglomeration of soft tallow and an astonishing rainbow. Mr. Innes[s], pray leave off such freaks, and paint as we know you *can* paint. Thus to trifle with yourself and the public is more than foolish: it is criminal.[103]

Inness was on the way to becoming one of America's greatest landscape painters, surpassing Durand in technique but perpetuating the older man's ability to capture the serenity of nature. That the Knick-

101. Quoted in E. Anna Lewis, p. 322. For additional comments on Durand, see below, Appendix III.

102. "National Academy of Design," *K*, XLII (July, 1853), 95.

103. "National Academy of Design," *K*, XLV (May, 1855), 533. Also see below, Appendix III.

erbocker writers failed to discover horizons for Inness' originality is hardly to their credit and marks the end of their critical pioneering.

The figures of Bryant, Street, Cooper, Willis, and the unnamed reviewers in the periodicals of New York stand out as having advanced the cause of American landscape painting. By revealing the power of nature they trod rather well-beaten paths, but by discovering the indigenous glories of the American topography and the capabilities of its painters they blazed real trails. Moreover, although they were obviously aware of shortcomings in native scenery and artists, they almost never sneered at future prospects. Their just criticism was not intended to destroy all hope, but to arrange defects and virtues in the proper perspective of optimism. To them the idea of progress was a reality. Great strides were desirable and yet to be made, but much had already been achieved.

CHAPTER V

LANDSCAPE: SIMILAR TECHNIQUES AND MUTUAL PUBLICATIONS

The Knickerbocker writers and the American painters used analogous methods to develop their landscapes. To some extent this overlapping of techniques arose from the social contact afforded by The Bread and Cheese Club and its successor, The Sketch Club. Members were usually artists who at some time in their lives painted landscapes, or authors who, like Bryant and Cooper, wrote about landscapes. What at first was merely fraternization soon became a broad spiritual affinity between large numbers of painters and writers, all striving for the same goals and employing similar procedures to reach them. It was only natural that they sometimes joined forces to produce landscape gift books.

Similar Techniques

Although individual authors undoubtedly had their own favorite painters' tricks,[1] the Knickerbockers and the Hudson River School resembled each other most in their use of the panoramic view, composition, accessories, and contrast. In some cases these techniques appear to be contradictory, but all were resolved in the largeness of their context and the multiplicity of their purposes. Motivated by religion, aesthetics, nationalism, regionalism, romanticism, and a dozen other forces, few American artists could have been satisfied with a single method of expression.

Little attempt will be made to discover the original ownership of these techniques. During the early nineteenth century, painters and writers were in such close contact and borrowed so freely from each other that an effective procedure could hardly have remained the property of any one group for more than a few years. Furthermore, almost all of the landscape methods employed by the Knickerbockers had not been invented by them, but were inherited from earlier poets, like Freneau, whose sun was setting as theirs was rising. To some extent the same thing might be said of the Hudson River School, since its techniques were foreshadowed in certain primitive paintings.[2] Suffice it to say, then, that the Knickerbockers and the American painters frequently saw nature through each other's eyes and sometimes forgot to distinguish between the pen and the brush.

THE PANORAMIC APPROACH. The panorama was one of the most interesting devices shared by the artists and writers. An importation from Europe, this technique had for its immediate purpose the inclusion of more landscape than an observer could take in without moving his head from side to side. This was accomplished at first by covering the walls of a rotunda with a series of canvases such as John Vanderlyn's "View of the Palace and Gardens of Versailles," exhibited in a circular structure called the New York Rotunda. As it progressed, however, the panorama encompassed larger areas, made possible by simply stitching paintings together and showing them as moving pictures. Several panoramas of this type, designed to celebrate the scenery

1. See, for example, Donald A. Ringe, "Chiaroscuro as an Artistic Device in Cooper's Fiction," pp. 349-57.
2. See F. Sweet, p. 14; Sears, p. xvii.

of the Mississippi River, are still preserved; and in many contemporary reviews we have descriptions of others.[3] Both moving and circular panoramas, as well as scenes of more modified wide-angle proportions, appear in the landscape works of the Knickerbockers and the Hudson River School.

The panoramic viewpoint was utilized by American artists for several reasons. First, it achieved drama and excitement by placing the observer in an unusual position. Paintings such as Doughty's "On the Banks of the Susquehanna" and Cole's "Destruction," from "The Course of Empire," appeal psychologically to the onlooker, who is flattered at being allowed to command acres of land temporarily his own. Like the eighteenth-century "spectator"—in the fourth book of Cowper's *Task*, for example—he enjoys an enlarged vision of life. Secondly, panoramas reflected the notion that America was vast beyond exhaustion, a place of horizons without limit.[4] Thus, as the frontier spread westward, the panorama followed. Trumbull's inclusive views of Niagara Falls, and Cole's near-boundless "Oxbow" were later supplemented with similar treatments of the West in the paintings of Bierstadt and Moran.

In Knickerbocker literature, sweeping descriptions of scenery were used for like reasons. Rip Van Winkle's perch high in the Catskills became a psychological release from the frustrations of an unhappy marriage. Readers of *The Alhambra* felt giddy but important as they were conducted to the tower of Comares and invited to gaze at the almost endless vistas to the north, the south, and the west.[5] Cooper, who believed that the lofty view "astonishes, and . . . excites the feel-

3. See Perry T. Rathbone (ed.), *Mississippi Panorama*. For a survey of the panorama in American painting, see Wolfgang Born, *American Landscape Painting: An Interpretation*, pp. 75-117. Several New York magazines took an interest in panoramas which were exhibited locally. See "The Departure of the Israelites from Egypt," *K*, V (Feb., 1835), 171-72; "Belshazzar's Feast," *K*, V (April, 1835), 359; "Moving Diorama," *K*, VI (July, 1835), 83; "Peristrephick Dioramas," *NYM*, XIII (July 25, 1835), 31; "Hannington's Peristrephic Diorama," *NYM*, XIII (Aug. 29, 1835), 71; "The New Panorama," *NYM*, XVI (Aug. 18, 1838), 63; "Catherwood's Panorama of Thebes," *NYM*, XVI (April 13, 1839), 335. Cf., however, the displeasure of an anonymous critic in "Monthly Record of Current Events," *Harper's New Monthly Magazine*, II (April, 1851), 705.

4. Born, p. 80.

5. Washington Irving, *The Alhambra*, pp. 124-32.

John Quidor

A BATTLE SCENE FROM KNICKER-
BOCKER'S HISTORY OF NEW YORK
(1838) (*M. & M. Karolik Collection,
Museum of Fine Arts, Boston*)

John Quidor

ANTONY VAN CORLEAR BROUGHT INTO
THE PRESENCE OF PETER STUYVESANT
(1839) (*Munson-Williams-Proctor Institute, Utica, New York*)

ings,"[6] mixed it with the panorama to describe the Valley of the Mohawk in *Notions of the Americans*,[7] Lake George in *The Last of the Mohicans*,[8] the Valley of the Susquehanna in *Home as Found*,[9] and the area surrounding the specklike ruins of Fort William Henry in *Satanstoe*.[10] Of course, the dramatic position of the onlooker could tend toward the sublime by placing him in vicarious danger and therefore introducing the Burkean element of terror. Most Knicker-bocker works came far from succeeding with this effect, however.[11] If anyone achieved true sublimity with the panorama it was Bryant, and his was of a different sort. "Thanatopsis," "The Prairies," and "The Flood of Years" contain an exciting mental liberation so closely integrated with the panoramic view that one cannot be sure which is the cause, which the effect. Surely these poetic visions are genuine panoramas of the mind, for they contain neither physical-spatial nor chronological boundaries. Completely free, the poet soars out of his own country into the past and future.

In addition to these various psychological uses, the literary pano-rama served as a way of impressing readers with the vastness of native scenery. Bryant employed it in "Monument Mountain" to prove that the American landscape was a huge melting pot large enough to blend the picturesque and the beautiful. Joseph Rodman Drake advised his friend Halleck to become a national poet by seating himself on "Appalachia's brow," where he could absorb the immensity of nature and stimulate his imagination.[12] Fortified with this counsel, Halleck adopted the technique to describe Weehawken and succeeded in filling his readers with a sense of patriotism as they cautiously peered over the edge of a cliff to see "ocean, and earth, and heaven, burst" before

6. *Excursions in Switzerland*, p. 186.

7. I, 248-49.

8. See Howard M. Jones, "James Fenimore Cooper and the Hudson River School," p. 249.

9. I, 141-43.

10. See James Fenimore Cooper, *Satanstoe*, pp. 101-2.

11. Some interesting approaches in poetry and prose were Richard Haywarde [Frederick S. Cozzens], "Thoughts from the Top of Trinity," *K*, XXXII (July, 1848), 38-40; Bryant, "Monument Mountain," *Poetical Works*, I, 103; Halleck, "Fanny," *Poetical Writings*, p. 130 (stanza xcv).

12. Joseph R. Drake, "To a Friend," *The Culprit Fay and Other Poems*, p. 42.

their eyes.[13] The nationalistic tone of such verses might be more accurately termed regionalistic, but it should be remembered that nationalism and regionalism meant the same thing in the days of the Knickerbockers, the microcosm standing for the macrocosm, and praise of many local scenes cumulatively proving the value of one vast, national landscape.

Two Knickerbocker writings were especially connected with the moving panorama. The first of these was *A Trip to Niagara* (1828), a three-act play written by William Dunlap "at the request of the Managers [of the Bowery Theatre], and intended by them as a kind of running accompaniment to the more important product of the Scene-painter."[14] Although it comprises an effective plea for tolerance on the part of foreign travelers toward America, the subject matter of *A Trip to Niagara* is subordinated to its panoramic background. At the beginning of the second act, the following paintings were shown as the players were made to journey up the Hudson:

DIORAMA, OR MOVING SCENERY

The steam boat is seen as passing up the river.

Scene   1. Harbour of New York. Governor's Island, Ships at anchor.
       2. Frigate at anchor. Jersey City.
       3. Hoboken.
       4. Weehawk.
       5. Palisades.
       6. Approaching storm.
       7. Storm.
       8. Boats passing through a fog.
       9. Clearing away and rainbow. Caldwell's landing. Boat stops.
     10. Highlands.
     11. Buttermilk Falls.
     12. West Point. Sun setting.
     13. Highlands continued.
     14. Newburgh by moonlight.
     15. Island near Newburgh.

13. Halleck, "Fanny," *Poetical Writings*, pp. 130-31.
14. Dunlap, *A Trip to Niagara*, p. iii.

16. Catskill Mountains in distance, and Mountain House.
17. Continuation of scenery.
18. Catskill landing.[15]

Apparently Dunlap restricted himself merely to writing the play: According to the advertisements, the scenery was painted by Jones, Gordon, and Reinagle, with the assistance of Haddock, White, and Leslie— obscure figures in the history of American painting.[16] *A Trip to Niagara* was quite popular, and on one occasion the diorama alone was presented as an afterpiece.[17]

A Pen-and-Ink Panorama of New York City (1853), written by Cornelius Mathews, was an extremely clever adaptation of the moving panorama for literary purposes. Regional in tone, this little book of essays, character sketches, and scenic views was designed to give its readers the feeling that they were actually present at the showing of a mid-century panorama. Thus Mathews addressed his audience with familiar patter:

In the little canvass I propose to open before you, ladies and gentlemen, I have attempted to paint a home picture. The seven colors of the rainbow have been pretty freely used, I may say, quite exhausted, by previous artists; there is little more to be done with them. We have had panoramas of the Thames, of California, the Mississippi, the Holy Land, gorgeous with all the tints of the palette. What, then, is left to me, that I too invite you to a panoramic exhibition? There is a single unemployed color, common writing-ink, and for a pencil, the old . . . grey goose-quill. With the aid of these, and your kind indulgence, I shall endeavor to body forth something for your entertainment, by unrolling before you the streets and characters of a great city. . . . In an hour or two we will accomplish lengths

15. *Ibid.*, pp. 26-27.
16. See George C. D. Odell, *Annals of the New York Stage*, III, 407. The Christian names of only two of these painters, Duke White and John L. Leslie, are certain. The original paintings from which the scenery was executed are attributed to Wall, probably William Guy Wall, in "Fine Arts: The Diorama at the Bowery Theatre," *The Critic*, I (Dec. 13, 1828), 104. See Born, p. 90, for possible far-reaching effects of this diorama.
17. See Odell, III, 408. An appreciative contemporary review was "Mr. Dunlap's Play of a Trip to Niagara," *NYM*, VI (Dec. 20, 1828), 191. Earlier instances of moving scenery on the New York stage are given in "A Trip to Niagara," *NYM*, VI (Nov. 22, 1828), 159.

and breadths of this town which it should take you, unaided, twenty years, more or less, to traverse. . . . I invite you, ladies and gentlemen, to bear me company.[18]

Mathews never allowed this illusion of reality to disappear. With each change of scene there was a carefully planned transition. For example:

In town again, with eyes sharpened by our holiday—let us follow our panorama as it moves along. Ladies and gentlemen, you have probably seen several historical paintings, and read a number of historical romances in your time with profound admiration! Will you be good enough to look this way at

THE NEW YORK FIREMAN.

Mark the picture before you. It is the morning of a wide and fierce conflagration. The clouds are dull and sullen. . . .[19]

The ending of the book is equally consistent: "Ladies and gentlemen, the Pen-and-Ink Panorama of New York City is closed—I am much obliged to you for your attendance, and hope to have the pleasure of meeting you again."[20] But the "audience" never gave this charming work the recognition it deserved.

The panoramic technique was employed quite sparingly by the Knickerbockers, who never used it to the extent that Walt Whitman did. In the novel it could exist only as a unit dependent on the more important ingredients of character analysis and plot development. In poetry it never replaced the popular microscopic point of view in the tradition of Burns's "To a Mouse."[21] On the other hand, the panoramic method was landscape's "Sunday best" and was useful for achieving a sense of vastness considered necessary for sublimity. Above all, it was employed by the Knickerbockers in much of their better

18. Cornelius Mathews, *A Pen-and-Ink Panorama of New York City*, pp. 5-7.
19. *Ibid.*, pp. 92-93. Also see p. 173.
20. *Ibid.*, p. 209.
21. See, for instance, Bryant's "To the Fringed Gentian," "To a Mosquito," and "The Yellow Violet," as well as C. F. Hoffman's "The Brook and the Pine," Edward Sanford's "Address to a Mosquito," and William P. Hawes's "Song of the Hermit Trout." The last two poems were collected in a useful anthology of writings by Gothamites: *The New-York Book of Poetry*, pp. 11-14, 46.

work and served well to express the exalted notions of nature which they shared with American painters.

COMPOSITION. In compositional techniques the writers of New York and the members of the Hudson River School were romantic realists, romantic because they arranged and selected their details for singleness of effect and mood, a unity which mirrored the all-ordering hand of God, and realists because they documented their landscapes with almost microscopic thoroughness, portraying each detail with infinite care and always applying that famous touchstone, truth to nature.[22] Coleridge's dictum that each part must be pleasurable but no single part more pleasurable than the whole was usually their ideal, yet it must be recorded that they sometimes failed to achieve it. The first third of Bryant's "Monument Mountain," for example, embodies such a minute portrayal of nature that the reader disregards Bryant's contention that all things were "mingled in harmony"[23] and asks himself instead: Is the story of the lover's leap, comprising the last two-thirds of the poem, an anecdote to embellish the landscape, or is the landscape description merely introduction to the anecdote? Is "Monument Mountain" primarily a descriptive or a narrative poem? Bryant seems to have lost his usual awareness of the whole, the sense of form which has helped him to survive even the close gaze of modern criticism.[24]

The painters also lapsed into compositional blunders at times. But the fact that these errors were caught and condemned by the reviewers of the day shows that an ideal of unity existed. Even offenses by the much-respected Thomas Cole were not allowed to go unnoticed. "Falls of Nunda," one of Cole's minor landscapes was put to rest by

22. See E. Clark, *History of the National Academy of Design*, p. 49. Paul Shepard, Jr., has analyzed 60 paintings of the Hudson River School by comparing them with the actual sites from which they were taken. His study shows quite conclusively that these artists were not literal transcribers of nature but that they frequently moved mountains, elevated foregrounds, depressed middle distances, and inserted waterfalls to suit their compositions. See especially Shepard, pp. 85-89, for a comparison of Kaaterskill Clove, an area in the Catskills and the site of Durand's "Kindred Spirits," with the painting itself.

23. Bryant, *Poetical Works*, I, 102.

24. See George Arms, *The Fields Were Green*, p. 19.

these remarks in *The New-York Mirror*: "This may be true to nature; but a more confused higgledy-piggledy picture we don't desire to see. Such a commingling of reds, and yellows, and browns, and mists, and cascades, and clouds, and cliffs! If it hadn't been for the house and the sky we should have thought the picture upside down."[25] Cole's pupil Frederick E. Church received like treatment from *The Knickerbocker* magazine. "CHURCH is much the same as ever," complained the reviewer; for "his pictures are frittered up in detail, which, though true by itself, yet lacks the unity and repose of nature."[26] Realism of parts was no excuse for confusion of the whole.

A few examples will serve to illustrate the methods by which the Knickerbockers composed for unity in their landscapes. The first is from Willis' *Pencillings by the Way*:

A lovely scene lay before me when I turned to look back. The valley . . . is as round as a bowl, with an edge of mountain-tops absolutely even all around the horizon. It slopes down from every side to the centre, as if it had been measured and hollowed by art; and there is not a fence to be seen from one side to the other, and scarcely a tree, but one green and almost un-broken carpet of verdure, swelling up in broad green slopes to the top. . . . St. Bris is a little handful of stone buildings around an old church; just such a thing as a painter would throw into a picture—and the different-colored grain, and here and there a ploughed patch of rich yellow earth, and the road crossing the hollow from hill to hill like a white band; and then for the life of the scene, the group of Italians . . . and the peasants in their broad straw hats, scattered over the fields.[27]

Here the unifying device is the mountains, enclosing the valley and framing the many details included in the description—the building, the church, the grain, the patches of ploughed earth, the road, and, finally, the human accessories. This technique of the "closed" scene had been used by the Hudson River School from its beginning and may be found in the watercolors of William Guy Wall, a forerunner of native landscape painters.[28]

25. "National Academy of Design," NYM, XIX (May 15, 1841), 159.
26. "National Academy of Design," K, XXXIX (June, 1852), 567.
27. Willis, *Pencillings*, p. 35.
28. See Donald A. Shelley, "William Guy Wall and His Watercolors," p. 37.

This urge to arrange is evident in Willis' declaration that "all . . . rivers, . . . to be seen to advantage, . . . should form the middle, not the foreground of the picture,"[29] and it is what makes Willis' description of the Silver Cascade almost as effective as the engraving of Doughty's picture which accompanies it: "The ear is suddenly saluted by soft dashings of this sweetest of cascades; and a glance upwards reveals its silver streams issuing from the loftiest crests of the mountain, and leaping from crag to crag, or spread in a broad thin sheet of liquid light over the edge of some projecting ledge, till it reaches the road, across which it passes, forming a still and transparent pool immediately beneath, before it joins the Saco in the depths of the gorge."[30] In both instances, in the letterpress and in the engraving, the cascade has been used to achieve totality of impression. All other details are subordinated to it.

To capture this unity the Knickerbockers sometimes rearranged the elements of an actual scene as any painter would. Thus Cooper explained that the landscapes of *The Deerslayer* were accurate "in all but precise position." He had carefully drawn rocks, shoals, rivers, bays, mountains, and "all the other accessories" from real models but had shuffled them around to some extent. An important shoal, for example, he had moved a little to the northeast.[31] Such procedures were just as allowable to Cooper and his fellow writers as they were to any member of the Hudson River School, for the goal of unity was common to both literature and painting. If neither group had sacrificed petty detail to this more important end, neither would have achieved true artistry. But such was not the case, and both groups by seeking unity through a blend of romantic and realistic techniques, naturally created arranged pictures with marked resemblances.

HUMAN ACCESSORIES. Both groups also employed man as an accessory in their landscapes. Minor gods and goddesses, sylphs, satyrs, and centaurs were no longer fashionable. Instead of such figures, nine-

29. Willis, *American Scenery*, I, 24.
30. *Ibid.*, II, 29.
31. James Fenimore Cooper, *The Deerslayer*, p. x. The wording of this passage is slightly different in the "New Edition."

teenth-century paintings and writings contained Indians, woodsmen, and townsfolk out for an airing. A few dehumanized landscapes were occasionally produced (Cole's "The Maid of the Mist" and Drake's "The Culprit Fay," for example), but these must be considered oddities at a time when man had become the chief landscape accessory.

Human beings were used in four different ways, each method strictly determined by the function of the picture. In the first place, man was introduced for technical purposes. He provided a foreground in Allston's "Moonlit Landscape"; he became a point of contact between spectator and scene, leading the eye into a "depth of space" in Morse's "View from Apple Hill";[32] he served to concentrate light and to develop the contrast of mild activity and static nature in Stanley's "Western Landscape." Among the writers, N. P. Willis made the most use of the human accessory for technical purposes, even going so far as to select the workers on his grounds at Idlewild for their picturesque appearances.[33] His acquaintance with many painters had given him a sharp, analytical eye.

Every new group changed and embellished the glorious combination of rock, foliage and water below me [at Trenton Falls], and I studied their dresses and attitudes as you would criticise them in a picture. The men with their two sticks of legs, and angular hats, looked abominably, of course. I was glad when they were out of the perspective. But the ladies of each party, with their flowing skirts, veils lifted by the wind, picturesque bonnets and parasols, were charming outlines as heighteners to the effect. . . . In the course of the morning, one lady came along . . . and, for her use, the gentleman who was with her carried a *crimson shawl*, flung over his shoulder. You would need to be an artist to understand how much that one shawl embellished the scene. It concentrated the light of the whole ravine . . . .[34]

This conviction of the picturesqueness of humanized landscape prompted Willis and the artist Bartlett to "people" one hundred and fifteen of the one hundred and nineteen engravings in their *American Scenery*.

32. Born, p. 36.
33. See Willis, *Out-Doors at Idlewild*, pp. 104-5.
34. Willis, *Rural Letters*, pp. 351-52.

A second type of landscape employed man to convey a sense of enjoyment, a method which is apparent in Henry Inman's "Picnic in the Catskills," Asher Durand's "Sunday Morning," and E. C. Coates's "View of New York Harbor." Here nature is pictured in its pastoral sense, as capable of transmitting simple pleasure apart from any spiritual therapy. In these scenes man is happy to have stolen away from the cares of the world. Alfred Billings Street's "A Forest Walk," although perhaps too closely resembling Marvell's "The Garden," is a telling example of this motif in the literature of New York:

> Here stretch'd, the pleasant turf I press,
> In luxury of idleness;
> Sun-streaks, and glancing wings, and sky
> Spotted with cloud-shapes, charm my eye;
> While murmuring grass, and waving trees
> Their leaf-harps sounding to the breeze
> And water-tones that tinkle near
> Blend their sweet music to my ear;
> And by the changing shades alone
> The passage of the hours is known.[35]

Although the artists and writers depicted men in groups as well as by themselves, the literary treatments of this subject often showed the author alone, passing freely amidst the scenes of nature, as in Drake's "Bronx" or Bryant's "Green River."

A third type of landscape arose as the poet or painter transformed man's simple enjoyment into a sense of wonder or awe in the face of nature's marvels. In such cases a single human being was usually employed, as in Cooper's *Leatherstocking Tales* or Doughty's "In Nature's Wonderland."[36] A few of the artists at times rejected such tricks and eliminated man entirely.[37] There was probably a national-

35. Street, *Poems*, p. 93.

36. The following pictures exhibit various degrees of this method: William Dunlap, "View of Niagara Falls," William Wall, "Hudson River from West Point," Thomas Doughty, "In the Catskills," Thomas Cole, "The Pass Called 'The Notch of the White Mountains,'" and William Bartlett, "Caterskill Falls."

37. See Thomas Cole, "Mountain Sunrise" and "Landscape with Tree Trunks," Thomas Doughty, "Mountain Torrent," Thomas Birch, "Upper Hudson," Asher Durand, "Monument Mountain" and "North Mountain Reservation, South Orange, New

istic motive behind this omission, a desire to exhibit the superiority of American over European scenery by showing that some areas in this country had never known the contaminating presence of man and civilization. "The Falls of the Mongaup" and "The Callicoon in Autumn," by Alfred Billings Street, present parallel examples of this method in Knickerbocker writings.

Finally, man was used as an accessory in landscapes of terror and desolation.[38] This was the most ambitious method because the painter or writer tried to create sublimity by injecting the element of horror into his art, in other words, by pursuing man with nature. Thus the painters portrayed man as either fleeing from nature (Catlin's "View on Missouri, Prairie Meadows Burning") or overcome by it (J. Shaw's "The Deluge"). The writers employed similar techniques for Gothic effects. In "A Forest Hymn," Bryant pictured himself as "annihilated" by a "mighty oak."[39] Willis personified the waters of Niagara as a dying man in order to lend the interest of the man-against-nature theme to his description of a scene which had already been exploited by others.[40] There were other examples of Gothic landscapes, such as "The Hunter's Flight" and "The Lost Hunter" by Alfred Billings Street and "Sonnet—Frost" by Park Benjamin. Perhaps the most effective was Bryant's "Midsummer" with its deliberately harsh sounds and spondee-impeded lines:

> A power is on the earth and in the air
> > From which the vital spirit shrinks afraid,
> > And shelters him, in nooks of deepest shade,
> From the hot steam and from the fiery glare.
> Look forth upon the earth—her thousand plants
> > Are smitten; even the dark sun-loving maize
> > Faints in the field beneath the torrid blaze;
> The herd beside the shaded fountain pants;

Jersey," John W. Casilear, "Moonlight," John F. Kensett, "Glimpse of Lake George," and William Hart, "Autumn in the Catskills."

38. For the literary influences on the American vogue of solitary and gloomy landscapes, see G. Harrison Orians, "The Rise of Romanticism," pp. 223-25. Other background is in Shepard, pp. 47-49.

39. Bryant, *Poetical Works*, I, 132.

40. See Willis, *American Scenery*, I, 33.

For life is driven from all the landscape brown;
 The bird has sought his tree, the snake his den,
 The trout floats dead in the hot stream, and men
Drop by the sun-stroke in the populous town;
 As if the Day of Fire had dawned, and sent
 Its deadly breath into the firmament.[41]

This sonnet is chiefly a landscape poem with man as an accessory even though his entrance is saved for the dramatic ending, the treatment progressing up a kind of ladder of being: first vegetable, then animal, then man—each in its turn overcome by nature. Through the religious terror introduced in the last two lines, the poet has striven for sublimity.

The painters and writers could at times give man a rather dignified place in their landscapes, at other times relegate him to diminutive proportions. These methods appeared simultaneously because of the wide variety of purposes behind nineteenth-century literature and art. Landscape was expected to please, instruct, soothe, spiritualize, and terrorize. Each function dictated a special technique and variations in the use of man.

CONTRASTED LANDSCAPES. Another device shared by writers and painters was the "before and after" technique of contrasting two or more landscapes in separate stanzas, chapters, books, or canvases. When Asher Durand exploited the device in "The Morning of Life" and "The Evening of Life" (1840), his friend Thomas Cole had already done so in "The Course of Empire" (1836), "The Departure" and "The Return" (1837), and "Past" and "Present" (1838). Cole devoted another four canvases to "The Voyage of Life" (1840) and was working on "The Cross of the World," a series of five pictures, when he died. Moreover, he had plans for at least three other groups: "Sowing and Reaping," "The World's Mirror," and "Future Course of Empire."

Alfred Billings Street and James Fenimore Cooper also experimented with this technique. In "A Contrast," a short poem of two

41. Bryant, *Poetical Works*, I, 172.

stanzas, Street presented a sharp double-picture of a frontier landscape and a civilized landscape. The first stanza might have been painted by any Hudson River artist:

> A LAKE is slumbering in the wild-wood depths,
> Picturing naught upon its polish'd glass
> But the long stretching and contracting shades
> That change as change the hours: its sullen tones
> Blending but with the forest's daylight songs
> And midnight howlings; o'er the leafy waste
> Curls a light thread of smoke—a hunter's fire;
> And mid the lilies' floating golden globes,
> Spangling the margin, where the ripples play
> And melt in silver, rocks his bark canoe.[42]

In the next stanza, however, we are told that years have passed and the scene is changed: much of the forest had been replaced with meadows; a village and gardens now stand where the hunter had camped; the sky is filled with the spires of churches, the domes of schools, and the roofs of houses. The single canoe has given way to "swift keels." In short, the hand of man has transformed a picturesque forest scene into the beauty of a cultivated and civilized landscape. But in contrasts such as these it was necessary to depict variety only amidst sameness; therefore, in the second stanza Street retained both the forest and the lake so that the reader might have familiar points of reference, the same context, in other words, in which to discover dissimilarities. There are not two landscapes; there is only an altered one.[43] This same retention of context may be found in "The Evening of Life." Durand pictured the aged shepherd sitting upon the base of a ruined column which, in "The Morning of Life," had probably been a section of the classical temple in the background.

Cooper's anti-rent series, comprised of *Satanstoe* (1845), *The Chainbearer* (1845), and *The Redskins* (1846), contains numerous examples of contrasted landscapes seen by three generations of the Littlepage

42. Street, *Poems*, p. 100.
43. *Ibid.* For a similar use of contrast, see Anthony Bleecker's "Trenton Falls, near Utica," collected in *The New-York Book of Poetry*, pp. 110-11.

family. Each novel has such contrasts *within* it,[44] but there are also contrasts *between* the novels. Thus a "before picture" in *Satanstoe* may have its "after picture" in *The Chainbearer* or even in *The Redskins*. For example, amid the heart of "a vast forest edifice" depicted in *Satanstoe*, Corny Littlepage discovers the scalped bodies of the surveyor Mr. Traverse and his two chainbearers. So carefully drawn is "this wide, gloomy" setting, in which "a sombre light prevailed, . . . rendering everything mellow and grave," that the Gothic landscape takes firm hold of the reader's memory.[45] The use of this same setting in *The Chainbearer* is, therefore, quite effective. Mordaunt Littlepage, Corny's son, is led like his father to this spot in the forest. It has changed in only one respect: it now contains a ruin—a human skeleton.

To show the evils of provincialism certain townscapes are also contrasted in this series. Rather cleverly, Cooper paints no townscapes in *The Chainbearer*, and as a result differences are greatly heightened. There is no easy transitional stage. First, in *Satanstoe* we see the New York of 1751, then the Albany of 1758; two books later—with a leap that takes us from the colonial period right into the middle of the nineteenth century—we come upon the same towns during the 1840's.[46]

But more important is the three-way contrast involving Ravensnest, the frontier settlement established by Herman Mordaunt, Corny Littlepage's father-in-law, and inherited successively by Corny's son Mordaunt and grandson Hugh Roger Littlepage. At first Ravensnest is nothing more than a few clearings in the wilderness, "neither very large nor very inviting."[47] Never an admirer of land filled with stumps and girdled trees, Cooper devoted only a few lines in *Satanstoe* to describing the terrain and an equal amount to the Old Nest House, which was later besieged by the Indians.[48] In *The Chainbearer*, how-

44. See Donald Ringe's analysis of *Satanstoe* in his "James Fenimore Cooper and Thomas Cole: An Analogous Technique," pp. 31-36.

45. Cooper, *Satanstoe*, II, 157-58.

46. For New York City, cf. *Satanstoe*, I, 32, 34-35, 100-2 to *Redskins*, I, 54-56; for Albany, cf. *Satanstoe*, I, 156, 161-65, 200 to *Redskins*, I, 74-75.

47. Cooper, *Satanstoe*, II, 74.

48. *Ibid.*, II, 77.

ever, he not only portrayed the landscape in full[49] but did so with the vocabulary of a painter. Looking down upon the scene, he saw "a foreground of open land, dotted with cottages and barns, mostly of logs, beautified by flourishing orchards, and garnished with broad meadows, or enriched by fields, in which the corn was waving under the currents of a light summer air." Several roads and a hamlet with its inn, store, school, and mills comprised the middle distance, and "the back-ground of this picture . . . was the 'boundless woods.' " The forest is represented as mysterious and therefore might be considered sublime. But more pertinent here are the abundant contrasts in the entire landscape with its indigenous mixture of the beautiful and the picturesque, the open and the closed, the light and the dark. Besides these internal contrasts there is the contrast between this view of Ravensnest and that found in *Satanstoe*. The stumps had now "nearly all disappeared from the fields," and Cooper delighted in their absence, compensating for it by picturing Herman Mordaunt's Old Nest House as a ruin, "mouldering, and . . . gone far into decay." The house had associations too, since it had once withstood an Indian attack. A third canvas was supplied in *The Redskins*. By this time Ravensnest had become a thriving frontier community. With dexterity, however, as if to avoid treating those inhabitants who had turned against their landlord, Cooper narrowed his focus from the panoramic sweep of *The Chainbearer* to a close-up of the Nest House and its immediate grounds. Here was a picture of aristocratic bliss, the original log Nest House having been replaced by one of stone, replete with stables, coachman, and extensive, parklike grounds, kept trim by a thousand grazing sheep.[50]

One of the purposes of the anti-rent novels was to prove that the property of the Littlepages, probably in reality Cooper's own property, had belonged to the family for at least three generations and that, as a result, the present landlord's title to it was indisputable. Therefore, it harmonized with Cooper's plan to give the Ravensnest area the stamp of age. This he neatly accomplished by decorating the grounds,

49. Cooper, *The Chainbearer*, I, 113-14.
50. Cooper, *The Redskins*, I, 118, 156-59.

so to speak, with two human ruins, the Indian Susquesus and the Negro Jaap, both of whom were over a century old and had been associated with all three landlords. Both, in fact, but especially the Indian, had been with Corny Littlepage and later with his son Mordaunt as they came upon the various landscapes in *Satanstoe* and *The Chainbearer*. Thus in all three novels they formed the continuing point of reference, the similarity in dissimilarity which rendered the contrast between the books meaningful. Furthermore, these two men were employed to enforce contrast within the single landscape itself. When put in with the soft, sylvan scenery of the Ravensnest of *The Redskins*, they achieved the same juxtaposition of the beautiful and the picturesque that belonged to a parallel landscape in *The Chainbearer*. One might compare the topography of *The Redskins* with that of the Englishman Richard Wilson's pictures if it were not for the abiding but subordinated wildness inherent in Cooper's scene.

Like Cole's landscapes of contrast, Cooper's books were saturated with theme; the idea behind the series which might be entitled "The Course of Ravensnest" was the recession and advance of men's minds. Each new generation of the landholding Littlepages frees itself from the shackles of provincial thinking while each new generation of renters is more tightly wrapped not only in the chains of provincialism but also in those of anti-rentism, to Cooper the vilest theory ever invented to destroy the rights of property. Thus the landscapes themselves, progressing always from a primitive to a civilized state, represent both parallel and contrast. In the case of the Littlepages, they parallel on the physical level a mental progression. In the case of the tenants, there is no parallel, only contrast between the attainment of material prosperity and the loss of spiritual integrity. To this irony of situation is added a final, telling contrast as Susquesus puts the anti-renters to shame by demonstrating that he, an uncivilized Indian, has recognized the rights of property, while they, supposedly civilized beings, have not. This talking ruin, already covered with the symbolism of antiquity, takes on even more meaning as a spokesman for democratic principles that protect the individual as well as the masses.

In *The Crater* (1847) one again finds Cooper using similar methods to puncture the belief in pseudo-progress. Since parallels between *The Crater* and Cole's "The Course of Empire" have been thoroughly analyzed elsewhere,[51] there is little need to discuss the subject here. Suffice it to say that Cooper, like Cole, adopted the role of prophet, declaring in *The Crater* that the present course of civilization would eventually call down the punishment of God, administered through nature, and that, like Cole, he developed his theme in a series of contrasted landscapes. Because he mentions "The Course of Empire" in the final chapter of this novel and because he praises Cole at another time for this series,[52] he undoubtedly borrowed his general design from the painter although other sources for ideas in *The Crater* have also been discovered.[53]

The Sea Lions (1849) contains further evidence of Cole's influence on Cooper. It, too, was composed of many different elements; the author drew upon various written accounts of Antarctic voyages as well as upon his own exposure to the sealing industry and familiarity with Alpine landscapes. Yet, as Thomas Philbrick suggests,[54] the framework for this novel was probably inspired by the second and third pictures in Cole's "Voyage of Life" series. Like the youth in these paintings, the hero of *The Sea Lions* (Roswell Gardiner) takes a voyage which symbolizes his spiritual progress, and while he moves from youth to middle age, he learns that his own powers are not enough to reach heaven, that he must also have faith. Cooper, in other words, was not only using Cole's methods but also repeating his conclusions.

Cooper and Cole were by no means the only Americans to be fascinated with the downfall of nations or to compare nature's mutation to man's. Some Americans, however, were so deeply imbued with democratic faith that they could interpret prophetic messages of empire's decay as visions of republic's bloom. To them it was the mani-

51. Ringe, "Cooper and Cole," pp. 18-30.

52. See Noble, p. 224.

53. See Harold H. Scudder, "Cooper's *The Crater*," pp. 109-26; W. B. Gates, "Cooper's *The Crater* and Two Explorers," pp. 243-46. Another possible germ of this novel is in Cooper, *Gleanings in Europe: Italy*, I, 224.

54. *James Fenimore Cooper and the Development of American Sea Fiction*, pp. 233-37.

fest destiny of the United States to prosper where other nations failed. A writer in the *Mirror*, for example, could optimistically interpret "The Course of Empire": "The climax in the course of man's progress, which Mr. Cole has here represented, is *that* which *has been*, and was founded on the usurpation of the strong over the weak: the perfection which man is hereafter to attain, will be based upon more stable foundations: political equality; the rights of man; the democratick principle; *the sovereignty of the people*."[55]

Yet Cooper and Cole stand alone as masters of the contrasted landscape because they were more deeply discontented and pessimistic than most of their fellow artists. Cooper's strong-mindedness is apparent in all his works, and his acute dissatisfaction with the America of his day is well known. Cole, however, has traditionally been thought of more or less as an ardent American and a cheerful romanticist. But, as Kenneth LaBudde has noted, Cole was at heart a pessimist about time and country:

Thomas Cole's criticisms of his society were probably shaped in part by the position it accorded him as an artist. His idea of the role he should play was not realized, and this contributed, no doubt, to his pessimistic frame of mind. Indeed, it may have been the largest single cause for the tenor of his outlook. He had hoped to have a volume of his verse published and he would have liked to have been recognized as an architect of monumental structures, but his major disappointment was not being able to be a painter of great art as he saw that art to be.[56]

Cooper and Cole, not close friends, not living for that matter in very similar environments, were kindred spirits nevertheless. Both were horrified by the increasing materialism of American society, and both found a panacea for it in Christianity. That both used parallel methods to develop their themes is, therefore, not surprising.

55. "The Third of Mr. Cole's Five Pictures," *NYM*, XIV (Nov. 4, 1836), 150. For equations of man's mutation and nature's, see Irving, *Bracebridge Hall*, p. 12; Prosper M. Wetmore, *Lexington, with Other Fugitive Poems*, p. 72; Halleck, "Twilight," *Poetical Writings*, pp. 36-37; Bryant, "Ruins of Italica," *Poetical Works*, II, 283; Willis, *American Scenery*, I, 33. Interest in the cyclical interpretation of history appears in B., "Downfall of Nations," *K*, VI (July, 1835), 44-53; Bryant, *Letters of a Traveller: Second Series*, pp. 15-16.

56. LaBudde, p. 159.

This survey of the techniques employed by Knickerbocker writers and American painters should prove, if nothing else, that these men were true artists, motivated by a high purpose. Whether they took the panoramic approach, used the human accessory, composed their pictures with a brand of selective realism, or created sharply contrasted scenes in order to criticize society, they did so with a single worthy goal in mind—to strengthen the bonds between God, man, and nature, and thus to fashion a spiritually functional art.

Mutual Publications

It was inevitable that with this much in common they would work on joint projects. The results of their co-operation were four gift books and a magazine, all devoted to landscape but varying in historical significance and commercial appeal. Such undertakings were for the aggressive, not the timid, since publication of any kind in the early nineteenth century was a precarious business, and sales were never insured.[57] Furthermore, the ineffectiveness of copyright laws gave pirated rather than native works a special attraction to publishers. Successful, original landscape books were therefore rare.[58] At least two such works, however, may be attributed to the Knickerbockers.

THE AMERICAN LANDSCAPE. The first joint production limited to native scenery, illustrated by an American, written by a Knickerbocker, and published in New York was *The American Landscape* (1830). Asher Durand engraved all but one of the seven illustrations for this pioneer volume. His friend Bryant composed most of the letterpress, which matched original paintings and drawings by Durand, Cole, Bennett, and Weir. The publishers planned extending "the work to ten numbers," each with "six views, in quarto, . . . to appear at intervals of six months, or oftener if possible."[59] But the first number proved to

57. MS letter, Irving to Cole, New York, Sept. 15, 1835, Cole Papers, NYSL, is an example of preliminary arrangements for the publication of such landscape books.

58. These are surveyed in Frank Weitenkampf, "Early American Landscape Prints," pp. 40-68.

59. A. B. Durand and E. Wade, Jun., "Prospectus of the American Landscape," in Bryant and Durand, *The American Landscape, No. I*, p. 4.

be the last,[60] although three of its engravings—"Weehawken," "Falls of the Sawkill," and "The Delaware Water-Gap"—were later reissued with their letterpress in *The New-York Mirror*.[61]

The reasons for the failure of *The American Landscape* are somewhat obscure. In many ways it promised success. Although it might be considered a continuation of *The Talisman* series, it abandoned the humor of these volumes[62] and approached its problem seriously. Its nationalistic tone was especially suitable to the temper of its day. The "Prospectus" read: "Nature is not less liberal of the characteristics of beauty and sublimity in the new world, than in the old"—an appealingly chauvinistic statement,[63] supplemented by Bryant's observation that native scenery contains "enough of the lovely, the majestic, and the romantic, to entitle it to be ranked with that of any country."[64] The text of *The American Landscape* was written by a man whose reputation was firmly established, and was illustrated by the country's leading engraver. Neither Bryant nor Durand could have been accused of hack work: the straightforward prose, hardly as lively as Willis' or Irving's, was nonetheless appropriate to the informative nature of the publication. The plates, although small, were carefully executed and are rather highly valued by some of today's art historians.[65] Lastly, both text and illustrations stressed aspects of American scenery that were most appealing in the early nineteenth century.

60. The *Mirror*'s statement that *The American Landscape* "was not put into circulation" appears to be inaccurate. See "Falls of the Sawkill," *NYM*, X (May 25, 1833), 369.

61. *NYM*, X (April 20, 1833), 329; X (May 25, 1833), 369; XI (June 7, 1834), 385 respectively. The engravings faced these pages of text. The *Mirror* also reprinted, without engravings, three other descriptions from *The American Landscape*, with several very short and minor additions and changes in wording: "Catskill Mountains," *NYM*, X (Oct. 17, 1832), 133; "Weehawken," X (Nov. 3, 1832), 142; and, with the third paragraph of Bryant's text omitted, "The Delaware Water-Gap," X (Dec. 1, 1832), 174.

62. Bryant II, pp. 180-81; MS letters, Bryant to Verplanck, New York, Feb. 23, March 5, 1830, Bryant-Verplanck Correspondence, Berg Collection, NYPL.

63. Bryant and Durand, p. 3.

64. *Ibid.*, p. 6.

65. See Virgil Barker, *American Painting*, p. 511; Larkin, p. 143; and, for the most specific analysis, Richardson, p. 169. The nineteenth century was apparently not quite so enthusiastic. See "The American Landscape," *NYM*, VIII (Jan. 8, 1831), 214; Durand, *A. B. Durand*, p. 73.

Lake Winnipiseogee was associated with the romantic Indian,[66] and Fort Putnam was described as a "venerable ruin of massive military architecture, . . . fraught with recollections of heroism, liberty, and virtue."[67] Above all, the popular concern for documentation was strictly adhered to; Bryant was careful to inform his readers of the exact point from which each picture was made, and "the proprietors" vowed that *"characteristic features will, in all cases, be truly and correctly copied."*[68]

But the fate of pioneer works was unpredictable, and the failure of *The American Landscape* seems to have been due mostly to external circumstances rather than to lack of merit. First, its small, gray plates could hardly compete with the larger, colored views of William Wall's *Hudson River Portfolio*, issued five years earlier than *The American Landscape.*[69] Secondly, it probably was not merchandised with any great enthusiasm by Elam Bliss, its publisher, who had already met with only limited success in the publication of The Sketch Club's *Talisman* series.[70] Thirdly, it appeared at a very precarious time. Although the fervor of the public was gradually being stirred up by the writers of the day, as yet the great wave of enthusiasm for nature which was to culminate in the National Park movement was only a promising ripple. The success or failure of landscape publications could hardly be predicted, and while one book might find buyers, another might not.

Had *The American Landscape* been published fifteen years later, it might have thrived. Bryant's dry comment that "it would be easier to find a series of good views of the scenery of China or Southern India, than of the United States"[71] would have been as true in 1845 as it was in 1830. No American book in the first half of the nineteenth

66. Bryant and Durand, p. 15.

67. *Ibid.*, pp. 11-12.

68. *Ibid.*, p. 4.

69. See Weitenkampf, p. 65.

70. This lack of enterprise became especially apparent when Bliss published Bryant's poetry in 1832. Finding approximately 100 copies of this edition still for sale, Bryant remarked: "Bliss *sells* as slow as Old Rapid in the play *sleeps.* Any other bookseller would have got off the whole before this time; but he is a good creature . . ." (letter to Dana, quoted in Godwin, I, 285).

71. Bryant and Durand, p. 6.

century covered the scenery of the entire United States. Perhaps *The American Landscape* would have done so, even with its modest regional beginning, had its life not been cut short by public apathy, but the need for such a publication was not yet felt by more than a few.

AMERICAN SCENERY. *American Scenery* (1840), written by Nathaniel Parker Willis and illustrated by William Henry Bartlett, was the most ambitious undertaking of the entire Knickerbocker period. Embodying two hundred and forty-six pages of text and one hundred and nineteen engravings, it was a bulky work, especially if its owner had its two volumes bound under one cover. The book's scope was limited to the northeastern part of the United States, but in this area was enough diversity of landscape to prevent the engraved views from becoming monotonous. The purpose of *American Scenery* was twofold: The illustrations were assembled to allow "those whose lot is domestic and retired" to enjoy the benefits of travel "at little cost and pains."[72] The letterpress was written to make each engraving meaningful by matching it with a legend, a poem, an anecdote, or a descriptive essay, chosen for its associational value.

American Scenery was a Knickerbocker production only in a limited sense. Willis, its editor, had been a New Yorker for almost a decade, but Bartlett, its illustrator, was an Englishman;[73] the book itself was published in London.[74] Only the two engravings made after pictures by Thomas Doughty cannot be traced to Bartlett's watercolors. On the other hand, because of its editorship, contents, and influence, the book is American in a very real sense.

Today, more than one hundred years after its publication, the value of *American Scenery* has been recognized but partially. True, it is an expensive book; a foxed copy now sells for about $25, but this is due

72. Willis, *American Scenery*, I, iv.

73. Information on Bartlett may be found in Bartlett Cowdrey, "William Henry Bartlett and the American Scene," pp. 388-400, and in Sears, pp. 1-2. Willis mentions Bartlett in *Rural Letters*, pp. 41-42, 114-17, 130; *Hurry-Graphs*, p. 78.

74. At a later date, however, a shorter, 92-page edition was published in America: N. P. Willis, *Picturesque American Scenery: A Series of Twenty-Five Beautiful Steel Engravings* (1883). In this edition, a few engravings after Thomas Moran and George L. Brown were added to those after Bartlett.

largely to the possibilities of grangerizing. When hand-colored and framed, its plates fetch from $6 to $30 and are sold even in department stores. *American Scenery* has retained its popularity because of Bartlett's illustrations, not Willis' text. This is unfortunate because the letterpress contains some of Willis' best writing, despite Henry Beers's remark that it is "hack work" of "little . . . purely literary interest."[75] What the author did not write for himself he compiled with skill from a wide range of chroniclers and poets. Actually, Willis imagined a worthy goal and achieved it, shaping *American Scenery* into a vast storehouse of association-enhanced landscape, and an authentic, colorful record of America's folklore, legend, and history. Equal credit should be given to Bartlett and Willis alike for this enterprise.

CANADIAN SCENERY. *Canadian Scenery* (1840),[76] another fireside travel work by Willis and Bartlett, was a two-volume companion of *American Scenery*, which it resembled in bulk, format, and, presumably, popularity. Since Willis borrowed most of the letterpress from various authorities on Canadian life and history, whom he acknowledged in a footnote of general indebtedness,[77] he can be praised only for his editorial acumen. Original or not, the text of *Canadian Scenery* is still valuable for its wealth of historical and legendary matter—two hundred and forty-four pages in all—much of it concerned with the North American Indian.[78] By uncovering its associations, Willis performed almost as great a service for the Canadian landscape as he had for the scenery of the northeastern United States.

The real charm of *Canadian Scenery* comes not from Willis' text, however, but from Bartlett's illustrations. This English artist seems to have felt more at home in Canada. His drawing appears bolder; his ability to capture the romance of a scene greater in this book than in *American Scenery*. "Raft in a Squall, on Lake St. Peter" surpasses in

75. Beers, p. 247.
76. Some background material for the writing of this book is given in Beers, pp. 244, 247-48.
77. See N. P. Willis, *Canadian Scenery*, I, 1 n.
78. See Daughrity, pp. 136-37.

its impact, most nineteenth-century engraved seascapes; "Les Marches Naturelles" and "A Forest Scene" place one solidly in the midst of nature, their moodiness heightened by contrast with the documentary quality of Bartlett's architectural and genre views. Because of its numerous fine engravings and authentic text, *Canadian Scenery* was a significant work, next to *American Scenery* the most ambitious effort at artistic collaboration in the Knickerbocker period.[79]

THE HOME BOOK OF THE PICTURESQUE. With *The Home Book of the Picturesque* (1852),[80] production of landscape gift books during the Knickerbocker period reached its climax. Its one hundred and eighty-eight pages encompassed letterpress by the leading writers of New York and engravings after pictures by major Hudson River School artists, so that everything about this book was either native or regional, including the publisher, George P. Putnam. One had to pay $7 for a cloth-bound copy, $10 for morocco, and $16 for a volume with India proofs,[81] but even these were bargain prices which allowed purchasers to support their country's arts.

The engravings were small but splendid vignettes executed by Henry Beckwith, John Halpin, Samuel Valentine Hunt, and John Kirk, all respectable practitioners of their craft. A list of the painters from whose pictures the engravings were made includes both the older and younger members of the Hudson River School: Thomas Cole, Asher Durand, and Robert Weir, plus Beckwith, who engraved his own picture of "The Bay of New York," Jaspar F. Cropsey, Thomas Addison Richards, Frederick E. Church, and Régis Gignoux. The superiority of *The Home Book of the Picturesque* was due, however, not to its inclusiveness or bulk (it contained only thirteen

79. Willis also worked with Bartlett on a book of Irish landscape but wrote very little of its text: N. P. Willis and J. Sterling Coyne, *The Scenery and Antiquities of Ireland*. A much smaller and less significant work, replete with wood engravings after various minor artists, was N. P. Willis (ed.), *Trenton Falls, Picturesque and Descriptive*. Willis was actually co-author of this book, not merely its editor. Thirty-three pages consisted of an essay written by John Sherman in 1827; the remaining 56 pages of text were Willis'.

80. Reissued as *Home Authors and Home Artists, or American Scenery, Art, and Literature* (n.d.).

81. See Thompson, p. 128.

plates), but to its consistently high quality of illustrations,[82] especially notable since, at the time of its publication, the usual American gift book was a congeries of secondhand engravings, pirated text, and trite sentimentality of the Botanical School type. No Fanny Fern wrote for this volume; the publisher therefore chose his pictures to explain the American landscape, not to provoke emotional outbursts over plagued heroines.

The letterpress was both varied and meaty, beginning in scholarly fashion with Elias Lyman Magoon's formal attempt to prove the spiritual benefits of landscape. Another selection, Fenimore Cooper's "American and European Scenery Compared," was a blunt essay, devoid of chauvinism, conceding "to Europe much the boldest scenery . . . [to] America the freshness of a promising youth."[83] A shorter piece contained Irving's desultory observations on national landscape and some recollections of his boyhood in the New York area. Bryant discussed "The Valley of the Housatonic," and Willis wrote about "The Highland Terrace, above West Point."[84] Representing the younger writers were Susan Fenimore Cooper, Bayard Taylor, Henry T. Tuckerman, Mary E. Field, and Alfred Billings Street. George Washington Bethune provided a fitting close to the volume with his "Art in the United States," predicting the establishment of a national gallery. Although no writer did his best work in these pages, each contributed to the anthology's over-all richness, due largely to the lively interest these authors took in the American landscape, an enthusiasm matched by the artists whose pictures they illustrated.

PICTURESQUE AMERICA. Years after the Hudson River School had declined and most of the Knickerbocker writers had died, William Cullen Bryant edited *Picturesque America* (1872), another landscape gift book which deserves mention here. The poet's contribution may be given in his own words: "I edited the work, it is true. Somebody must edit such a publication, and I do not see why I should not do it as

82. For some background material, including a letter to Putnam from his close friend John F. Kensett, who was displeased with the engraving of his picture, see George H. Putnam, *George Palmer Putnam: A Memoir*, pp. 192-93.

83. *Home Book of the Picturesque*, p. 69.

84. This essay was reprinted in Willis, *Out-Doors at Idlewild*, pp. 1-25.

well as another. Every part of it, except a few of the first sheets, passed through my hands; and I do not remember that I was ever more weary of any literary task, for the mere description of places is the most tedious of all reading. It was my business to correct the language, omit superfluous passages, and see that no nonsense crept into the text; and this I did as faithfully as I knew how."[85] In this mass of letterpress, over eleven hundred large pages, Bryant must have been happy to come upon essays by Thomas Bangs Thorpe, John Esten Cooke, and Constance Fenimore Woolson.

Although he did not select the hundreds of excellent illustrations in *Picturesque America*, Bryant was probably delighted with those which recalled friendships of earlier days: James M. Hart's "The Adirondack Woods" had the delicate serenity of Asher Durand's "Monument Mountain," and J. D. Woodward's "Connecticut Valley from Mount Tom" was reminiscent of Thomas Cole's panoramic "Oxbow." The old spirit—druidical, topographical, associational—lingered on the pages of this belated Knickerbocker book. Its old editor, destined to live only six more years, having once failed with *The American Landscape*, was too tired to be proud of the acclaim which met his latest effort.

Picturesque America was the first major landscape publication edited by a Knickerbocker writer to treat of the entire United States and, in this sense, was quite new. *The American Landscape, The Home Book of the Picturesque*, and even *American Scenery* had been limited to the northern and eastern part of this country. *Picturesque America* with its descriptions and views of the Rocky Mountains, the Golden Gate, and the coast of Florida, achieved a coverage that the pioneer works had been denied because of insufficient public support and the immaturity of native publishing. Unfortunately, few of the Knickerbockers still lived to enjoy this eloquent tribute to America's vastness.

Paradoxically enough, this study of nature demonstrates the importance of man. Certain techniques were used and gift books were

85. Letter from Bryant to Dr. Dewey, quoted in Godwin, II, 347.

published so that man might benefit from the experience of those who had devoted their lives to analyzing scenery. Panoramic and compositional techniques, for example, taught that even in vastness God can create and men can find unity, harmony, and order. Human accessories in painted and printed views allowed man to look at himself in a mirror to discover his relationship to nature, which could delight, awe, and terrorize. By paying special attention to landscapes of contrast he could learn that his own life and the lives of his empires have, like nature, periods of blight and bloom. Finally, the publication of attractive landscape gift books helped him to review the lessons he had been taught by the Knickerbockers and their fellow artists, who never lost sight of the fact that they were men talking to men—about nature.

CHAPTER VI

GENRE

Definition of the Term

According to Oliver Larkin the art of "genre" is an attempt "to interpret man to himself by showing how he behaves on simple and present occasions."[1] Larkin's definition of this vague term rules out landscape for landscape's sake, for man is the center of attraction in the world of genre, the landscape serving as his backdrop. Because genre interprets behavior, and behavior implies action, a portrait could not strictly be termed genre, nor could a character sketch unless seasoned with anecdote. Moreover, the phrase "simple and present occasions" certainly denies the rank of genre to most histories although some historical pictures and writings may be called semi-genre, for they stress the everyday affairs of the past rather than its extraordinary incidents and reduce aristocratic heroes to common and even comic characters.

The treatment of genre materials may be serious or humorous, and it may range from neoclassic satire to complete objectivity to romantic

1. *Art and Life in America*, p. 214.

sentimentalism. The satire need not be harsh, like Hogarth's or Swift's, for the humanitarian who respects his characters while admitting their vices often seeks to reform them with gentle humor. Nor need the sentimentality be extreme, in spite of the fact that, to the romanticist, emotionalism "was a form of emancipation . . . an enlargement of his feelings, a freeing of his inner responses . . . [a force which] widened the expression of individual thoughts and moods."[2] Attitudes toward genre subjects therefore encompassed both the romantic and the neoclassic—and much that lies between.

But although genre materials did not go unnoticed amid the elegance of eighteenth-century neoclassicism, it was the dominant romanticism of the next century that turned the spotlight on the common man and thus made it possible for genre to play its most important role in art. America especially reflected this change of emphasis. The political theories of the Federalists, with their neoclassic dependence on a natural aristocracy and on checks and balances to restrain majorities, gave ground in successive stages to a romantic faith in the middle and lower classes. Under Jacksonian democracy, for example, neither aristocratic lineage nor special training was deemed necessary for those who would hold public office. Anticipating this faith in the potential of the common man was the reliance of the Methodists, Baptists, and Disciples on an untrained ministry to serve the frontier. Contrary to the Puritans, who had believed in the leadership of the elite, the Baptists at first refused to establish seminaries; even after relenting they held that a theological education was not essential to the spreading of Christianity.[3] Nevertheless improved primary and secondary education for all Americans was the goal of such environmentalists as Horace Mann, and it was this romantic spirit that, reviving Puritan intellectualism, eventually brought learning to the middle and lower classes. Supplementing the schools were the various schemes for adult education, including debating societies, the lyceums, and library associations. Moreover, there were hundreds of utopian movements which

2. Orians, "The Rise of Romanticism," p. 192.
3. William W. Sweet, *Religion in the Development of American Culture*, pp. 182-83.

drew their numbers from and aimed to reform the common people.[4] In short, during the second quarter of the nineteenth century, Americans were attending primarily to the interests of the common man, while the literary and visual arts were not only reflecting but causing this attention.

Genre in American Literature

Genre had made its first appearance in American literature during the eighteenth century, the age of neoclassic satire. It had been lacking in the writings of the Puritans, who constantly focused on man's relationship with God and, even in the neoclassic period, it would not affect the serious epics of the Connecticut Wits. Yet it was an important ingredient of such mock-heroic efforts as Barlow's *Hasty Pudding*, Trumbull's *The Progress of Dulness*, and Brackenridge's *Modern Chivalry*, filled with the quixotic antics of Teague O'Regan and many another ordinary man. Dwight's *Greenfield Hill*, replete with village worthies, and Hopkinson's familiar essay "On White-Washing" also qualified as genre pieces.

In its very beginning the Knickerbocker literature of the next century treated genre situations and characters, although frequently in historical settings. The authors of *Salmagundi* (1807) snickered over their contemporaries, but in *A History of New York* (1809) Irving applied much the same method to bygone days. Humbling the great and exalting the low, he found common denominators for everyone. Even the gods were not spared. His pen reduced Venus to "a blear eyed trull," Mars to "a drunken corporal," and Apollo to "a bandy-legged fifer, playing most villainously out of tune."[5] The proud governors of New Amsterdam were given the foibles of the man in the street, that is, of the Dutchman on the stoop, who in turn was described in meticulous and loving detail.

In 1825 Bryant noted that America was as rich as any country in material for native fiction, and that the activities of nature's noblemen

4. For these and other examples of the connection between romanticism and the rise of the common man, see Harvey Wish, *Society and Thought in America*, I, 283-478.

5. Diedrich Knickerbocker [Washington Irving], *A History of New York*, II, 136.

were more substantial stuff on which to build literature than the "magnificent levees of princes, . . . the bright assemblies of fashion, . . . [or] the glittering dances and pranks of fairies." What Bryant called for was "something . . . which is natural, the uneffaced traits of strength and weakness, of the tender and the comic, all which the pride of rank either removes from observation or obliterates."[6]

These natural traits as they appeared in the writings of the Knickerbockers may be divided conveniently into urban and non-urban. As New York City grew in population, certain occupational groups took on enough identity to attract the pens of local wits. The Croakers— Halleck and Drake—addressed a poem to "Dear Simon! Prince of pastry cooks!"[7] M'Donald Clarke wrote of "Luke, the Broadway Baker"[8] and of the clam boy "with his ricketty wagon and old blind horse."[9] Cornelius Mathews, moved by the spirit of regionalism to discover the unique aspects of New York, carefully described the city's firemen, newsboys, and seamstresses.[10] Did the garbage man escape this ingathering of society's lower ranks? No, he was caught in an essay by Edward Sanford,[11] a minor Knickerbocker but a master of euphemisms. With unparalleled delicacy and with tongue firmly in cheek, Sanford identified his subject as the man who "receive[d] from the tenants of the underground apartments of the houses where he had the honor to call, those superfluous vegetable particles which are discarded—especially in warm weather—from the alimentary preparations of well-regulated families."[12] In such descriptions of urban characters, there is obvious satire, but, although the writers admitted the shortcomings of each sitter, they also tried to make their readers see him as he really was, recognize his share of dignity, and accept him as a useful member of society.

6. Bryant, Review of *Redwood*, by Catharine M. Sedgwick, *North American Review*, XX (April, 1825), 252.
7. Halleck, *Poetical Writings*, pp. 303-5.
8. Clarke, *Poems*, pp. 135-36.
9. "The Clam Cart," *ibid.*, pp. 280-82.
10. *A Pen-and-Ink Panorama of New York City*, pp. 93-101, 182-95, 109-120. "The genuine Newsboy, in his full development and activity, we fancy, does not exist, except in New York" (*idem*, p. 182).
11. "A Charcoal Sketch of Pot Pie Palmer," in *The Atlantic Club-Book*, II, 251-67.
12. *Ibid.*, II, 258.

Non-urban traits and characters, having already enjoyed a longer tradition than urban subjects in literature, were now in greater demand than ever; for the celebration of homespun virtues was part of the New-World attack on the loose morality of English and continental romanticism as represented by the works of Bulwer, Schiller, Byron, and Godwin.[13] In New York perhaps Samuel Woodworth wrote the most effective verse in praise of rural values. With "The [Old Oaken] Bucket" he created a popular symbol of nostalgia for the simple, pure life of the cottager. In "The Needle," a later poem of the same meter, he denounced "the gay belles of fashion" in order to applaud women to whom "home and its duties are dear."[14] But it was prose rather than poetry which best displayed the dignity and substance of sailors, frontiersmen, and rustics. Cooper, whose sympathies with the common man were definitely limited by his hatred of mediocrity, nevertheless furnished prototypes in Long Tom Coffin of *The Pilot* and Natty Bumppo of the *Leatherstocking Tales*. Equally valid but less memorable homespun heroes were Sybrandt Westbrook and Bosh Blivins, supplied respectively by Paulding in *The Dutchman's Fireside* and Willis in *Paul Fane*.

With such characters the Knickerbockers easily disproved the notion that only high society can ennoble fiction, and by sometimes turning their attention to middle- and lower-class activities—whether ordinary or extraordinary, urban or non-urban—they enriched a tradition which met and mingled with a similar current in American painting.

Genre in American Art

Native genre painting began in the Colonial Period, which has been mistakenly represented as an age of artists practicing a single branch of art, portraiture. Actually, during this period genre found its way onto cards, banners, chimney-backs, embroideries, wall-panels, and fire-boards. Occasionally it was painted on canvas or, like John Greenwood's lively "Sea Captains Carousing at Surinam," on bed-ticking. Landscapes were mixed with genre in the form of hunting

13. See Orians, "The Rise of Romanticism," pp. 174-77.
14. *The Poetical Works of Samuel Woodworth*, I, 122.

177

scenes and peopled topographical views. There are, however, few sur-
viving examples of genre painting from this era, the descendants of
the colonials apparently preferring to dispose of the anecdotal pictures
cluttering their attics as so much trash but to save the family portraits
as precious heirlooms.[15]

Until 1830 there were no native specialists in genre. Copley's
"Brook Watson and the Shark," Peale's "Exhuming the Mastodon,"
Krimmel's "Fourth of July Celebration," Sargent's "Dinner Party,"
and Fisher's "Going Fishing" were scattered efforts, works by men
who usually painted portraits. The first American artist to make a
career of depicting genre scenes was William Sidney Mount, whose
"Rustic Dance," painted in 1830, was his initial contribution to this
field.

After 1830 many native artists specialized in recording the ordinary
aspects of the life around them. George Caleb Bingham pictured
ruddy-faced checker players and gleeful raftsmen; David Gilmour
Blythe found humor in the crush of city folk at a post office window;
Tompkins H. Matteson captured the fright and frenzy of boys attacked by hornets; Richard Caton Woodville painted a sailor's wedding; and Francis W. Edmonds showed the joys of harmless "spark-
ing" while mother washed the dishes. Although these and other
painters treated their subjects with a great amount of realism, they
generally selected the smiling aspects of life, either ignoring or de-
emphasizing not only sex and brutality but also hard work. In most
of the pictures from this period we see Americans at play and at rest.[16]

Critical Appraisal of Genre

As journalistic art critics, the Knickerbockers spilled more ink over
architecture and landscape paintings than over these pictures of every-
day life. Perhaps the writers did not know what to say about genre,
what principles to judge it by, or how to explain themselves techni-

15. James T. Flexner, *American Painting*, pp. 148-75, especially pp. 152-53, 166-75.
16. Lloyd Goodrich, *American Genre: The Social Scene in Paintings & Prints* (*1800-1935*), pp. 6-7.

Thomas Cole

SCENE FROM THE LAST OF THE MOHICANS
(1827) (*The New York State Historical
Association, Cooperstown, New York*)

Thomas Cole

LAST OF THE MOHICANS

(*The Wadsworth Atheneum, Hartford*)

cally in a critical jargon which they would be forced to invent for themselves. One could call landscape "sublime" or "picturesque"; but what could one say of a figure painting that commemorated no historical event, was not an exact likeness of a cherished relative, and did not even pretend to be a topographical record? Consider *The Knickerbocker's* comment on an anecdotal painting of the day: "The picture has one great merit,—it tells the story."[17] To the nineteenth-century critic this was the crux of genre: it told to men the story of a man or men. But it did not tell the story of great men, as did historical painting. And it did not stimulate the onlooker to thoughts of God, as did landscape painting. Thus it had to be judged on its story-telling values. If a particular genre painting fulfilled the demands of such criteria, it might even be called a great painting, but its greatness might never equal that of the other branches of design.

The Knickerbockers favored the work of Mount, a Long Islander, above all native genre pictures. True, there were a few complaints. "All his faces are too much alike,—not only in the same picture, but in all his pictures," mentioned the "Editor's Table" of *The Knickerbocker*. "His gentlemen and ladies, or rather lads and lasses, are all of the same family."[18] A reviewer for the *Literary World* thought that the coloring in Mount's work was deficient.[19] But such whispers went unheard in the general chorus of praise. Writers in the *Mirror* called Mount's "Farmer's Nooning" a "truly American" picture[20] and singled out the painter's rare talent for putting expression in the hands of his figures.[21] "Let Mr. Mount stick to nature, . . ." another critic suggested. "He is in the right path."[22] Reviewers for *Arcturus*, the *Literary World, Harper's*, and *The Knickerbocker* could be just as

17. "Editor's Table: The Fine Arts: National Academy of Design," *K*, V (June, 1835), 555.

18. "National Academy of Design," *K*, V (June, 1835), 555. Also see *idem*, IX (June, 1837), 622.

19. "National Academy Exhibition," *LW*, III (May 27, 1848), 328.

20. "The National Academy of Design," *NYM*, XIV (June 17, 1837), 407.

21. "William S. Mount," *NYM*, XIV (Dec. 24, 1836), 206.

22. "National Academy of Design," *NYM*, XIII (June 25, 1836), 414. Also see *idem*, XIII (June 18, 1836), 406, and XV (June 9, 1838), 398. But cf. *idem*, XIX (May 22, 1841), 167. In "The National Academy," *NYM*, [n. s. V] (May 1, 1847), 59, Mount is called "at once the best and the worst of our artists."

enthusiastic,[23] a writer in the last-named magazine even going so far as to call Mount "the American Teniers."[24]

To acquire an accurate view of the critical scene one must see how a New York magazine could shift from generous praise of a native son to almost malicious condemnation of another genre painter. The Knickerbockers did not always damn by omission. Witness the *Literary World*'s appraisal of George Caleb Bingham's "Jolly Flat Boat Men": "a vulgar subject, vulgarly treated, . . . drawing . . . faulty and the composition artificial,—altogether a most unworthy and unfortunate selection." Even more condemnatory were the same reviewer's remarks on Bingham's "Raftsmen Playing Cards": ". . . disagreeable, a monotonous, dull, dirty pink pervades every part; and in texture there is the same monotony. Flesh, logs, and earthen jugs have the same quality of substance, the same want of handling . . . ; we would rather see the figures as hard as statues than see light, shade, color, and texture swept into a muss of soft confusion. In composition, Mr. B. should be aware that the regularity of a pyramid is only suitable to scenes of the utmost beauty and repose. . . ."[25] This is Gothamite criticism at its harshest.

The Knickerbockers could both praise and condemn native genre painters; but, in the final evaluation, the range of their critical remarks, however judicious, is no more important than the paucity of them. What the writers did say may have been fair, but they did not say enough. Practical criticism of genre was scattered and brief; abstract principles were seldom applied to the form, and a real critical

23. See "The Fine Arts: Exhibition of the Academy," *Arcturus*, II (June, 1841), 61; "The Fine Arts," *LW*, I (June 5, 1847), 419; "Monthly Record of Current Events," *Harper's New Monthly Magazine*, II (Feb., 1851), 417.

24. With a qualification, however: Mount's ". . . rustic scenes, while they have all the nature and humor of the Dutchman, are entirely free from his occasional grossness" ("Editor's Table: The Fine Arts: National Academy of Design," *K*, V [June, 1835], 554-55). For further praise of Mount in *K*, see IX (June, 1837), 621-22; XXIV (July, 1844), 75; XXVII (June, 1846), 556; XXIX (June, 1847), 572. But cf. an anonymous critic's unfavorable notice of Mount's "Webster among the People," in *K*, XLV (May, 1855), 531.

25. Both quotations are from "The Fine Arts: The Art-Union Pictures," *LW*, II (Oct. 23, 1847), 277. Another genre painter, Albertus D. O. Browere, was made the target of a reviewer's barbs in "American Academy of the Fine Arts," *The* (New York) *American Monthly Magazine*, I (Aug., 1833), 401.

ferment never developed. As we shall discover, the Knickerbockers contributed more to native genre by supplying its artists with material than by praising them.

From Pictures to Words

Before disclosing this process, however, we must first examine the influence of genre pictures on the literature of New York, for, although the Knickerbockers usually wrote letterpress from which illustrations were later made, the process was sometimes reversed, the designs being made first, the letterpress after. Because engravers needed a great deal of time to work on a plate, pictures for gift books had to be submitted long before the publisher's deadline, so that, if a writer did not compose his letterpress before the artists made their sketches, he was forced to write on their subjects, which may or may not have suited his fancy and abilities. Litterateurs in The Sketch Club were used to impromptu writing, and therefore it is not surprising to find in *The Talisman*, their annual, at least seven instances of letterpress composed to match pictures.[26] Sands' "Weehawken" and Halleck's "Red Jacket" respectively illustrated engravings of a drawing by Neilson and a portrait by Weir, but no less than five pieces, including the sonnet on Cole, were written by Bryant to accompany designs by artist-friends.[27]

Other Knickerbocker productions, some of them non-fictional, bear the same marks of composition. Gulian Verplanck wrote prose sketches for engravings of paintings by Robert Weir.[28] James Kirke Paulding and other authors performed similar services for *The New-York*

26. See Bryant II, pp. 132, 139, 156, 172-73. Cf. Thompson, p. 38.

27. In *The Talisman* for 1828: "Sonnet" accompanying Henry Inman's "William Tell"; "Drummond, a Tale of the Dismal Swamp" accompanying Henry Inman's "Dismal Swamp." In *The Talisman* for 1830: "Song: Innocent Child and Snow-White Flower" accompanying Henry Inman's "Child and Lily"; "To the River Arve" accompanying John Neilson's "View on the River Arve"; "Sonnet: To Cole the Painter" accompanying Thomas Cole's "View near Ticonderoga."

28. See Verplanck, "Bourbon's Last March," *NYM*, XII (Oct. 11, 1834), 113-14, especially 113 n.; July, p. 243; Verplanck, "View of Washington's Headquarters," *NYM*, XII (Dec. 27, 1834), 201-2, accompanying "Washington's Head-Quarters. Newburgh, N.Y.," facing p. 201; "An Autumnal Evening," *NYM*, XII (March 28, 1835), 305-6, accompanying "Evening. A Scene in the Highlands N.Y.," facing p. 305.

Mirror by matching drawings of New York buildings with quaint stories of the city's Dutch past.[29] Less ambitious magazines sometimes printed material of this type without the picture which inspired it,[30] and this practice was usually followed also in collecting the works of the Knickerbockers. N. P. Willis, for example, because he frequently edited and contributed to gift books, derived many of his verses and sketches from engravings.[31] But in the collected edition of 1882 there are no illustrations other than a portrait of the author; nevertheless the artistic source of many of the poems may be detected in various ways. Sometimes it is obvious in such titles as "Upon the Portrait of the Hon. Mrs. Stanhope" or in the note "Written for a picture" which is appended to "The Soldier's Widow." At other times it must be discovered by means of internal evidence, as in the case of "The Torn Hat," the text of which proves to be a clever reverie on Thomas Sully's famous picture of the same name.[32]

On the whole, this process of occasional verse and prose hardly did much to raise the level of Knickerbocker literature. Bryant's best poems for *The Talisman* series were usually those which were not written to accompany engravings.[33] The same might be said for most Knickerbocker productions of this type—keeping in mind the exceptions, however, such as Halleck's "Red Jacket," which may be numbered among the author's happier efforts. The letterpress achieved individuality and quality largely when the writers contented themselves with a few vague references to the engraving and then soared

29. See, for example, Paulding's "Knickerbocker Hall, or the Origin of the Baker's Dozen," *NYM*, VIII (Jan. 1, 1831), 201-3, accompanying Alexander Davis' "Old Dutch House in William-Street," p. 201; "Old Times in New-York," *NYM*, XIII (April 30, 1831), 337-38, accompanying J. Burford's "View of New York, from Jersey City," facing p. 337.

30. See, for example, B. B. T. [Benjamin B. Thatcher?], "The Seaman's Daughter: Suggested by Fisher's 'Portrait of a Girl,' at a Late Fair in Boston," *K*, V (Feb., 1835), 123.

31. See his prose in *The Ladies' Souvenir*, pp. 13-14, 49-50, 103-4, 119-20, 204-5.

32. These and the following art-derived verses may be found in *Poems of Nathaniel Parker Willis* (1882): "On the Picture of a 'Child Tired of Play,'" "Chamber Scene: An Exquisite Picture in the Studio of a Young Artist at Rome," "Saturday Afternoon," "Psyche before the Tribunal of Venus," "On the Picture of a Girl Leading Her Blind Mother through the Woods." For additional items and comments, see Daughrity, pp. 114-15, 133-34.

33. Bryant II, p. 174.

off on the wings of their own fancies. In this way the authors were able to reduce the restraining effects of the visual arts on their writings.

From Words to Pictures

Reaching a far wider audience than the artists, the Knickerbockers supplied a greater amount of anecdotal material than they borrowed. It was more logical for a painter to base a picture on a book known to thousands of readers than it was for a writer to base a poem, an essay, a novel, or a short story on a painting that had never been copied, that could be seen only in a private collection or in the exhibitions of the academies. Therefore, native artists of the early nineteenth century borrowed freely from the most popular American, British and Continental authors. The annual catalogues of the American Academy, the National Academy, and the Pennsylvania Academy, for example, listed hundreds of paintings on subjects from the works of Shakespeare, Cervantes, Burns, Goldsmith, and Byron. Quotations from these works were frequently printed under such listings. It is primarily these quotations, carefully indexed by Bartlett Cowdrey and Anna Wells Rutledge, which enable us to discover the literary influences on American art.

Of course, the writings of the Knickerbockers provided a vast field for book illustrators. The works of Irving and Cooper proved the most fertile sources, but books by Morris, Paulding, Bryant, Willis, and other New Yorkers were also embellished, usually by their artist-friends. As a result, a complete check list of these illustrations, which include plates, figures, marginal drawings, title-page vignettes, and decorated letters, would be large indeed—far too large for inclusion here.[34]

34. In the following selective list of illustrated books, the illustrators' names are given after the date of publication:

George Pope Morris: *The Little Frenchman and His Water Lots, with Other Sketches of the Times* (1839)—David Claypoole Johnston; *The Deserted Bride and Other Poems* (1843)—John G. Chapman and Robert W. Weir; *The Deserted Bride, and Other Productions* (1853)—Felix O. C. Darley and Robert W. Weir. A letter from Morris to Weir, thanking Weir in a very enthusiastic manner for the "exquisite designs" published in the last-named volume, is printed in I. Weir, p. 131.

James K. Paulding: *A Christmas Gift from Fairy Land* [ca. 1838]—John G. Chapman. "It is one of the most beautifully illustrated books published in this coun-

One illustrator nevertheless deserves special mention because he was so closely connected to the Knickerbockers and their writings. He is Felix O. C. Darley, a member of The Sketch Club and the artist with whom we associate Irving and Cooper almost as readily as we associate Cruikshank with Dickens. Darley illustrated the new editions of *The Sketch-Book* (1848), *Wolfert's Roost* (1855), and other works by Irving as they were issued by Putnam's at mid-century. More important were his *Illustrations of Rip Van Winkle* (1848) and *Illustrations of the Legend of Sleepy Hollow* (1849), published by the American Art-Union for distribution to all its members. Each of these two volumes matched Irving's text with six large etchings in outline. Ranging from the robust to the delicate, yet always distinctively American, these twelve pictures have been called "the high-water mark in illustrations for Irving down to their date, and perhaps for the hundred years following."[35] Darley's illustrations for Cooper were even more ambitious, for they amounted to nearly three hundred and fifty drawings reproduced as woodcuts and steel engravings in the edition of Cooper's novels published by W. A. Townsend from 1859 to 1861. The sixty-two steel plates were later reissued with appropriate passages from the novels as a single volume entitled *The Cooper Vignettes* (1862). Out of this great number of drawings it is impossible to decide upon the best or even a representative picture, but certainly "Tom Coffin on the Wreck of the *Ariel*," a scene from *The Pilot*, is one of the most memorable.

However, it is not our purpose here to dwell on illustrations meant for books. The influence of the Knickerbockers on the visual arts is

---

try in the first half of the century" (Sinclair Hamilton, *Early American Book Illustrators and Wood Engravers*, p. 90). Also see W. I. Paulding, pp. 272-73.

William Cullen Bryant: *Poems by William Cullen Bryant: with Illustrations by E. Leutze, Engraved by American Artists* (1847)—Emanuel Leutze.

Nathaniel Parker Willis: *Poems of Early and After Years* (1848)—Emanuel Leutze.

Cornelius Mathews: Ben Smith [Cornelius Mathews], *The Motley Book* (1838)—William Page. See Taylor, pp. 18, 248.

Lewis Gaylord Clark: *Knick-Knacks from an Editor's Table* (1852)—Frank Bellew. See Hamilton, p. xxxix.

35. George L. McKay, "Artists Who Have Illustrated Irving's Works," p. 39. The entire article (pp. 38-40) is a well-balanced survey of its topic. For Darley's work on Cooper's novels, see Theodore Bolton, "The Book Illustrations of Felix Octavius Carr Darley," pp. 171-73.

much more impressive when we discover that it extended to paintings as well as drawings. In other words, American artists based some of their major works on Knickerbocker literature.

Irving's stories inspired a wide variety of painters.[36] *The Sketch-Book* evoked Henry Inman's "Dismissal of School on an October Afternoon";[37] Asher Durand's "Rip Van Winkle Visiting the Haunted Glen in the Catskills";[38] George W. A. Jenkinson's "Ichabod Crane and the Headless Horseman";[39] Thomas Cole's "Landscape, Sleepy Hollow"; Daniel Huntington's "Ichabod Crane and Katrina Van Tassel"; and Charles Bird King's "Rip Van Winkle Returning from a Morning Walk." Full of burlesque and exaggeration, *A History of New York* was equally popular with the artists. From it were taken Albertus D. O. Browere's "Capture of Fort Casimir," John W. Ehninger's "Peter Stuyvesant and the Cobbler," and Asher Durand's "The Wrath of Peter Stuyvesant," which was reproduced as an engraved frontispiece in *The Knickerbocker* magazine for 1839. Scenes from *A History of New York* were also painted by Charles Loring Elliott, who found this brief experiment with narrative art, undertaken early in his career, a means of commanding the attention of a public indifferent to his portraiture.[40] Among the other works by Irving, only *The Life and Voyages of Columbus* proved especially fertile to the artists, but the resultant pictures were history rather than genre.

The most enthusiastic painter of anecdotes from Irving was John Quidor. It was not friendship that prompted this eccentric genius to base at least seventeen pictures on Irving's works, for he and the author were not close friends, if, indeed, they were even acquainted.

36. All examples of Irving's influence on genre painting which are not attributed in footnotes to other studies have been taken from the carefully annotated "Checklist of Irving Illustrations" in Prown, pp. 118-33, the fullest treatment of its subject. Further material on these paintings is in *idem*, pp. 60-66. Also see "An Illustrated Washington Irving Miscellany," pp. 41-55, which combines passages from Irving with reproductions of the pictures they inspired.

37. For analyses of this picture, inspired by "The Legend of Sleepy Hollow," and of several paintings which Inman based on "Rip Van Winkle," see William A. Gerdts, "Inman and Irving," pp. 420-23.

38. *PAFA*, p. 67.

39. See Henri Dorra, "Parallel Trends in Literature and Art," pp. 31-33.

40. See L. Gaylord Clark, "Charles Loring Elliott," pp. 652, 654.

"It seems rather to have been a case of spiritual affinity reinforced, perhaps, by the fact that Quidor had been born and raised on the Tappan Zee near Irving's own country."[41] Most of these pictures—including the "Embarkation from Communipaw" at the Detroit Institute of Arts—were taken from *A History of New York* and *The Sketch-Book*, but Quidor also used a source which other artists ignored: from Irving's *Tales of a Traveller* he painted "The Devil and Tom Walker," "Tom Walker's Flight," "Wolfert's Will," and a masterpiece of eerie coloring entitled "The Money Diggers." By working only from stories with an American setting, Quidor called attention away from Irving's feeble imitations of Gothic romances and focused it on his indigenous and more vigorous tales.

Quidor's paintings vary considerably in adherence to the details and tone of their literary sources. At times he worked up his scenes from the barest outlines, going far beyond the details supplied by Irving although never contradicting them. Such was the case with "Antony Van Corlear Brought into the Presence of Peter Stuyvesant," a painting at the Munson-Williams-Proctor Institute. Quidor based this picture on little more than one sentence in *Knickerbocker's History*: "Whereupon he [Antony the Trumpeter] put his instrument to his lips and sounded a charge, with such a tremendous outset, such a delectable quaver, and such a triumphant cadence that it was enough to make your heart leap out of your mouth only to be within a mile of it."[42] With the exception of Peter and Antony none of the ten figures in the painting are in the passage from which it derives. Nor is the dog. Nor does Irving describe the room. Even more important, the fantastic visual rhythms of the painting—rhythms of human legs and table legs, of waving arms, of pipe and gun, of cane and horn—are all Quidor's inventions, as are the varied expressions of the listeners. Obviously Quidor was not a slavish imitator. In some cases he substituted unrestrained caricature for Irving's controlled subtleties so that, as E. P. Richardson has observed: "The odd, humorous characters of Irving's invention were transposed by Quidor's fancy . . . to

41. John I. H. Baur, *John Quidor: 1801-1881*, pp. 11-12.
42. [Irving], *A History of New York*, II, 13.

another plane. Irving's imagination was genial: Quidor's pictures have a pungent flavor, composed of riotous, uncouth grotesquerie and the remoteness of dreams."[43] However, there is an exception to this statement; in parts of *A History of New York* Irving's imagination was anything but genial. For example, in Book VI he cut up the Dutch families one by one, ridiculing their hard-sounding names and rotundity of figure, denying their valor, laughing at their heroes, and reducing their battle with the Swedes to one of the most farcical episodes in all literature. Nor was he ruled by restraint:

The heavens were darkened with a tempest of missives [he wrote]. Carcasses, fire balls, smoke balls, stink balls and hand grenades, jostling each other, in the air. Bang! went the guns—whack! struck the broad swords—thump! went the cudgels—crash! went the musket stocks—blows—kicks—cuffs—scratches—black eyes and bloody noses swelling the horrors of the scene! Thick-thwack, cut and hack, helter-skelter, higgledy-piggledy, hurley-burley, head over heels, klip-klap, slag op slag, hob over bol, rough and tumble! . . . The earth shook as if struck with a paralytic stroke—The trees shrunk aghast, and wilted at the sight—The rocks burrowed in the ground like rabbits, and even Christina creek turned from its course, and ran up a mountain in breathless terror![44]

In one of the cruder passages Peter Stuyvesant, knocked to the ground by Risingh the Swede, is saved only by falling on "a cushion softer than velvet, which providence, or Minerva, or St. Nicholas, or some kindly cow, had benevolently prepared for his reception."[45] All this confusion and burlesque Quidor crowded into a painting called "A Battle Scene from Knickerbocker's History of New York." True to the original, he included such accessories as the falling geese, the rainstorm, and "the valiant men of Sing-Sing, who assisted marvelously in the fight, by chaunting forth the great song of St. Nicholas."[46] The heart of the picture contains the decisive moment of the battle: the gallant Peter is about to topple Risingh, his mortal enemy,

43. Richardson, p. 184.
44. [Irving], *A History of New York*, II, 142-43.
45. *Ibid.*, II, 149.
46. *Ibid.*, II, 141.

with a stone bottle of "true dutch courage."[47] As usual, Quidor had painted boisterously, but Irving had been boisterous too; so that, with all its bizarre effects, Quidor's "Battle Scene" almost perfectly matched Irving's original. After writing *A History of New York*, Irving began to mellow and his writing became more refined in tone. Therefore, *The Sketch-Book, Tales of a Traveller*, and the rest of Irving's later works lacking the youthful abandon which made a classic of *A History of New York*, appear quite out of harmony with the scenes that Quidor derived from them. Yet, all Quidor's adaptations of Irving's stories are interesting in themselves, proving that true genius impresses itself even on borrowed materials.

James Fenimore Cooper also provided subjects for paintings.[48] Of course, the *Leatherstocking Tales* were more popular with the artists than his other works although *The Pathfinder* proved an exception, being rather curiously ignored in spite of such paintable episodes as the blockhouse attack and Natty's proposal to Mabel Dunham. Several of the pictures inspired by these books may still be seen today. For example, George Loring Brown's "Leather Stocking Kills the Panther"—a scene from *The Pioneers*—is in the Karolik Collection of the Museum of Fine Arts in Boston; and two other paintings from the same novel are owned by the New York State Historical Association at Cooperstown. In one of these, John Quidor's "Leatherstocking Meets the Law," Natty has just thrown Squire Hiram Doolittle to the ground and is now brandishing his rifle at an amused Billy Kirby while Hector, his dog, stands by. The other painting, Tompkins H. Matteson's "The Turkey-Shoot," concentrates on a scene which helped to make *The Pioneers* one of America's earliest local-color novels. Especially interesting for its comprehensiveness, this picture provides us with close-ups of Chingachgook, Billy Kirby, Oliver Effingham, Brom the Negro, Elizabeth Temple, her father, and Leatherstocking —all against an authentic background. Matteson himself lived in the vicinity of Otsego Lake, the setting of *The Pioneers*.

47. *Ibid.*, II, 150.
48. Stearns, pp. 34-37; Beard, pp. 116-19, 126-27, n. 25; I. Weir, pp. 48-49; *PAFA*, pp. 183, 50, 63, 253.

Two of the finest pictures of scenes from the *Leatherstocking Tales* were the work of Thomas Cole. These paintings, owned by the Wadsworth Atheneum and the New York State Historical Association, are actually versions of the same subject—an episode in Chapter XXIX of *The Last of the Mohicans*. Both pictures show a rocky platform in a spectacular mountain setting. Here the Delawares have gathered in a circle to watch their ancient chief Tamenund decide the fate of the prisoners claimed by the crafty Magua. The figures are small in these paintings, but we can nevertheless detect Duncan Hayward and Leatherstocking (probably with their arms tied), Magua holding the fainting Alice Monro, and Cora, her dark-haired sister, imploring mercy of Tamenund. The paintings are faithful not only to the chapter from which they came but also to the general vastness of setting throughout the book. Cole's breadth of vision was equal to Cooper's. There are, however, some differences between the two paintings although each is a stirring picture in its own right. In the one owned by the Wadsworth Atheneum the beams of the rising sun are still quite faint, there is a strange, gigantic shaft of rock behind the circle of Indians, and the prisoners are standing on Tamenund's right. In the one owned by the New York State Historical Association the sun is a good deal brighter, there is a huge boulder teetering behind the circle of Indians, and the prisoners are spaced more or less evenly in front of Tamenund.

American artists also painted episodes from a few of Cooper's other novels. As early as 1824 his friend William Dunlap exhibited a scene from the stage version of *The Spy*, and Asher Durand later drew upon this novel for his "Last Interview between Harvey Birch and Washington." *The Pilot* inspired James Hamilton to depict the wreck of the *Ariel*—a painting of great boldness and power if it was anything like the engraving of it reproduced in Thomas Philbrick's book on Cooper's sea novels. Cooper's other narratives, even those stories with a great amount of action, seem to have attracted little attention from the painters; nevertheless, since the pictures mentioned above are but a sampling of those located and unlocated and since his novels have been frequently illustrated with figures and plates, we must agree with Thomas S. Cummings that Cooper "furnished an abundant harvest" for the artists.[49]

Subjects for genre paintings were also provided by other Knickerbockers. A scene from *The Dutchman's Fireside*, by Paulding, inspired the brush of Robert W. Weir;[50] Bryant's verse supplied topics for such artists as James Henry Beard and Victor Gifford Audubon;[51] and Clement Clarke Moore's "A Visit from St. Nicholas" was translated into Weir's several pictures of Santa Claus,[52] who is easily recognizable even without his beard. In 1834 the annual show of the National Academy was graced with a painting called "The Old Oaken Bucket," representing the middle stanza of Samuel Woodworth's famous poem. The work of Frederick S. Agate, this picture was carefully described by a writer in the *Mirror*, who contrasted it to the engraved frontispiece of Woodworth's *Melodies*, first published in 1826:

It [the painting] is very different . . . and is much more animated, there being two additional figures introduced, which are admirably grouped with that of the young rustic, who has just returned from the field in his shirt-sleeves, and who is drinking from the moss-covered bucket, just drawn from the well. We allude to a couple of dogs, which are gazing wistfully at their master, as if anxious to partake of the pure and refreshing fluid which he seems so much to relish. The iron-bound, oaken bucket, is drawn up by a windlass, instead of a sweep and pole, and the curb is adorned with creepers and wild flowers.[53]

49. Cummings, p. 229.

50. Weir mentions having begun this picture in MS letter, Weir to George P. Morris, West Point, Jan. 20, 1835, Verplanck Papers, NYHS.

When John Wesley Jarvis painted a sign for an oyster house, he used a scene from Paulding's *John Bull*. See Dickson, p. 134.

51. For these and other artists, see Stearns, pp. 32-33. Joseph Mozier based a statue called "Truth" on Bryant's "Battle Field." See MS letter, J. Mozier to Bryant, Rome, July, 1854, Goddard-Roslyn, NYPL.

52. See two articles by R. W. G. Vail: "Santa Claus Visits the Hudson," pp. 337-43, which contains a colored reproduction of one of these paintings; "An Encore for Santa Claus," pp. 326-30. For proof that Weir's paintings of Santa Claus were inspired as much by Verplanck, Paulding, and Irving as by Moore, see Charles W. Jones, "Knickerbocker Santa Claus," pp. 357-83.

53. "Agate's Picture of the Bucket," *NYM*, XI (June 7, 1834), 391.

Because such poems as "The Bucket" attracted artists, it is probable that another popular effusion, George Pope Morris' "Woodman, Spare that Tree!" also inspired a painting or two. As yet, however, none has been found.[54]

Glad to insure the success of their works by depicting material already established in popularity, the artists sometimes created pictures that had their own identity. The delightful paintings of John Quidor, for example, prove that genuine talent was not always hampered by literary origins. In effect, this process of picturing ready-made themes added one more facet to the diversity of American genre art, which should be appreciated all the more because it encompasses the work of artists as unlike as Mount, Inman, Weir, Quidor, and Woodville.

54. William S. Mount decided to paint the subject but apparently never went beyond completing a preliminary oil sketch. See Bartlett Cowdrey and Hermann W. Williams, Jr., *William Sidney Mount*, p. 11, n. 56.

CHAPTER VII

THE HOUSE AND ITS ENVIRONS

Architecture

ENTHUSIASTIC AMATEURS. On a late afternoon in December, 1829, James Fenimore Cooper ordered dinner in a state of bewilderment. He had just come to Rome with his family, and upon entering the Eternal City he had seen so many famous landmarks from the carriage window that his head was still swimming with impressions of the Coliseum, the Arch of Titus, the Forum, and many another segment of the Roman kaleidoscope. He ordered dinner but could not wait for it: there was an hour of daylight left in which to see St. Peter's. Taking his son Paul by the hand and procuring a guide, he hastened forth. Neither the Tiber nor the Tomb of Adrian could distract him. He walked on, looking straight ahead, until he stood before St. Peter's. "The laquais would have me stop to admire some of Michael Angelo's sublime conceptions, [he later recounted,] but I pressed forward. Ascending the steps, I threw out my arms to embrace one of the half columns of the facade, not in a fit of sentimentalism, but to ascertain its diameter, which was gigantic. . . . Pushing aside the door in common use, I found myself in the nave of the noblest temple in which any religious rites were ever celebrated."[1] This episode illustrates the zeal with which Cooper studied architecture—an ardor not surprising to those who have read *Home as Found* or *Notions of the Americans* or who know that, with the help of Samuel Morse, he revamped his house at Cooperstown, changing it into a design-it-yourself Gothic mansion.

Other Knickerbockers also showed a love for architecture, but neither so intense nor so articulate a love as Cooper's. Irving achieved much of his reputation by changing castles, abbeys, and other exotic architecture into settings for his works. In the remodelling of Sunnyside, his own home, he was equally successful and only slightly less romantic. He transformed this famous "snuggery" into an "English cottage" without destroying "the strongly marked symptoms of its Dutch origin," including the "quaint old weather cocks and finials, the crow-stepped gables, and the hall paved with Dutch tiles."[2] Verplanck showed interests of a quite different kind when, addressing the American Academy of Fine Arts, he debunked the imitative architects of his day and anticipated the functionalist doctrines of Greenough. Younger Gothamites such as Willis and Fay also commented on contemporary architecture not only in their own books but in the *New-York Mirror*, which they helped to edit. One of their fellows, the humorist Charles F. Briggs or "Harry Franco," delivered a lecture on Sir Christopher Wren with such seriousness that his friends, expecting his usual sarcasm, were disappointed.[3] On the whole, the devotion of these writers to architecture was remarkable even during an age of lawyer-poets and sailor-novelists, and frequent cross-fertilization between the arts. Amateurs the Knickerbockers were, but amateurs with enthusiasm enough to put their ideas into print and practice. Besides, they were professionals in their own fields—arts very closely related to architecture—and they shared a common body of

1. Cooper, *Gleanings in Europe: Italy*, II, 65.
2. Downing, pp. 409-10. Although the English watercolorist George Harvey was his architect, Irving himself planned such parts of the house as the sash windows, the kitchen gable, and the recess in one of the bedrooms. See Irving, "A Letter from Irving to His Architect," pp. 47-48.
3. See Perry Miller, *The Raven and the Whale*, p. 107.

aesthetics with the architects. Their ideas therefore deserve careful study.

ESTIMATES OF URBAN ARCHITECTURE. On first thought one might suspect that such confirmed romantics ignored urban architecture to concentrate on rural architecture as part of the landscape. But such was not the case. In America, as in England, romanticism had traditionally been tempered and the extremism of its continental varieties was frowned upon. Thus Bryant, America's foremost nature poet, could write a "Hymn to the City" in which God makes his presence known even among the huddled buildings, "the work of human kind." Here the concept of pantheism has been extended to inform all of nature, both rural and urban, but primitivism, another romantic doctrine, is at the same time denied, for the message of the poem is that man need not forsake civilization to find his Maker. On this side of the Atlantic there was in addition a realistic strain which compelled Americans to acknowledge their immediate environment so that if a man lived or worked in the city, he did not pretend to live or work in the country. Perhaps, too, the New Yorkers, bred in a city founded by the urban Dutch, were not likely to belie their heritage. Whatever the reason, they wrote a great deal about their own urban architecture and that of other cities. For the purposes of analysis, their remarks will be subdivided respectively into comments on dwellings, public buildings, theaters, and churches.

Since the Knickerbockers were romanticists as well as realists, they did not ignore the architectural relics of their city. Antiquarianism, which was to become popular in America after 1815,[4] had touched their literature as early as 1809, when Irving wrote *A History of New York*, yet this spirit was not enough to preserve the city's old Dutch architecture. Only a few original buildings remained, and there was little hope of their weathering the first half of the nineteenth century. In 1827 *The New-York Mirror* began to feature these ruins in a series entitled "Antiquities of New York," the work of several authors and artists. Small engravings of drawings by Alexander J. Davis

4. See Orians, "'The Rise of Romanticism: 1805-1855," pp. 192-93.

headed the columns, which usually included the date the building was erected, its architectural characteristics, and humorous stories about the Dutch people who had built it. More often than not, the writer would first bewail the tearing down of these few remaining examples of the Knickerbocker past and then take subtle thrusts at the new idea of progress which demolished them only for the pleasure of creating something new in their place.[5] Refusing to claim that such buildings merited attention purely as architecture, the magazine took approximately the same stand as Theodore Fay, who believed that these Dutch relics were "clothed with associations half ludicrous, half melancholy."[6] Thus readers who were not stimulated aesthetically were at least made aware of a fast-vanishing heritage, a new addition to the nonclassical past glorified by romanticism.

Another urgent subject for the Knickerbockers was the domestic architecture of their own day. Those associated with the *Mirror* exhibited a sense of social justice, a romantic humanitarianism, in deprecating the shoddy building practices of the times. In 1831, for example, Theodore Fay cited whole blocks of buildings which were "constructed carelessly, of very worthless materials, and inadequately put

5. The following articles in *NYM* contain such conservative statements: Samuel Woodworth, "New-York Antiquities: History of the Old Stuyvesant Mansion," IX (Dec. 31, 1831), 201; Anon., "Buildings of 1646," V (Dec. 8, 1827), 174; and Anon., "Dutch Architecture: Old Dutch House in Pearl-Street," VIII (March 19, 1831), 289. Cf. "Dutch Architecture: The Old House in Broad-Street," VIII (July 10, 1830), 1—the most extensive analysis of Dutch building types in New York as they were treated by the *Mirror*.

Two engravings which were accompanied by short stories but not by illustrative texts, are entitled "Old Dutch House in William-Street: Built 1648.—Modernized 1828," VIII (Jan. 1, 1831), 201, and "Antiquities of New-York: Old Dutch House in New-Street," X (Feb. 2, 1833), 241.

For descriptions and pictures of New York antiquities other than those of Dutch origin, see the following articles in *NYM*: "French Church du St. Esprit," VIII (July 17, 1830), 9; [Samuel Woodworth], "Antiquities of New-York: German Church in Frankfort-Street, Corner of William," IX (Nov. 26, 1831), 161; "Antiquities of New-York: The Walton Mansion-House.—Pearl Street," IX (March 17, 1832), 289; and John Pintard, "Antiquities of New-York: A Brief History of Federal Hall," IX (Nov. 19, 1831), 153. The article in the issue for Nov. 26, 1831 is attributed to Woodworth in Kendall B. Taft, "Samuel Woodworth," p. 103.

The architectural relics of New York were also noticed in other publications: William Leggett, "Miscellany: Old Dutch Buildings," *The Critic*, I (April 25, 1829), 394-95, and William Cullen Bryant, in *The Home Book of the Picturesque*, p. 160.

6. Theodore Fay, *Views in New-York and Its Environs*, p. 40.

together." He noted, however, that such cases were the exception, not the rule.[7] Two years later an anonymous writer for the *Mirror* had similar comments to make: "Many [of the city's dwellings] are supported almost entirely upon a range of stone pillars, of a size unwarrantably small and dangerous . . . . Upon these pillars rises an edifice of six stories . . . ." He also criticized "mortar . . . made of sand and gutter water; bricks . . . half baked and loamy; and rafters placed against walls, instead of being properly inserted and secured."[8]

But more extensive observations on contemporary housing had appeared in Cooper's *Notions of the Americans* (1828). While the novelist conceded that New York had a fresh and lively air, that the houses of the poorer people were "rarely [as] old and tottering" as comparable dwellings in Europe, and that the city's better houses were furnished "quite above ordinary standards, even in England,"[9] he found certain major defects in New York architecture: (1) the awkward outside flight of steps or stoops; (2) the "narrow, ill-arranged" facades; (3) the lack of dressing rooms; (4) the "narrow, crowded, and inconvenient" interior stairs; and (5) "the bad division of the principal apartments on the different floors," especially that which made the dining room one of the best rooms in the house.[10] Years later Cooper bitterly satirized stoops in *The Monikins*,[11] noting elsewhere that he had replaced such hazardous objects with an entrance tower in his own house.[12] Cooper's remarks, which considered virtues and vices together, represent the only genuinely substantial analysis of the city's housing to come from the pen of a Knickerbocker.

Public buildings in New York received the same critical treatment at the hands of the writers, and no edifice more so than the City Hall, a rather Frenchified structure begun in 1803 and designed by John

7. Fay, pp. 39-40.

8. "City Improvements," *NYM*, XI (Nov. 30, 1833), 175. Also see "Careless Building," *NYM*, XI (May 31, 1834), 383.

9. Cooper, *Notions*, I, 130-31, 144. Cooper's ideas were echoed in Fay, p. 40.

10. Cooper, *Notions*, I, 145-50.

11. II, 139-40. In this same book (II, 140-41), Cooper scoffed at the iron *chevaux-de-frise* in front of New York houses, which were probably the same as the "odious" awning posts he mentioned in *Homeward Bound*, II, 246.

12. *Home as Found*, I, 168.

McComb, Jr., and Joseph F. Mangin.[13] True, Cooper thought that "at first [this building] strikes one more agreeably than many a better edifice," and Willis could even call it "beautiful," but this praise was offered grudgingly, for there were too many faults to be ignored. Most of all, the City Hall was "defective in elevation" (as Willis phrased it). Cooper was probably thinking of this structure when he dryly observed in *The Monikins*: "The houses of the private citizens . . . overtop the roofs of all the public edifices, to show that the public is merely a servant of the citizen."[14] Moreover, because of the two types of stone used in its construction it had, in Cooper's words, a "party-coloured appearance" which the Knickerbockers found quite disagreeable even though this variegated effect was by no means unusual in New York, the early Dutch settlers having often built houses of brick, stone, and wood combined.[15] Perhaps the shotgun attack in the *Mirror* best summarizes most of the objections: "The front is deformed with a mass of gingerbread work, the height is too small for the breadth, the belfry or steeple is altogether too small, and the red freestone behind is a horror."

Other governmental buildings, such as the Custom House (1833-41),[16] received their just due in the *Mirror*, where they were pictured and described,[17] but ultimately the Knickerbockers' enthusiasm over them was eclipsed by the general ill treatment afforded the City Hall.

Playhouses in New York were given special consideration by the *Mirror*, where articles describing these structures in detail were matched with handsome engravings. The Lafayette Theater (1825) was declared "the largest and most splendid [building] ever erected for theatrical purposes in the United States," and was praised for its

13. Quotations in this paragraph are taken from the following analyses of the City Hall: "The New Custom-House," *NYM*, XII (Aug. 23, 1834), 57; Cooper, *Notions*, I, 131; Willis, *American Scenery*, I, 104. Also see Fay, pp. 13-14.

14. II, 141.

15. See Hugh Morrison, *Early American Architecture*, p. 101.

16. See "The New Custom-House," *NYM*, XII (Aug. 23, 1834), 57. Now known as the Federal Hall Memorial Museum, this magnificent structure combining a Roman dome and Greek porticoes was the work of Town and Davis, Ross, and Frazee.

17. For remarks on the Old Jail, see *ibid.*; Fay, pp. 13-14; John Pintard, "Public Buildings: The Old Jail," *NYM*, IX (Sept. 10, 1831), 73-74. The Hall of Record is discussed in "Public Buildings: The Hall of Record," *NYM*, IX (Sept. 17, 1831), 81.

galleryless interior and effective ventilation.[18] But it was for the new Bowery Theater (1828) that the *Mirror* held the most affection, finding it ". . . at once simple and elegant. There is no confusion of ornaments, no blending of styles, no discordance of proportions; but, while the separate parts are beautiful in themselves, the *tout ensemble* delights the spectator with its Doric simplicity and grandeur." There were other features to praise as well: the fireproof exterior, covered with stucco in imitation of marble; the outward-opening doors, designed for quick egress in case of panic; and the substitution of a drapery for the drop curtain which had made the actors look ludicrous to the audience.[19] The *Mirror* did not go into theoretical, romantic rhapsodies over this theater (as the engraving would seem to indicate) without also considering the practical merits of the building.

Though commendatory, this estimate of the theaters of New York was judicious, for in a comparatively short time they had markedly improved, especially in ventilation and lighting. No longer valid was Irving's observation, made in 1802, that a New York playhouse with its "dismal subterranean passage that leads from the pit" and its "ragged bridewell-looking antechamber" is little better than a dungeon.[20]

Two other important public buildings discussed by the Knickerbockers had been designed by Martin E. Thompson—the United States Branch Bank (1822-24) and the second Merchant's Exchange (1825-27), both Greek revival in style. The bank was characterized by the *Mirror* as a "chaste edifice" of marble, "constructed in the most substantial manner, and . . . fire-proof throughout."[21] Indeed it was substantial: its front is now one of the facades of New York's Metropolitan Museum. Thompson's Merchant's Exchange was described in great detail by the *Mirror*, the author especially admiring its Ionic

18. "Lafayette Theatre," *NYM*, V (Oct. 6, 1827), 102. This theater was destroyed in 1829 and never rebuilt.

19. "Public Buildings: The New Bowery Theatre," *NYM*, VI (Aug. 23, 1828), 49-50. Between the time of this article and the end of 1866, the "fireproof" Bowery underwent four major fires. See Charles Sotheran, "The Theaters of New-York," pp. 480-82.

20. Irving, *Biographies*, p. 32.

21. "Public Buildings: United States Branch Bank," *NYM*, VII (Sept. 26, 1829), 90.

vestibule, its low-set basement, and its all-marble facade with recessed portico.[22] Modern critics have upheld the *Mirror*'s enthusiasm.[23]

In the New York of the Knickerbockers, churches were plentiful and diverse. The clean lines of the modern skyscraper were not to dominate the horizon for almost a century to come, so that many an undwarfed tower, steeple, and weathercock jutted into the sky line of the city and attested to a religious eclecticism expressed in equally varying architectural idioms. Georgian and Gothic were the two most fashionable styles, but a number of old Dutch churches still stood. When a writer in the *Mirror* called these buildings "handsome" and "elegant,"[24] he was more polite than accurate; as the illustration which accompanied his text proves, they were venerable, not beautiful. At least, however, they usually had more integrity of design than the Jew's Synagogue, which with its combination Georgian facade and Gothic tower represented a fourth popular type of religious architecture in New York—the composite.

The city's Gothic churches elicited favorable comments from most of the Knickerbocker journalists. Although the second Trinity was called a "pitiful specimen of economy" by Irving and Paulding,[25] and the third Trinity was thought by Willis to be so poorly situated that its steeple looked like a column,[26] writers in the *Mirror* found Christ's Church (1823) "imposing"[27] and St. Thomas's (1824-26) "the best specimen of the gothic style . . . in the city,"[28] but soon to be sur-

22. "Public Buildings: Merchant's Exchange," NYM, VII (Sept. 26, 1829), 90. Also see Fay, pp. 25-26.

23. See, for instance, the credit given to Thompson in Hamlin, pp. 135-36, and Ada Louise Huxtable, *Classic New York*, pp. 68, 127, n. 32. Anonymous comments on other public buildings were scattered throughout NYM: "Columbia College," VI (Dec. 6, 1828), 169-70; "The Rotunda," VII (Sept. 26, 1829), 89; "The Bloomingdale Asylum for the Insane," XI (Feb. 1, 1834), 241; "The New-York University," XII (Sept. 13, 1834), 81; and "Masonic Hall," VII (Sept. 26, 1829), 90.

24. "Views of Public Buildings," NYM, VII (March 20, 1830), 290.

25. *Salmagundi*, pp. 269-70. The dates of these structures are as follows: first Trinity, 1696-98, steeple, 1711; second Trinity, attributed to Josiah Brady, 1791; third Trinity, designed by Richard Upjohn, 1846.

26. Willis, *Prose Works*, p. 721. Willis thought that it should have been set "*sidewise upon the street.*" Also see *idem*, p. 585.

27. "Public Buildings," NYM, VII (May 15, 1830), 354.

28. "Public Buildings of the City: St. Thomas's Church, Corner of Broadway and

passed by St. Patrick's (1809-15).[29] On the whole, the Knickerbockers seemed to appreciate their Gothic churches. If they were perhaps not critical enough, they might be partially excused by the fact that they had so few churches of this type to compare with each other. Novelty often invites praise, even when not deserved.

Enthusiasm for New York's classical churches was more or less limited to detailed analyses in the pages of the *Mirror*, books by the Knickerbockers containing little or nothing on this subject. Several churches were singled out as noteworthy:[30] St. Paul's Chapel (1764-66)—the work of Thomas McBean—for its "graceful columns"; St. Mark's (1796) for its brick spire added by Martin E. Thompson in 1827; St. John's Chapel (1803-1807) for its "perfectly light and elegant" appearance created by John and Isaac McComb; and Alexander J. Davis' L'Eglise du St. Esprit (1832-34) for its functional design. As a writer in the *Mirror* observed, there was a pleasing fitness in the dipteral portico which Davis had given this church. Besides providing "additional stability," it created "shelter from the north and east (which is very desirable in the winter season,)" and made the building unusually deep and narrow to match the dimensions of its site. Whether this explanation was written by Davis himself, who had drawn the picture from which the accompanying engraving was made, it is difficult to ascertain. The article was not signed, but it shows a concern for the practicalities sometimes ignored by the writers of these "reviews," so much were they interested in correctness.

What the Knickerbockers did say about New York's churches, whether Gothic or Georgian, was in praise of them. The Dutch

Houston-Street," *NYM*, VI (June 20, 1829), 393. See Fay, p. 54, for additional material on this church, designed by Josiah Brady.

29. "Public Buildings," *NYM*, VII (May 15, 1830), 354. Although St. Patrick's, the work of Joseph Mangin, had been consecrated in 1815, it was not considered complete even as late as 1830: "The front of the building is faced with hewn brown stone, and several niches are open for statues, which are to be placed when the whole is finished, when it will undoubtedly be the most impressive-looking edifice in the city." Destroyed by fire in 1869, it was later rebuilt.

30. Quotations and summaries in this paragraph are taken respectively from the following sources: Fay, p. 8; "Public Buildings," *NYM*, VII (May 15, 1830), 354; H., "Public Buildings: St. John's Chapel, New York," *NYM*, VI (April 11, 1829), 313; "L'Eglise du Saint Esprit," *NYM*, XII (Nov. 29, 1834), 169.

buildings they commended with reservations; a few other churches they were proud of as architecture. And, from the general tone adopted by these writers, it is safe to conclude that they agreed with Theodore Fay, who observed that increasing leisure was bringing with it a change for the better, from the oversimplicity of the old Dutch churches to the relative elegance and tastefulness of the more modern edifices.[31]

When the Knickerbockers turned to the architecture of other cities, they tended to contrast it to their own. Philadelphia, for example, received this kind of treatment in Cooper's *Notions of the Americans* and Willis' *American Scenery*. "I found Philadelphia remarkable for its regularity of construction, its neatness and its quietude," Cooper observed.[32] Yet he seemed to regret that it looked duller than New York, which he attributed to the fact that Philadelphians did not paint the bricks on their houses. Twelve years later Willis noticed this same lumpish peculiarity, but he thought that it was owing to a general want of ornament in the city's architecture, to a Quaker fondness for severe simplicity which was appropriate enough in public buildings, but not suited to dwellings.[33]

Public buildings, especially banks, were in fact the architectural glory of Philadelphia; Cooper and Willis agreed that these structures were far superior to New York's. In 1807 the Salmagundians had poked fun at the current pride over Benjamin Latrobe's masterpiece, the Bank of Pennsylvania (1799), which, they said, was being "estimated as one of the wonders of the world."[34] However, in 1828 Cooper was serious when he remarked: "There are certainly a hundred buildings in Europe of a very similar style, and of far more laboured ornaments; but I cannot remember one, in which simplicity, exquisite proportion, and material, unite to produce so fine a whole."[35]

31. See Fay, pp. 56-57. But cf. Cooper, *Notions*, I, 133, and "The New Custom-House," *NYM*, XII (Aug. 23, 1834), 57, in which the anonymous author declares that few churches in New York "are grand and imposing; and several of the neatest among them are ruined with stucco."

32. *Notions*, I, 301.

33. *American Scenery*, II, 73.

34. William Irving *et al.*, *Salmagundi*, p. 228.

35. *Notions*, I, 302.

If not a wonder of the world, this bank was at least the second finest modern edifice he knew of, excelled only by the Bourse of Paris. Another Philadelphia building, William Strickland's Bank of America (1818-24), also received extravagant praise, Willis declaring that this Greek revival structure needed only the stains of time on its white marble to become "the model of one of the most graceful temples of antiquity."[36] In fact Willis was so enthusiastic over this architect's work that he also included a view of Strickland's Philadelphia Exchange (1832-34) in *American Scenery*.

Willis praised the community spirit of Philadelphia's citizens, which gave the city a noticeable air of superiority, especially in "all that ministers to the comfort of the inhabitant—such as excellence of markets, abundance of water, cleanliness of streets, . . . &c."[37] As a symbol of this spirit he and Cooper singled out Philadelphia's Fairmount Waterworks, Latrobe's synthesis of classical simplicity and useful beauty, although Willis lamented the "absence of any grand design in the whole" of the water works, which left them without a "general fine effect."[38]

The architecture of the United States Capitol was never wholly accepted as beautiful by the Knickerbocker writers. And indeed there was good reason for this coolness. As Verplanck stated in 1824, the Capitol had at first been designed in the French style predominant during the days of Louis XIV, an architecture characterized by Verplanck as "that corruption of the Roman, or rather Palladian . . . which delights in great profusion of unmeaning ornament . . . to supply the place of unity and dignity." It is true that Latrobe and others had attempted to masculinize the building and make its details contribute to a more massive effect, and that they had succeeded in the "great" Portico, Loggia, and Hall of Representatives. Yet Verplanck maintained that the harm had already been done: ". . . the Capitol still betrays the vices of its primitive design. It not only wants unity of effect as a whole, but is subject to more serious objections in its parts,

36. *American Scenery*, II, 73. This building is often called The Second Bank of the United States.

37. *Ibid.*, II, 53.

38. *Ibid.*, II, 72. Also see Cooper, *Notions*, I, 303.

arising from absence of congruity and convenience for their several purposes. All these defects would have been avoided, and much would have been gained in economy and utility, as well as grandeur, had a more cultivated taste prevailed over the commencement of the work."[39] Such was the case against the Capitol in 1824.

In 1828 another important analysis was made of this building, this time by Cooper in *Notions of the Americans*. His displeasure was concentrated on the western front of the Capitol:

The Capitol is composed of a centre and two wings. The former is something more than 150 feet square, or nearly square, and the latter are each just 100. The several parts are in a line on the eastern front, and consequently the wings are thrown back on the western. This irregularity of the western facade is a great defect: it impairs the unity, and consequently the majesty, of the edifice. There are too many angles, those fatal blots on the beauty of architecture. There is another serious defect in the building as seen from the west: the centre is not only a story higher, but it is also a story lower than the wings. On this side the edifice stands on the brow of the hill. In order to profit by the formation of the ground, a basement, which is below the level of the earth to the east, but not to the west, has been constructed beneath the centre. But this basement necessarily comes into view; and the fact of its being painted white, coupled with its airy situation, gives the whole construction the air of a mighty ostrich which is just extending its little wings from the centre of its clumsy body, not to fly, but to scud across the plain beneath. The effect of a fine colonnade is much weakened by this substructure. . . . Some plan is in agitation to conceal this superabundance of foundation; but it is rare indeed that a capital defect in a building is successfully repaired by any second hand expedients.

The eastern front of the Capitol promises to be beautiful: it possesses unity of design, perfect simplicity of outline, and a noble colonnade.[40]

Cooper's graphic powers were seldom to serve a better purpose than this debunking of architectural pretentiousness.

Because by the end of the 1830's the Capitol had undergone some

39. Gulian Verplanck, "An Address Delivered at the Opening of the Tenth Exhibition of the American Academy of the Fine Arts, May, 1824," *Discourses and Addresses*, pp. 131-32.

40. Cooper, *Notions*, II, 19-20.

changes, both Cooper and Willis found a certain new grandeur in its general outline even though its details were rather unimpressive.[41] The mellowing process had chiefly been accomplished through an improvement in the landscaping, but, as fine as the Capitol now looked, Cooper's *Home as Found* still warned against a false national pride which could ever dare to compare it with St. Peter's, the Louvre, or the cathedral at Milan.[42]

The Knickerbockers commented on the architecture of other American cities almost as fully but much less significantly. New Haven, Boston, Albany, West Point, Charleston, Richmond—all were covered by these amateur students of architecture,[43] who were able to maintain a critical attitude even in an age of outspoken nationalism and regionalism.

THE WAR ON WHITE PAINT. In reviewing the architecture of various cities two of the Knickerbockers, Cooper and Willis, crusaded against the peculiar American addiction to painting buildings a dazzling white which clashed with the surrounding landscape. Willis recommended green goggles as protection against the "Dover Cliff porticoes" of "Mount Blanc hotels" but was quite serious in labeling white paint an enemy of nature lovers: "Oh, those chalky universes [hotels in this case] in rural places! What miles around, of green trees and tender grass, do they blaze out of all recognition with their unescapeable white-paint aggravations of sunshine, and their stretch of unmitigated colonnade! You may as well look at a star with a blazing candle in

41. See Cooper, *Correspondence*, I, 373-74; Willis, *American Scenery*, II, 55.

42. Cooper, *Home as Found*, I, 127. There are other Knickerbocker comments on various facets of Washington architecture. For observations on the President's House ca. 1828, see Cooper, *Notions*, II, 22; ca. 1840, Willis, *American Scenery*, II, 32-33. For enthusiastic praise of Latrobe's Hall of the House of Representatives, see Cooper, *Notions*, II, 31-32, and Verplanck, *Discourses*, p. 132. But cf. [Willis?], "American Rural Architecture," *The Corsair*, I (June 29, 1839), 249.

43. For comments on buildings in New Haven, see Cooper, *Home as Found*, I, 129-30; Willis, *American Scenery*, II, 9-10. For Boston's buildings, see Willis, *American Scenery*, I, 44, 57. Willis also covered Albany in *idem*, I, 24. Weir's house and Church of the Holy Innocents were the particular objects of Willis' praise of West Point architecture in *Hurry-Graphs*, pp. 115, 154, and were also described by W. B. Gibson in *Home Book of the Picturesque*, pp. 151-53. Bryant spoke of the architecture of Charleston and Richmond in *Letters of a Traveller*, pp. 76, 81.

your eye, as enjoy a landscape in which one of these mountains of illuminated clapboard sits a-glare." He called for the philanthropist and the satirist to war against this "national foible" and menace to "overworked optics,"[44] as he himself was doing.[45] But, after all, fashion was the opponent and, as late as 1852, his fellow scribbler Cooper was still unable to announce an overwhelming victory for taste, only a "great improvement."[46]

Cooper had been slow in discovering just exactly which side he should take in this battle between a paint-mad American public and the lovers of the subdued and harmonious. Brought up in an area where houses were kept fresh and gay-looking, where bricks were painted red and lined with white, Cooper could not but feel a sense of pride in the lively appearance of New York. As a result, his enthusiasm was reflected in *Notions of the Americans* (1828), one of his earlier works. In it he wrote as if he liked fresh paint—even white paint—admired green blinds, and was not greatly upset with red-and-white facades.[47] Indeed he thought that the particular charm of the country's landscape was due not only to the "brilliancy of the climate" and to the "exterior ornaments of the houses" but also to the "freshness of the paint."[48] But residence in Europe and cultivation of a sense of the picturesque almost completely reversed Cooper's views on this matter. How different was his tone in *The Monikins*, written only seven years later! Here he again spoke of red bricks lined with white, but this time to condemn the resultant accentuation of detail, which he ironically pronounced as sublime as the multiplication table.[49] Having become accustomed to the subdued hues of stone buildings in France, he now found "every structure" at home "flaring and tawdry" and admitted that his early regional taste had been "corrupted."[50]

44. Willis, *Rural Letters*, pp. 338-39.

45. See Willis, *Pencillings*, pp. 102, 167, in which the author preaches against the use of paint on ruins. Also see *idem*, pp. 34, 108; *A l'Abri*, p. 59; *Hurry-Graphs*, pp. 122-23. Cf. *Rural Letters*, p. 317.

46. Cooper, in *Home Book of the Picturesque*, p. 60.

47. See Cooper, *Notions*, I, 60-61, 130-31, 301.

48. *Ibid.*, I, 143.

49. Cooper, *The Monikins*, II, 153-54.

50. Cooper, *Gleanings in Europe: France*, p. 72.

Behind Willis' and Cooper's campaign against garish exteriors were two basic ideas, one much emphasized in the nineteenth century, the other in the twentieth. There was, in the first place, a certain amount of primitivism in their reasoning. Whatever was natural was to be sought in architecture and landscape gardening. According to Cooper, for example, "we are never dissatisfied with the natural tints of stone, for the mind readily submits to the ordering of nature. . . ." Marble is white, but other stones and wood are not. Therefore, to make something that which it is not, is to succumb to the artificial and the unnatural—a sin against the harmony of creation. To Cooper, as to Willis, white facades in a country of wood structures were to be shunned. In the second place, and reinforcing this primitivistic motive, was the idea that house and environs should be one, that unity of effect and architectural integrity are twin goals, reflecting the harmony in nature. Such a notion condemned all violent contrasts as sins against the picturesque; for instance, combinations of red bricks and white linings, or green shutters and white walls were equally to be avoided. Furthermore, as Cooper wrote, "a fence that looks as if it were covered with clothes hung out to dry, does very little toward aiding the picturesque." The war against white paint, in other words, was not to stop with the house alone, but was to be carried out against its accessories as well.[51]

It is interesting to note how closely these ideas approximate those of Willis' neighbor and acquaintance, Andrew Jackson Downing, who exerted a major influence on nineteenth-century architects. Downing also thought that white was anathema for houses, and he added another reason for his judgment—that dazzling, white houses were never to be found in landscape paintings. A modern historian writes that "Downing [had] absorbed much of this from Uvedale Price. . . ."[52] Is it possible that Price's *On the Picturesque* was also the source from which Cooper and Willis drew their ideas? Neither of them seems

---

51. Cooper, in *Home Book of the Picturesque*, pp. 58-59, 54; Cooper, *Home as Found*, I, 143, 146-47, and *Gleanings in Europe: France*, p. 30. Bryant also seems to have favored more somber architectural coloring. See his *Letters of a Traveller*, pp. 242, 320.

52. Vincent J. Scully, Jr., "Romantic Rationalism and the Expression of Structure in Wood: Downing, Wheeler, Gardner, and the 'Stick Style,' 1840-1876," p. 127.

to have mentioned it, yet there is a chance that at one time they might have come across this book in which Price condemned both white walls and brightly painted bricks because they take the element of surprise out of the picturesque and destroy the calculated effects of mysterious light and shade by their conspicuousness.[53] Whatever the sources of their ideas, Willis and Cooper had consciously joined forces with Downing in a fight against a fashion that was annihilating the individuality of American buildings by making them all look alike— at least in color. Together with Downing these writers were paving the way for a closer synthesis of the house and its environs, a development which is now reaching fruition in some modern architecture.

GREEK, GOTHIC, OR FUNCTIONAL? Fashion was again their opponent but their chief weapon was functionalism when Cooper, Willis and Verplanck turned to architectural types such as Greek and Gothic. The most emphatic denial of the modish Greek revival architecture of the 1830's was published in *Home as Found* (1838), one of those many books in which Cooper expressed his growing petulance with America. Cooper did not like his country's mania for Greek buildings, or "whited sepulchures" as he called them,[54] primarily because, with his aristocratic leanings, he was always suspicious of popular taste and failed to see how public sentiment and individualism could harmonize. Must a man who builds a Gothic house be considered eccentric— simply because he is following his own preference?[55] A fashion-mad nation was lining the entire Hudson River with white porticoes, and even breweries and markets were being made to look like the Parthenon. The quality of these structures angered Cooper just as much as their quantity. Because they had been drawn by good imitators but incompetent planners, they had become architectural monstrosities, with facades dazzling the eyes of the beholder and interiors frustrating all occupants, their ill-arranged rooms running counter to the best principles of functional living.[56] And to Cooper a "Grecian abor-

53. Price, pp. 129-33.
54. Cooper, *Home as Found*, I, 135.
55. *Ibid.*, I, 21-22; Cooper, *Gleanings in Europe: France*, p. 358.
56. Cooper, *Home as Found*, I, 22, 128-35.

tion" of this type was even worse than a Gothic failure.[57] Bad taste, lack of invention, and a preponderance of structures better "suited to heathen worship than to domestic comfort" were the result of consulting books rather than convenience.[58]

Cooper even questioned the authenticity of the so-called "republican motives" for Greek and Roman revival architecture. He denied the theory that one republic should build in the same manner as other "republics," chiefly because he saw that there was no more affinity between America and Greece or Rome than that "between a horse-chestnut and a chestnut-horse."[59] This was the same man who had once praised such classical structures as Latrobe's Bank of Pennsylvania and the Hall of the House of Representatives, but Cooper now saw different issues involved than the pleasure of beholding two particularly beautiful buildings. Now he was shocked at a national catering to fashion, at an ignorance of functionalism, and at a false republicanism which put imitation before invention. This was Cooper's case against the Greek. Willis, it must be mentioned, shared his dislike.[60]

For criticism of Gothic architecture, therefore, one must turn neither to Cooper not Willis but to Gulian Verplanck and an anonymous writer in *The New-York Mirror*. Verplanck, addressing the American Academy in 1824, claimed that those who strove to build impressive Gothic structures usually failed because their reach was far greater than their grasp. They were attempting to reduce the large scale of a Catholic church which had been designed to encompass a huge stage of "solemnity, pomp, impression and varied rich ceremonial" to the small scale required by a Protestant church which needed none of these things, which in fact frowned upon them all. Thus Verplanck admonished his audience: "If we imitate the architects of

57. *Ibid.*, I, 145.
58. *Ibid.*, I, 128.
59. *Ibid.*, II, 106. Also see *idem*, I, 21.
60. See Willis, *Rural Letters*, pp. 326-27, and *Hurry-Graphs*, p. 123, for dissatisfaction with the Greek revival. Willis himself lived in a Gothic cottage designed by Calvert Vaux. See T. Addison Richards, "Idlewild," pp. 145-66, containing 26 illustrations of the house and grounds; Calvert Vaux, *Villas and Cottages*, frontispiece and pp. 246-55, containing floor plans as well as text by Vaux and a letter from Willis.

the middle ages, we should take them as our masters throughout, and apply the same style of construction and decoration on the same scale that they did; and, therefore, in our places of worship, we should be content with copying their simpler and less adorned chapels and halls, and smaller parochial churches, without making the vain attempt to exhibit the vast proportions, the numberless and exquisite minuter beauties, and the infinity of picturesque combinations of Salisbury Cathedral, or York Minster, in the cheapest and least durable materials, and within the limits of a few square yards."[61] Such was the situation in 1824, when the Gothic revival was still in its early stages and as yet had found expression mostly in scattered churches throughout the country. It became fashionable certainly by the 1840's, however, even to build houses in the Gothic manner, and just as Cooper had attempted to put a halt to the excesses of the mature stages of the Greek revival, *The New-York Mirror* tried to check the absurdities of a ripened Gothic revival which had also spread into the field of domestic architecture.

The author of the articles in the *Mirror* damning Gothic dwellings cannot be definitely identified. They are unsigned reviews of William H. Ranlett's *The Architect*, but because they appear in the section entitled "Notes on New Books," they could quite possibly have been written by Hiram Fuller, the successor to Willis and Morris as editor of this periodical. Whoever the author was, he was anti-Goth to the core. Certainly he knew that he was fighting a losing battle, that the Gothic tide was now widening into an eclecticism that would embrace a swirling mass of Persian, Moorish, Elizabethan, and other non-indigenous types. Nevertheless he bitterly attacked the public for its lack of national pride. "They are," he wrote of these angular and lavishly trimmed buildings, "the most costly and least convenient houses that can be built, but the great objection to them is that they are not genuine expressions of the spirit of the people, but, on the contrary, are ridiculous affectations. . . ." Moreover, they were anachronistic: "there can be nothing more grotesque, more absurd, or more affected," he continued, "than for a quiet gentleman, who has made

61. Verplanck, *Discourses*, pp. 132-33.

his fortune in the peaceful occupation of selling calicos, and who knows more of the middle ages than they do of him, to erect for his family residence a gimcrack of a Gothic castle, with turrets, and pointed windows, and portcullises, and battlemented roofs, as though he anticipated an attack upon his hen roost from some Front de Boeuf, in his neighborhood."[62] This reviewer's "common-sense attitude," as Talbot Hamlin has called it,[63] when combined with the equally judicious observations of Gulian Verplanck, comprised the case against early American Gothic architecture and the foolish love of imitation which ignores practical considerations.

If these Knickerbockers tended to berate two of America's main styles of building, what did they accept, or what did they substitute for the ideas they had so bluntly refuted? The first positive contribution came from Verplanck. In his 1824 address to the American Academy he announced his doctrine of modified functionalism: "Without assenting in full to that metaphysical theory, which resolves all beauty into the perception of utility, still, though use be not efficient cause, it is the inseparable companion of true taste, and the same faculty which regulates the proportions of the column, or the composition of the frieze, presides with equal care over the minutest arrangement conducing to personal convenience or pleasure."[64] To Verplanck this functional approach was all-inclusive, a "sound architectural science" which "may be traced as distinctly in the increased comforts of the hospital, the improved commodiousness of the prison or penitentiary, and the bold and secure lightness of the bridge, as in the splendour of the palace, or the massive dignity of the cathedral."[65] Yet it was precisely of this attention to function that native architects, with their meagre imitations of old-world Greek and Gothic prototypes, had been too negligent: "Most of our architects," observed Verplanck, "are very deficient in . . . that power . . . of giving expression to buildings, of making their appearance announce their uses. . . ."[66] Thus in plain

62. "Notes on New Books," *NYM,* [n. s. V] (Oct. 17, 1846), 26.
63. Hamlin, p. 325.
64. Verplanck, *Discourses,* p. 135.
65. *Ibid.*
66. *Ibid.,* p. 133.

Jesse Talbot

CASCADE BRIDGE, ERIE RAILROAD
(*The Home Book of the Picturesque,* 1852)

Robert W. Weir

CHURCH OF THE HOLY INNOCENTS
(*The Home Book of the Picturesque,* 1852)

CITY-HALL, NEW-YORK.

Alexander J. Davis
(*top left*) OLD DUTCH HOUSE
IN NEW-STREET, NEAR
WALL-STREET
(*The New-York Mirror,* 1833)

(*top right*) OLD DUTCH HOUSE
IN PEARL-STREET
(*The New-York Mirror,* 1831)

(*below*) CITY-HALL, NEW-YORK
(*The New-York Mirror,* 1828)

and simple terms Verplanck called upon his countrymen to adopt a principle of form-follows-function.

Not far behind Verplanck was Cooper, who began to impart similar ideas to the public as early as 1828. His *Notions of the Americans*, published in that year, is by no means a complete statement of principles, but nevertheless behind many of its scattered evaluations of buildings and building-types, a concern with the relationship between purpose and form is evident. He praised the Hall of the House of Representatives for its simple and neat beauty, which, "though so totally destitute of any personal decorations," had been designed with "the benefit of comfort" in mind.[67] He pointed out a possible function of the stepped gables of Dutch houses: they might allow the inhabitants to ascend to the roofs to regulate their iron weathercocks.[68] He noted that most New York churches were "constructed internally, with direct reference to the comfort of the congregation."[69] He discussed the "ill-arranged" facades of New York houses, concluding that these exteriors should be stripped of "inappropriate ornament," and so designed as to "convey a proper idea of the more substantial comforts . . . and . . . neatness that predominate within."[70] He campaigned for the introduction of dining rooms which would be "convenient to the offices, suited to the habits of the family, plain in . . . ornaments, and removed from the ordinary occupations of those who enjoy . . . [them]."[71] He especially complained of houses and furnishings not in keeping with the climate, although he admitted that the extreme fluctuations of American temperatures created a partially insolvable problem: "A people in whose country the heats of Florence and the colds of St. Petersburg periodically prevail, may well hesitate between a marble fountain and a Russian stove. I am not certain, that, considering their pursuits, and the peculiarity of climate, they are very wrong in their present habits. But I shall for ever protest against the use of carpets, while the thermometer is at 90°. . . .

67. Cooper, *Notions*, II, 31-32.
68. *Ibid.*, I, 129-30.
69. *Ibid.*, I, 133.
70. *Ibid.*, I, 145.
71. *Ibid.*, I, 146.

The perspiration stands on my forehead while I write of them!"[72]
Cooper was to outgrow many of the things he said in *Notions of the
Americans*—for instance, he would definitely reverse his ideas of archi-
tectural coloring—but he never abandoned his functionalist principles.

He was still applying them in 1838, this time through the medium
of fiction in *Home as Found*, one of his social novels. Explaining his
own renovations at Otsego, he wrote: "I have consulted comfort; and
that I would maintain, in the face of Vitruvius himself, is a *sine qua
non* in domestic architecture." And again: "No architecture, and especially no domestic architecture, can ever be above serious reproach,
until climate, the uses of the edifice, and the situation, are respected
as leading considerations."[73]

What could be more tempting than to see in these statements the
source of Horatio Greenough's ideas? They are remarkably similar,
even in their omissions; neither Cooper nor Greenough wrote about
the development of balloon-frame or cast-iron construction, although
these innovations, introduced in the 1830's and 1840's, were technical
advances of the utmost importance.[74] Besides, Cooper was Greenough's patron, elder, and friend—an ideal combination for influence
—and there must have been a great many opportunities for them to
talk about architecture when they were together in Paris. On the
other hand, as Nathalia Wright has shown,[75] Greenough could have
evolved his theory of functionalism from many sources, including
builders' manuals, eighteenth-century rhetorics and books on taste,
classical and Renaissance treatises, romantic concepts of organic form,
and his own study of anatomy and sculpture. With such possibilities
it is hardly likely that Cooper made any noteworthy contribution to
the evolution of Greenough's ideas. Instead, like Emerson, he must
have listened eagerly to his young friend's theories and then passed

72. *Ibid.*, I, 151.
73. Cooper, *Home as Found*, I, 129, 74, 87, 167-69.
74. In his *Architecture, Ambition and Americans*, pp. 149-50, Wayne Andrews
complains of this blind spot in Greenough's architectural vision. The resemblance
between the functionalist passages in *Home as Found* and the writings of Greenough
is noted in Harold Small's "Bibliographical Appendix" to Greenough's *Form and
Function: Remarks on Art*, p. 137.
75. *Horatio Greenough: The First American Sculptor*, pp. 177-91.

them on to others in conversation and print. However, in his own time Cooper may have been just as effective as Greenough in spreading the gospel of functionalism. Though Greenough was a writer to be reckoned with—a true master of metaphor—he was often obscure and he obviously never commanded the large transatlantic audience enjoyed by Cooper. Thus at first his carefully developed essays probably reached fewer people than Cooper's scattered remarks. Not until the twentieth century did Greenough begin to achieve the audience he deserved.

Before leaving this subject we should mention the functionalist ideas disseminated in *The Corsair* for June 19, 1839, by an anonymous writer who was probably N. P. Willis, co-editor of the magazine.[76] A building must "answer the purpose" for which it is intended, he declared; this is "the first, if not the highest end, in all kinds of structures." Yet he saw that architecture must also measure up to a high standard of taste, that neither the pretentious town mansions nor the new-style country villas of America had done this, and that the Greek revival, failing in the "preposterous" feat of making "a private residence . . . resemble a Grecian temple," had become "a most ridiculous caricature of the structures of antiquity." But what did he recommend as a substitute for such imitations? "A combination of the old fashioned Dutch North-river mansion, with the modern English cottage"—after the manner of Irving's Sunnyside. The author's reasons for this choice show careful thought and some knowledge of functionalism. Although he maintained that the rural architecture of England is a model of "comfort, picturesqueness, and perfect adaptability to the climate" and as such should furnish "some valuable hints" for wouldbe American builders, he also cautioned his readers:

76.“American Rural Architecture,” *The Corsair*, I (June 19, 1839), 249. Several reasons make it fairly safe to attribute this article to Willis: (1) It appeared in his own magazine; (2) he generally contributed "art notes" to the earlier numbers of *The Corsair* (see Beers, p. 242); (3) this article was an expanded version of another article of the same title appearing in *The New-York Mirror*, also co-edited by Willis—*NYM*, XV (Aug. 26, 1837), 71—(4) the *Corsair* article was purportedly a review of architectural books by Frederick Catherwood and A. J. Downing, whom Willis often mentioned in his writings; (5) Willis was extremely interested in rural architecture, as can be seen in his *Out-Doors at Idlewild*.

...we say hints, merely, for perfect in itself as is the modern English gentleman's cottage . . . its plan and elevation require considerable modification to make it suitable to our climate. . . . The steep roof, for instance, is admirably fitted to shed our winter snows, but the deep troughs . . . are as exceptionable from the lodgment they afford to the snow. The ground plans are generally far better than those common among us. But then the bed chambers would be almost insupportable when our summer sun beats down upon the roof.

To offset the effect of the sun on the western and southern sides of the house, the author suggested a piazza constructed "like an arcade beneath the upper story of the building."[77] If the dwelling were to have pillars, he thought they might be made of cast iron and fashioned after the unique Indian-corn, tobacco-leaf and cotton-plant columns in the Capitol at Washington, where they "hardly become the dignity of a public building. . . ." In all, this writer showed some concern for the practical problems of architecture and tried to recommend solutions which combined beauty and utility.

With these theories Verplanck, Cooper, and the anonymous author in *The Corsair* demonstrated their allegiance to one of the more subtle aspects of romanticism: the idea that form or outward structure should grow naturally from within (from the character and uses of the material) instead of being applied from without in neoclassic fashion. Thus they joined such English romantics as Coleridge, Wordsworth, and Carlyle as well as their American contemporaries Emerson, Thoreau, and Greenough.[78]

EVALUATION OF THE KNICKERBOCKERS' COMMENTS ON ARCHITECTURE. Just how much did the Knickerbockers contribute to the advancement of sound architecture in America? They helped stop unsound architecture. They did not erect great American buildings. They drew no plans; they were not architects in the accepted sense. But they were critics—exercising their right to condemn, to warn, to praise, and to

77. Glenmary, Willis' home, which is pictured in *American Scenery*, has such an arcade—another reason for attributing this article to him.
78. See Richard P. Adams, "Architecture and the Romantic Tradition: Coleridge to Wright," pp. 47-48.

encourage—and they wrote of what they had seen. For the most part they praised with reservations: the old Dutch buildings, humorous but venerable heirlooms; New York houses, superior to English dwellings but ill-arranged; New York City Hall, agreeable, even beautiful, but lacking elevation; New York theaters, once depressing, but now splendidly functional; New York churches, ranging from "the best" to "elegant" to "a pitiful specimen"; Philadelphia's buildings, magnificent banks, but dull-looking houses; the United States Capitol, a certain grandeur, but mean detail.

Although many of the Knickerbockers were judicious reviewers, some of them went even further. Cooper and Verplanck, by advocating functionalism, stepped from the status of reviewer to that of theorist; in doing so they made the Knickerbocker contribution to American architecture more substantial and more positive. The Knickerbockers left us no buildings, but they left us words—wise words at that.

Landscape Gardening

Comments by the Knickerbockers on adorning houses through landscape gardening were sparse, reflecting the general ignorance of this art in America. But it was a native defect of which they were always aware.[79] As early as 1820 Irving declared that gardening, the natural expression of praiseworthy virtues, was an art as dignified as painting;[80] in 1824 Verplanck complained that American villas were not landscaped to match the pretension of the owners or the scales of the houses themselves;[81] and in 1838 Cooper lamented that gardening was of all the ornamental arts "perhaps the least known" in America.[82] The writings of New Yorkers also contained other aspects of the subject. Irving, for example, used gardens in the settings for some of his sketches[83] and Bryant and Cooper wrote just enough on

79. See, for instance, Cooper, *Homeward Bound*, II, 246.
80. Irving, *The Sketch-Book*, pp. 90-100.
81. Verplanck, *Discourses*, p. 134.
82. Cooper, *Home as Found*, II, 114.
83. See Irving's *Bracebridge Hall*, p. 108, *Wolfert's Roost*, pp. 258-59, *Sketch-Book*, pp. 276-77, *Crayon Miscellany*, p. 161.

landscaping to indicate that they preferred it in its natural form.[84] Yet only one Knickerbocker—N. P. Willis—made a substantial contribution to the literature of landscape gardening.

Willis carried on a one-man campaign for improvement in American landscaping technique because he believed that the embellishment of grounds was an art equal to architecture; like Cooper, he realized that America, a country especially suitable for striking effects, was paradoxically far behind other nations in this art.[85] With two country seats, Glenmary and Idlewild,[86] to practice on during his lifetime, Willis was personally involved in landscape gardening. The subject furnished him excellent impromptu material for his chatty familiar essays, written to meet a myriad of periodical deadlines. Later collected as *Out-Doors at Idlewild* and *Rural Letters*, two of his best books, these essays are important, for they reached a large audience.

Turning in disgust from the freakish creations of such English landscape architects as Capability Brown,[87] Willis found a hero in Andrew Jackson Downing, a designer of natural-looking scenery equalled only by Frederick Law Olmsted's. In his essays Willis not only frequently mentioned Downing's theories but also let it be known that Downing was his cherished neighbor.[88] Later, reflecting on the great loss brought about by Downing's early death, Willis remarked: "Downing's genius was our country's one solitary promise of a supply for [the] . . . scarcity of beauty coin in our every-day pockets. He was the one person who could be sent for . . . to look at fields and woods, and tell what could be made out of them."[89] Willis and Downing had held similar notions of the essential ingredients of rural beauty. Both

84. Cooper, *Gleanings in Europe: France*, pp. 180-81; Bryant, *Letters of a Traveller*, pp. 26, 327. Cooper's grounds at Otsego are described in Willis, *Out-Doors at Idlewild*, pp. 127, 130.

85. Willis, *Pencillings*, p. 12, *Out-Doors at Idlewild*, pp. 112, 211-12.

86. The grounds at Idlewild are described in T. Addison Richards, "Idlewild," pp. 145-66.

87. Willis debunked Brown in *A l'Abri*, pp. 56-57; and in *Out-Doors at Idlewild*, pp. 63, 91, Willis punned on Brown's name.

88. For Willis' references to Downing, see *Rural Letters*, pp. 175, 354, *Hurry-Graphs*, p. 140, *Out-Doors at Idlewild*, pp. 58, 115, 167, 213. Willis described Downing's house and grounds in *Rag-Bag*, pp. 121-24.

89. Willis, *Out-Doors at Idlewild*, p. 213.

preached the gospel of restraint; both advocated restoring and enhancing, not disguising and disfiguring. Thus Willis wrote: "I am making an experiment at Idlewild—seeing how far a place can be improved by originating nothing—taking advantage only of what Nature has already done . . .";[90] and again: "I have Downing's horror of tree-trimming—let me here record it . . .";[91] and in another place: "I am slow to condemn; . . . the death-blow to a living tree, however necessary, makes my blood start. . . ."[92] Like Downing, Willis gave thought to his projects because he believed: "You get such large effects with so little labor . . ." if you think before you shovel.[93] In *Rural Letters* Willis included a whole chapter on the practicalities of landscaping.[94] How to choose a location, where to build the house, how long to make the gravel road, how to keep the grounds trim ("sheep . . . are cheaper 'help' than men . . .")—all these subjects are discussed in Willis' delightful "while-I-hold-you-by-the-button" manner and show the author to be a curious mixture of common sense and romantic idealism.[95] Other writings and passages contain more practical hints on improving and "marrying" brooks,[96] making a shelf road,[97] cutting an "eye-path" to the village spire,[98] trimming out a wood,[99] and designing a "pig-tight" gate that would also reflect the owner's personality.[100]

In all, these thumbnail treatises on the art of cheaply and tastefully embellishing the environs of a house represent the sole Knickerbocker contribution of any length to this field. Moreover, they uniquely mix two romantic traditions. The first—its English branch embracing Uvedale Price, Walter Scott, and Humphrey Repton, its American Andrew J. Downing, Edgar Allan Poe, and Frederick Law Olmsted—

90. *Ibid.*, p. 53.
91. *Ibid.*, p. 115. Also see *ibid.*, p. 113.
92. *A l'Abri*, p. 94. Also see *Out-Doors at Idlewild*, p. 106.
93. Willis, *Out-Doors at Idlewild*, pp. 54-55.
94. Willis, *Rural Letters*, pp. 175-87.
95. For the reference to sheep, see *ibid.*, p. 187.
96. Willis, *Out-Doors at Idlewild*, pp. 226, 69-70; *A l'Abri*, pp. 15-16.
97. Willis, *Out-Doors at Idlewild*, p. 72.
98. Willis, *A l'Abri*, p. 45.
99. *Ibid.*, pp. 95-96.
100. Willis, *Out-Doors at Idlewild*, p. 65. Also see *idem*, pp. 64, 66, 90, 99.

is the tradition of romantic landscape gardening, informed by primitivism and designed to please chiefly the emotions and the imagination. The second tradition is the romantic or informal essay, practiced in England by William Hazlitt, Leigh Hunt, Charles Lamb, and Thomas De Quincey, in America by Theodore Fay and Lewis Gaylord Clark, in both countries by William Cox and Washington Irving. The triumph of Willis' essays is that when he advocated personal, informal gardening, he did so in personal, informal essays, his style thus perfectly matching his subject.

City Planning

In their many travels throughout their own country and abroad, various Knickerbockers took time to observe the physical make-up of certain key cities. Thus Cooper wrote of London squares and parks,[101] and of the "grand" streets of Washington, D.C., which were out of keeping with the mean houses lining them and which, with their oblique crossings and resultant acute angles, left a "gore" of unsalable narrow land.[102] Willis also lamented the "irregular and ill-defined geography" of Washington but at the same time claimed that the "chess-board regularity" of Philadelphia fatigued the eye.[103]

It was William Cullen Bryant who had the most to say—and do—about city planning. Throughout his *Letters of a Traveller* (1850), which were originally published in the *Evening Post*, his interest in ecological matters is apparent. After noting the open squares and wide, tree-lined streets of Savannah, Georgia, then the newly planned Princes Park of Liverpool and Loudon's Arboretum at Derby, Bryant soon let his fellow New Yorkers realize that he was writing all this for their benefit, that he wanted them to see the value of open ground for themselves and their already-crowded city. In London he observed: "These parks have been called the lungs of London . . . [and] will probably remain public grounds as long as London has an exis-

101. Cooper, *Gleanings in Europe: England*, pp. 99-113.
102. Cooper, *Notions*, II, 9, 21.
103. Willis, *American Scenery*, II, 50, 73. Also see *idem*, I, 54, and *Prose Works*, pp. 614, 721.

tence."[104] Bryant regretted that the early citizens of New York had not provided for public grounds in the middle of the island, but he reminded his readers that there was still time to save their city from the evils of "sultry summers and the corrupt atmosphere generated in hot and crowded streets." Manhattan, he noted, still had "unoccupied lands which might . . . be procured for the purpose, and which, on account of their rocky and uneven surface, might be laid out into surpassingly beautiful pleasure grounds"; meanwhile, he warned, "the advancing population of the city is sweeping over them and covering them from our reach."[105] A few writers have mistakenly named Andrew J. Downing as the originator of the plan which eventually evolved into New York's Central Park,[106] but as early as 1836, thirteen years before Downing proposed the park, Bryant was emphasizing to Parke Godwin the urgency of the situation, the immediate need to buy up available ground before it would be too late. And, in the *Evening Post* for July, 1844, Bryant advocated Jones' Woods as the best site. Even though another location, which Bryant also recommended, was ultimately chosen, his suggestion stimulated discussion of the matter; the project was finally begun in 1856, more than a decade after Bryant's initial proposal.

As Ernest Eaton has pointed out, Bryant's efforts were well-timed indeed. The city was just about to attain proportions that would have made a truly "central" park difficult if not impossible to develop, and business groups powerful enough to exert "strong economic pressure against *The Evening Post*" were beginning to unite in opposition. Nevertheless Bryant went ahead, and the citizens of New York should be thankful that he did.[107] This was, in fact, a double achievement for Bryant because it started an extensive chain reaction. When Frederick Law Olmsted finished Central Park, so admired were his masterly

104. Bryant, *Letters of a Traveller*, p. 169. This letter originally appeared in the *Evening Post* for June 24, 1843. See Ernest R. Eaton, *William Cullen Bryant, First Advocate of Central Park*, New York, p. 2.

105. Bryant, *Letters of a Traveller*, pp. 169-70.

106. Allan Nevins, *The Evening Post*, p. 193, names these authors and refutes their claims for Downing's priority. Also see Eaton, p. 3.

107. Eaton, p. 7. Also see Nevins, pp. 196-201; Frederick Law Olmsted, Jr., and Theodora Kimball, *Frederick Law Olmsted: Landscape Architect*, II, 22-23.

designs that city after city began to develop parks of their own, either by hiring Olmsted himself to design them or by imitating his plans. In a way, then, many of the country's urban landscapes may be traced ultimately to Bryant's deep interest in human ecology and public health.[108]

Covering acres and acres of magnificently landscaped ground, Central Park is a monument to Bryant just as much as is another New York Park which bears his name. Unfortunately, because Willis' Idlewild is not open to the public, there is no similar tribute to the only other Knickerbocker who wrote at length about the architecture of landscape. Yet the accomplishments of both authors represent the best of constructive romanticism. Willis made landscape gardening into an idiom for simultaneously expressing the personalities of men and nature; Bryant converted it into a means of humanitarianism.

108. See James M. Fitch, *American Building*, p. 134. Other passages of ecological interest may be found in Bryant, *Letters of a Traveller*, pp. 174, 176, 232, 241, 245, 257, 260, 321; *Letters of a Traveller: Second Series*, pp. 54, 125-28, 258.

CHAPTER VIII

CONCLUSION

The connection between the Knickerbockers and the fine arts has now been examined in detail, stress having been put on the close personal association between author and artist, on the role played by literary magazines in promoting the fine arts, and on the place of landscape, genre, and architecture in the writings of the Gothamites. It now remains to summarize and rearrange this material by considering (1) the artists' services to the writers and influence on their works, (2) the writers' services to the artists and influence on their works, and (3) the writers' contribution to the modern study of American art.

The first type of service comprises acts of friendship by which the artists showed their esteem for the Knickerbockers. We recall Greenough presenting Willis to society in Italy and acting as proofreader for Cooper, Morse taking Cooper's side in journalistic disputes, Rand and Cole writing letters of introduction for Bryant, Durand finding space in his studio for poor McDonald Clarke, and the artists of the Century Club giving Bryant a portfolio of nearly fifty pictures to celebrate his seventieth birthday. But unless we cite less important gestures—Morse finding a place in which Cooper could live upon his return from Europe, Weir naming one of his children after Verplanck —we have exhausted our record. Certainly this is due in part to the lack of adequate biographies of nineteenth-century American artists, but it is also due to the status of these artists. They were usually in a position to receive from, not give to, the writers.

Nevertheless art did exert a powerful influence on Knickerbocker literature, for the artists were able to do its authors one favor that eclipses all the rest: they instructed these writers in the fine arts. As far as we know, only Willis and Irving took formal art lessons. Yet for men whose profession was closely related to the visual arts formal instruction was not necessary. The Knickerbockers learned quickly and well in the congenial atmosphere of The Sketch Club, in strolls through galleries and visits to dealers, and in relaxed conversations with their artist-friends everywhere. Thus Allston, Leslie, and Wilkie taught Irving; Allston and Weir taught Verplanck; Morse and Greenough taught Cooper; Downing, Harding, and Alexander taught Willis. Almost every Knickerbocker treated in this study could have truthfully said with Bryant: "Among the artists of our country are some of my oldest and best friends. In their conversation I have taken great delight, and derived from it much instruction."[1]

An intimate acquaintance with artists—and the knowledge which came from this acquaintance—strongly determined both the matter and manner of Knickerbocker writings. This literature virtually teemed with art material ranging from short allusions to chapter-length orations and serialized essays in magazines. There were philosophical treatments of patronage, functionalism, and art institutions; surveys of the fine arts in various cities and countries; biographical sketches of painters, sculptors, and architects; reviews of art books and local exhibitions; and essays on the practicalities of city planning and landscape gardening. Moreover, the Knickerbockers wrote occasional poetry and prose inspired by art objects and in some cases published to accompany engravings in gift books and magazines. Although this

1. Quoted in Godwin, II, 220.

letterpress was seldom of a high order, it does serve to remind us that literature can have a subordinate function, that words are sometimes written to illustrate, not to be illustrated. Finally there were short stories, novels, and plays about artists, most of them composed by N. P. Willis, who anticipated Henry James in this type of fiction.

The manner in which the Knickerbockers treated their material just as convincingly demonstrates the strong influence of the visual arts. Who but a lover of drawing would call his masterpiece *The Sketch-Book* and himself "Geoffrey Crayon"? And what other group of authors so consistently drew upon the world of art for allusions, metaphors, and similes—even when writing about an entirely different world? We find this art vocabulary everywhere, even in Cooper's frontier novels.

Most of all, when the Knickerbockers discussed the fine arts, they did not stutter and stammer, but spoke out confidently, forcefully, and perceptively in the manner of professionals or at least well-informed amateurs. This tone is an extremely important influence stemming from personal acquaintance with artists and with their galleries, schools, clubs, studios, and homes. Without it the Knickerbockers' writings on art would not have sounded authentic. Without it they would have gone unread.

Turning now to the ways in which the Knickerbockers served and influenced the fine arts, we may begin with another aspect of the topic treated in the last few paragraphs, the transfer of ideas from one profession to another. We have already seen that the writers learned a great deal from their artist-friends, but the process was not that simple, for the writers also reused the ideas passed on to them orally by the artists, transforming conversation into various forms of literature, such as essays and novels. Theories of functionalism, for example, and warnings against white paint, unnatural landscape gardening, and the excesses of the Greek and Gothic revivals had certainly come to the writers from the artists, but they took on a new existence in print, and reached a much wider audience than they had at first enjoyed as the property of these artists. The two-directional nature of the relationship is apparent: the artist helped the writer by giving him

new ideas, but the writer helped the artist by restating and popularizing these ideas. Only a few artists were articulate enough to capture
many readers with their own pens.

Because the Knickerbockers commanded such a wide audience,
they were also able to serve the fine arts in a second way, namely, by
providing subject matter for hundreds of drawings and paintings.
Friends borrowed from friends—Durand, for example, took the themes
for at least five of his pictures from Bryant's poems—but friendship
was not necessary: Quidor painted over a dozen episodes from Irving's
works although he had apparently never even met Irving. More important was the status, the popularity, of the source, and the Knickerbockers avoiding not only the harsh doctrines of lingering Puritanism
but also the mystical innovations of Transcendentalism, were popular
writers. For this reason the artists borrowed freely from their works—
especially from their narrative writings—glad to insure the success of
their canvases by using pretested subjects and themes. The result was
a genre painting with healthy roots in a native soil which had been
nourished by anecdotal literature. Landscape painting was also served
by the Knickerbockers. However, although stories in genre paintings
are rather easily traced to their literary sources, scenery usually defies
such documentation, and therefore only a few landscape paintings
derived from print can be cited. Borrowing of landscape techniques is
also hard to determine, for such descriptive devices as the panorama
seem to have appeared simultaneously in books and pictures. Nevertheless we may be as certain of indirect literary influence on landscape
painting as we are of direct literary influence on genre painting. It
is safe to assume that few American artists would have specialized in
landscape, or been so successful in specializing, had the writers not
pointed to the religious, therapeutic, and didactic values of nature.
Nor would paintings of native scenes have become so popular had not
the writers dignified the American landscape by enumerating its merits
and finding remedies for its defects.

The Knickerbockers also served American art by making it known
to their readers. The bulk of this publicizing was accomplished by
the editors—Morris, Willis, Clark, Bryant, Hoffman, and the Duyck-

incks. Their magazines contained surveys of architecture, full reviews of annual and special exhibitions, and a multitude of news items recounting the activities of painters and sculptors. But artists and their works were mentioned in other places as well, in personal essays, for example, and even in novels. This publicity was greatly needed. By themselves pictures, statues, and buildings, unable to be mass-produced like books, accumulated an appreciative audience at a slow rate. The writers were able to speed up this process.

Their fourth service to the fine arts may be classified as public and private patronage. Immediately the Rotunda paintings come to mind: Verplanck failed with Allston and Morse but helped to get commissions for Weir and Inman; Paulding recommended Chapman, who also received a commission; Cooper and Morris contributed money to a subscription for a painting from the disappointed Morse; and Irving, upon Inman's death, asked Congress to give one of the Rotunda panels to Powell. If we add to this the successful campaign of Cooper, Willis, and Verplanck to procure the Washington statue for Greenough, we find the Knickerbockers shaping the early career of governmental patronage and at the same time helping their friends. Although there were better American artists than those ultimately commissioned, the former were either not available or not acceptable to Congress; the Knickerbockers should therefore be praised for recommending second-, not third-, best artists.

But public patronage, because it divides responsibility for commissions among so many people, is an imperfect index to the aid which the Knickerbockers gave their friends. Private patronage is more significant in this study. For example, the credit for lending money to Greenough and Rand must go, not to Congress or a committee, but respectively to Cooper and Bryant. The sources of patronage are equally clear in the case of private commissions. Just as important as the fact that Verplanck found buyers for some of Weir's paintings is the fact that he bought a number of Weir's paintings himself. Other commissions should be remembered, especially those which Cooper gave to Morse, Cole, and Chapman, and those which Morris, as editor of the *New-York Mirror*, lavished on dozens of painters and engravers.[2] No masterpieces resulted from any of this patronage, but some of these commissions were well-timed indeed. Verplanck was one of Cole's earliest patrons, and Cooper rescued Greenough from poverty and disappointment in Italy by paying him to carve the "Chanting Cherubs."

Lastly the Knickerbockers supported various art-institutions. Thus Clement Clarke Moore was a patron of the American Academy, and Gulian Verplanck was one of its vice-presidents. But the help given to its young rival, the National Academy, was more spirited and important. Bryant served on the faculty of the National Academy, and he allowed it to use the *Post* as a battleground in its paper war. Cooper meanwhile bought casts from the antique and other gifts for this new organization, headed by his friend Morse. And the editors of literary magazines regularly stimulated public interest in both academies as well as in the American Art-Union by printing comprehensive reviews of their exhibitions.

The Art-Union was aided in other ways by the Knickerbockers. Four writers were on its Committee of Management, and, while their individual contributions cannot be evaluated, their mere participation in a movement to give art to the public is worth noting. More can be said about the poet-presidents of the Art-Union. Wetmore's term, marked by strained relations with the National Academy, hints that one Knickerbocker injured the cause of native art. But Bryant's influence was undeniably healthy, for during his presidency he maintained peace with the National Academy and in his speeches made the Art-Union a symbol of democracy, insisting that popular taste can often be good taste and that both artist and public benefit from a wide distribution of original paintings. Bryant's part in founding and guiding the Metropolitan Museum, another means of giving art to the masses, occurred outside the chronological limits of this study; nevertheless it should be recalled as proof that the close relationship between

2. Although these commissions for the *Mirror* smack of corporate rather than private patronage, we must remember that Morris hired the artists himself and that they applied directly to him for approval and payment. Moreover, when these engravings and the original paintings and drawings were exhibited at the National Academy, Morris, not his magazine, was usually listed in the catalogues as their owner. See, for example, *NADER*.

the Knickerbockers and the fine arts did not die with the Knicker-bocker era but with the last Knickerbocker.

Today, when the literary critics are reassessing the work of these authors, let art historians be reminded of its great and lasting value. Passages from Bryant's eulogy on Cole are quoted now and then, while Cooper's and Irving's letters on various artists are well-known sections of the famous survey written by their friend Dunlap. Even more useful is the vast amount of art-material in the literary magazines—a mountain of opinions, facts, and documents which every historian working in this area should explore. Moreover, the many engravings which the Knickerbockers published in their books and journals have taken on values far beyond their original functions. The architectural views which appeared in the *Mirror*, for instance, are sometimes the only known reproductions of buildings long ago destroyed. Nor should we forget the usefulness of the exhibition reviews listed below in Appendix II: They not only epitomize nineteenth-century taste but also serve as an excellent means of identifying paintings from that era. By providing this kind of source material the Knickerbockers helped future generations to understand their own.

Certainly there is also a sociological meaning behind this inter-action of the visual and literary arts. For well over a century New York City has been noted for its ability to change and grow, but equally celebrated have been its commercialism, cosmopolitanism, and conviviality. All these traits, forming in combination the personality of New York,[3] had a profound effect on the Knickerbocker period. The city's commercial success produced a growing number of patrons on the one hand and an influx of artists and writers on the other. Following the Gothamite fondness for conviviality, these groups became fast friends and soon found themselves even more closely associated in joint efforts to record the ever-changing manners, cus-toms, scenery, architecture, and people of their city—a rapidly shifting kaleidoscope resulting in part from the size and cosmopolitanism of New York.

But although this interaction of the arts in a unique environment

3. Still, p. 90.

was the first large-scale relationship of its kind in the United States, it cannot have been totally without parallel. There were groups of artists and writers in Boston, Philadelphia, Charleston, Cincinnati, and Chicago; like New York, each of these cultural centers had distinctive personality traits which could have produced co-operation between these groups. Whether they did or not is a problem for future research. But the solution promises to come soon as interdisciplinary studies gather momentum and as scholars make increased use of the Archives of American Art; it will come sooner if more tools like *American Literary Manuscripts* are compiled to help locate unpublished materials.

When this work is completed—when all the major cities are covered and every historical period is examined—will it then be clear that American writers and artists never ceased joining forces? Let us hope so, for such co-operation proved, in the Knickerbocker period, of great benefit to both groups. Their works gained a wider range and a larger audience, and in each other they found not only friends but champions.

APPENDIXES

ADDITIONAL ARTIST-WRITER

FRIENDSHIPS

This appendix is designed neither to replace nor repeat the notes in Chapter II but to supplement them. For this reason the friendships documented there will not be documented here, and vice versa. Moreover, such important pairs as Irving and Allston, Verplanck and Weir, Cooper and Greenough, Bryant and Cole will not even be mentioned below; they have already been fully treated in Chapter II. Instead this appendix presents evidence which, although too disparate and fragmentary to form coherent stories, will nevertheless provide valuable supplementary material for future studies of artists and writers, whether as individuals or friends. It does not, of course, obviate the use of the index to this book.

Under each author listed below are given the names of his friends and acquaintances (in alphabetical order) and the documentation for their relationships.

CHARLES F. BRIGGS

William Page: Taylor, pp. 27, 46, 55-56, 85-86, 90.

WILLIAM CULLEN BRYANT

Washington Allston: Bryant praised him in MS letter, Bryant to Richard H. Dana, New York, Aug. 4, 1843, Dana Papers, MHS. Also see MS letters, Bryant to Mrs. Frances F. Bryant, New York, Aug. 5, 1829, Bryant to Richard H. Dana, New York, April 17, 1830, Goddard-Roslyn, NYPL; Bryant II, pp. 56, 223.

John James Audubon: Godwin, I, 369-70, II, 41; Bryant II, p. 201.

Edward S. Bartholomew: Godwin, II, 73.

Albert Bierstadt: MS letter, Bierstadt to Bryant, Studio Building [New York], June 5, 1862, Goddard-Roslyn, NYPL.

George Loring Brown: Bryant, *Letters of a Traveller*, p. 238. Brown gave Bryant a landscape painting. See MS letter, Geo. L. Brown to Bryant, Studio, Friday Morn, Bryant-Godwin, NYPL.

Henry Kirke Brown: Bryant, *Letters of a Traveller*, pp. 238-40; Godwin, II, 11-12. Brown executed a bust of Bryant *ca.* 1851 and was invited to Bryant's home in the 1850's, 1860's, and 1870's. See MS letters, Brown to Bryant, Brooklyn, June 28, 1854, Newburgh, June 22, 1865, Sept. 3, 1876, Bryant-Godwin, NYPL; Godwin, II, 58. Asked to accompany Bryant, John Durand, and others to Havana and Mexico, Brown declined in MS letter to John [Durand?], Newburgh, Jan. 22, 1872, Charles Henry Hart Collection of MS Letters, Archives of American Art.

John G. Chapman: Bryant and Chapman met at Paris in 1849, at Rome in 1853 and 1858. For evidence of their friendship see Godwin, II, 73, 111, and the following MS letters: Bryant to Chapman, New York, March 27, 1845, Bryant to [Mrs.] Frances [F. Bryant], Paris, Sept. 17, 1849, Bryant to Julia Bryant, Paris, Sept. 19, 1849, Chapman to Bryant, Rome, Jan. 29, 1858, Goddard-Roslyn, NYPL; Chapman to Bryant, Florence, Nov. 7, 1849, Rome, Feb. 10, 1858, Feb. 25, 1858, June 11, 1869, Bryant-Godwin, NYPL. Mr. William P. Campbell in a letter dated Washington, D.C., July 2, 1963, has listed other evidence, including MSS, which corroborates the Bryant-Chapman friendship. This material is to be incorporated in his forthcoming Ph.D. dissertation on Chapman for Harvard University.

Thomas Crawford: Godwin, II, 73, 111.

Andrew Jackson Downing: MS letters, A. J. Downing to Bryant, Newburgh, Saturday, Sept. 30, no year, Bryant-Godwin, NYPL; Bryant to Mrs. Frances F. Bryant, n.p., Oct. 13, 1847, Goddard-Roslyn, NYPL; Godwin, II, 38.

William Dunlap: MS letter, Bryant to Ric[hard H. Dana], New York, Nov. 26, 1838, Goddard-Roslyn, NYPL; Cummings, p. 153; Nevins, p. 125.

John Frazee: Bryant II, p. 223.

Henry Peters Gray: Godwin, II, 11.

Horatio Greenough: Bryant met Greenough as early as 1828 (Bryant II, p. 149). Greenough asked to be remembered to Bryant in MS letter, Horatio Greenough to S. F. B. Morse, n.p., May 15, 1828, Morse Papers, Vol. X, LC. When Bryant went to Paris in 1834, he presented Greenough with a letter of re-introduction from Morse. See MS letter, H. Greenough to Samuel F. B. Morse, Paris, Aug. 24, 1834, Morse Papers, Vol. XI, LC, and Mabee, p. 161. Asked for his opinion of the statue of Washington, Bryant advised Greenough to execute it "according to your own notions of what is true and beautiful" (quoted in Godwin, I, 310). Also see MS letter, Greenough to Bryant, Florence, Feb. 24 [1835], Goddard-Roslyn, NYPL. Greenough was entertained at Roslyn in July of 1848 and pronounced the scenery "all glorious" (Greenough, *Letters*, p. 153). In 1845 Bryant visited Greenough's studio in Florence and wrote about the sculptor's "The Indian and the Hunter" to the *Evening Post*. See Bryant, *Letters of a Traveller*, pp. 235-36. When Greenough planned a series on the treason of Arnold, the capture of Major André, and the hanging of Nathan Hale, he again asked Bryant's advice. See MS letter, Greenough to Bryant, Florence, May 7, 1851, Bryant-Godwin, NYPL. In 1851 Greenough and Bryant were working together on rousing the public to build a monument honoring Cooper. See MS letter, Greenough to Bryant, Cambridge, Mass., Feb. 7, 1852, Bryant-Godwin, NYPL; Godwin, II, 62. But in the next year Bryant, then in London, was informed of Greenough's death: MS letter, Frances F. Bryant to Bryant, New York, Dec. 17 [1852], Goddard-Roslyn, NYPL.

Richard S. Greenough: Godwin, II, 73.

George Harvey: John Rand introduced Bryant to Harvey by letter: MS letter, Rand to Bryant, London, Sept. 17, no year, Bryant-Godwin, NYPL. Harvey consoled Bryant on the death of Bryant's wife and mentioned having been entertained at Roslyn in MS letter, Harvey to Bryant, London, Aug. 20, 1866, Bryant-Godwin, NYPL.

Thomas Hicks: Godwin, II, 58.

Harriet Hosmer: Godwin, II, 111; MS letter, Hosmer to Bryant, Rome, April 7 [1868 or 1869], Goddard-Roslyn, NYPL.

William Morris Hunt: Godwin, II, 11.

Daniel Huntington: MS letters, Bryant to Mrs. Frances F. Bryant, Paris, Dec. 9, 1852 (on microfilm erroneously placed among letters dated 1832), Goddard-Roslyn, NYPL; Huntington to Bryant [New York], Dec. 26, 1865, Huntington to Miss Bryant [New York], June 24, 1878, Bryant-Godwin Collection, NYPL.

Charles Cromwell Ingham: Bryant, *Prose Writings*, I, 232.

Henry Inman: Bryant, *Orations*, pp. 16-17; Wilson, p. 114; MS letter, Bryant to Richard H. Dana, New York, Feb. 17, 1837, Goddard-Roslyn, NYPL; Bryant II, pp. 226-27, 231.

Eastman Johnson: Godwin, II, 300; Sears, pp. 52-53.

John F. Kensett: Godwin, II, 300, 329.

Charles R. Leslie: Godwin, II, 47, 224.

Emanuel Leutze: MS letter, Bryant to Mrs. Frances F. Bryant, Vienna, Sept. 10, 1845, Goddard-Roslyn, NYPL; Godwin, II, 11. Leutze accepted Bryant's invitation to attend a meeting of The Sketch Club at the poet's home in MS letter, Leutze to Bryant, n.p., Thursday morning, Goddard-Roslyn, NYPL.

Samuel F. B. Morse: Bryant, "Reminiscences of Miss Sedgwick," p. 441. Bryant's contribution to the erection of the Morse statue in Central Park was especially generous. See Mabee, pp. 373-74. Also see Bryant, "The Electric Telegraph: Speech at a Dinner Given to Samuel Breese Morse, December 29, 1868" and "The Morse Statue: Address Delivered on the Unveiling of the Statue of Samuel Finley Breese Morse, June 10, 1871," *Orations*, pp. 325-30, 361-68.

William S. Mount: Cowdrey and Williams, p. 5.

Joseph Mozier: Godwin, II, 73.

William Page: Godwin, II, 73, 111; MS letter, Page to Bryant, n.p., n.d., Goddard-Roslyn, NYPL; Taylor, p. 260.

Hiram Powers: Bryant, *Letters of a Traveller*, pp. 164-65, 236-37; Godwin, II, 3, 11; MS letter, Hiram Powers to Bryant, Florence, March 23, 1852, Goddard-Roslyn, NYPL. A photograph of Bryant and Powers together is reproduced in Paul R. Baker, *The Fortunate Pilgrims*, facing p. 128.

Randolph Rogers: Godwin, II, 73.

Thomas Prichard Rossiter: MS letter, Rossiter to Bryant [New York], Nov. 27, no year, Bryant-Godwin, NYPL.

James D. Smillie: MS letter, Smillie to Bryant, New York, June 1, 1870, Goddard-Roslyn, NYPL.

William Wetmore Story: Godwin, II, 73, 111.

Thomas Sully: Godwin, I, 173.

Ithiel Town: Larkin, *Art and Life in America,* p. 96.

John Vanderlyn: Godwin, II, 208; Bryant, *Letters of a Traveller,* p. 222; MS letter, Bryant to Mrs. Frances F. Bryant, Paris, August 5, 1845, Goddard-Roslyn, NYPL.

William G. Wall: MS letter, Bryant to Mrs. Frances F. Bryant, Paris, Aug. 4, 1845, Goddard-Roslyn, NYPL.

LEWIS GAYLORD CLARK

Charles Loring Elliott: L. Gaylord Clark, "Charles Loring Elliott," *Lippincott's Magazine,* II (Dec., 1868), 652-57; MS letter, C. L. Elliott to Dear Robert, Hoboken, Nov. 28, 1861, Charles Henry Hart Collection, Archives of American Art. "Editor's Table," *K,* XXVI (Aug., 1845), 192; XXXIX (June, 1852), 564; XLII (July, 1853), 94-95; XLV (May, 1855), 529-30; XLVI (Nov., 1855), 550; Clark, *Knick-Knacks,* pp. 136-38, 268.

Henry Inman: Clark claimed to be "an intimate personal friend" of Inman even before meeting Elliott. See Clark's "Charles Loring Elliott," *Lippincott's Magazine,* II (Dec., 1868), 652-53. Clark's magazine often contained praise of Inman: "Henry Inman," *K,* IV (Nov., 1834), 410; an obituary notice of Inman in "Editor's Table," *K,* XXVII (Feb., 1846), 179; Clark, *Knick-Knacks,* pp. 137-38, 157-58.

Thomas Bangs Thorpe: Thorpe's "Lewis Gaylord Clark," *Harper's New Monthly Magazine,* XLVIII (March, 1874), 587-92.

MCDONALD CLARKE

John William Casilear: See below, under Durand.

Lewis P. Clover: Clover contributed reminiscences of Clarke to J. Durand's *A. B. Durand,* pp. 87-90.

Asher B. Durand: *Ibid.,* p. 87; MS letters, Sandy [McDonald] Clarke to A. B. Durand, Providence, July 13, 1833, San[dy] Clarke to A. B. Durand, Newport, Aug. 26, 1833, S. Graham to A. B. Durand, Providence, Jan. 24, 1834, Durand Papers, NYPL. In the letter of July 13 Clarke asked to be remembered to "Sir Thomas Twibill, Casalier, Paradise, [and] Young"—all of whom were probably working with or under Durand at the time.

William Page: J. Durand, *A. B. Durand,* p. 88.

John Wesley Paradise: See above, under Durand.

George W. Twibill: Possibly this is the "Sir Thomas Twibill" mentioned in Clarke's letter of July 13, and inquired after in his letter of August 26 (see Durand, above).

JAMES FENIMORE COOPER

John G. Chapman: Dunlap, *Arts of Design*, III, 245; Cooper, *Letters and Journals*, I, 389-90, 404, 430, 431, II, 14, 115, 117; MS letter, Chapman to Cooper, Rome, May 3, 1830, Cooper Collection, YUL.
George Cooke: Cooper, *Letters and Journals*, II, 54, 62, 117.
Robert W. Habersham, Jr.: *Ibid.*, II, 311, 361.
Charles Robert Leslie: *Ibid.*, I, 254, II, 409, 410.
Gilbert Stuart Newton: *Ibid.*, I, 254.

EVERT A. DUYCKINCK

Sanford Gifford: Mize, p. 282.
Daniel Huntington: MS letters, Daniel Huntington to Evert Duyckinck, n.p., Jan. 19, 1850, Huntington to Geo. L. Duyckinck, 48 E. 20th, Feb. 27, 1851, Huntington to Evert A. Duyckinck, 48 E. 20th, June 21, 1851, Huntington to Duyckinck Bros., 48 E. 20th, April 9, 1857, Duyckinck Papers: Literary Correspondence, NYPL.
Charles Lanman: Mize, p. 282.
William S. Mount: *Ibid.*, pp. 257, 276-79, 281-82, 284.
William Page: *Ibid.*, pp. 282-84.
Robert W. Weir: MS letter, Weir to Mr. [W. I.] Paulding, West Point, Nov. 26, 1867, Duyckinck Papers: Literary Correspondence, under Halleck, NYPL.

THEODORE FAY

William Dunlap: *Arts of Design*, III, 224.
Horatio Greenough: *Ibid.* and MS letters, Bryant to Greenough, Pisa, Feb. 27, 1835, Greenough to Bryant, Florence, Feb. 24 [*ca.* 1835], Goddard-Roslyn, NYPL. Greenough's studio is described in Theodore S. Fay, "The Minute-Book," *NYM*, XII (Sept. 13, 1834), 84; *Idem* (Jan. 10, 1835), 220.
John Rand: "Mr. Fay is located near us in London. he [*sic*] is very friendly to me and thinks very highly of your portrait" (MS letter, Rand to Bryant, London, Aug. 21, 1835, Bryant-Godwin, NYPL).

FITZ-GREENE HALLECK

Henry Inman: Adkins, pp. 264, 275, 385, 391-92.
Samuel F. B. Morse: *Ibid.*, pp. 148, 152, 226, 372-73.
Robert W. Weir: Irene Weir, pp. 41-42.

HENRY WILLIAM HERBERT

E. W. Clay: Judd, I, 84, 97.
Henry Inman: *Ibid.*, I, 25, 68-70, 93.

CHARLES FENNO HOFFMAN

Christopher Pearse Cranch: Scott, pp. 75, 84.

WASHINGTON IRVING

John James Audubon: Herrick, II, 153; Williams, II, 53.
Chester Harding: Harding, pp. 118, 146.
George Harvey: "A Letter from Irving to His Architect," *American Collector*, XVI (Oct., 1947), 47-48; George Harvey, "The Fine Arts: A Few Hints on the Philosophy of Size in Its Relation to the Fine Arts," *K*, XXIII (Feb., 1844), 158.
John Wesley Jarvis: *Letters of Washington Irving to Henry Brevoort*, p. 21; Dickson, pp. 135-36.
Charles Lanman: Williams, II, 204, 389.
Emanuel Leutze: P. M. Irving, II, 196.
Samuel F. B. Morse: Mabee, p. 25.
Ithiel Town: Larkin, *Art and Life in America*, p. 96.
John Vanderlyn: Dunlap, *Arts of Design*, II, 160; Prown, pp. 9, 135; *Letters of Washington Irving to Henry Brevoort*, p. 48; Williams, I, 403.
Robert W. Weir: Irene Weir, pp. 33-34.

CLEMENT CLARKE MOORE

William S. Mount: Patterson, p. 161.
Robert W. Weir: *Ibid.*, p. 114.

GEORGE POPE MORRIS

William S. Mount: Cortland P. Auser, "The Contribution of George Pope Morris to American Journalism," pp. 178, n. 64, 275-76, 356, 422. To Auser's calendar of unpublished sources should be added MS letter,

Morris to Mount, New York, Dec. 18 [18]51 [1857?], Mount Papers, Suffolk Museum.

Robert W. Weir: Auser, pp. 179-80, 276, 350, 354, 356, 422; MS letters, Weir to Morris, West Point, Jan. 20, 1835, Verplanck Papers, April 14, 1835, Miscellaneous Letters, NYHS. Morris dedicated *The Little Frenchman and His Water Lots* to Weir.

JAMES KIRKE PAULDING

Asher B. Durand: Paulding, *Letters*, pp. 132-33, 169; J. Durand, *A. B. Durand*, p. 120.

Horatio Greenough: MS letter, Greenough to Bryant, Florence, May 7, 1851, Bryant-Godwin, NYPL; William I. Paulding, *Literary Life of James K. Paulding*, pp. 271-73; Paulding, *Letters*, pp. 191-92, 194.

John Quidor: In Thomas Bangs Thorpe's "New-York Artists Fifty Years Ago," *Appleton's Journal*, VII (May 25, 1872), 574, Paulding is said to have taken "a great deal of interest" in Quidor, his friend Jarvis' pupil.

James Renwick: Paulding, *Letters*, pp. 35, n. 2, 43, n. 4, 231, n. 15.

Robert W. Weir: MS letter, Robert W. Weir to Mr. [W. I.] Paulding, West Point, Nov. 26, 1867, Duyckinck Papers: Literary Correspondence, under Halleck, NYPL.

Joseph Wood: Wilson, p. 153, and [James Kirke Paulding], "Sketch of the Life of Mr. Joseph Wood," *Port Folio*, New (Third) Series, V (Jan., 1811), 64-68, where Wood is called "the first artist in his line, in the United States" (p. 68).

JOHN HOWARD PAYNE

Washington Allston: Dunlap, *Arts of Design*, II, 318; MS letter, Wa[shington]. Allston to Samuel F. B. Morse, Boston, Oct. 28, 1829, Morse Papers, Vol. X, LC.

John James Audubon: Overmyer, p. 324.

George Catlin: Overmyer, p. 297.

Thomas Cole: MS letter, Payne to Cole, 67 Varick Street, Tuesday [*ca.* Feb. 1-15, 1843], Cole Papers, NYSL.

William Dunlap: Overmyer, p. 286.

Anna Marie Freeman: Mize, pp. 281-82.

John Wesley Jarvis: Dickson, p. 148.

Charles R. Leslie: Overmyer, pp. 115, 122, 226; Dunlap, *Arts of Design*, II, 318; Leslie, pp. 145-47, 190-91, 195, 199; MS letter, Leslie to Payne,

London, Feb., 1815, Charles R. Leslie folder (Miscellaneous Papers), NYPL.

Samuel F. B. Morse: Dunlap, *Arts of Design*, II, 318; Morse, *Letters and Journals*, I, 118; Overmyer, p. 115.

John Rand: John Howard Payne may have been the "Mr. Payne" who wrote letters of introduction for John Rand. See MS letters, Rand to Bryant, London, Jan. 6 [or 5], 1834, Jan. 25, 1834, Bryant-Godwin, NYPL.

John Trumbull: Overmyer, pp. 117, 119, 283, 291, 395.

Benjamin West: Overmyer, p. 115.

GULIAN VERPLANCK

Thomas Cole: LaBudde, "The Mind of Thomas Cole," p. 166. Verplanck was one of Cole's earliest patrons, for in 1825 he commissioned Cole to paint two pictures of Trenton Falls. See Cole's MS notebook for 1825, an unpublished sketchbook entitled "Thomas Cole / 1825 / New York" (Cole Papers, DIA), pp. 30, 36. Also see MS letters, Thomas Cole to Verplanck, Catskill, May 17, 1844, July 15, 1844, 20 Greene St. [New York], Wednesday [*ca.* 1834], Verplanck Papers, NYHS.

William Dunlap: MS letters, William Dunlap to Verplanck, New York, Jan. 26, 1826, Jan. 11, 1833, Jan. 15, 1838, and Feb. 19, 1838, Verplanck Papers, NYHS; July, pp. 117, 261; Cummings, p. 153.

Asher B. Durand: MS letter, A. B. Durand, William Cullen Bryant, and J. F. Kensett to Verplanck, New York, Dec. 28, 1854, Bryant-Verplanck Correspondence, Berg Collection, NYPL.

John Frazee: MS letters, Frazee to Verplanck, New York, Feb. 18, March 26, April 14, April 27, 1832, Jan. 16, Jan. 24, 1833, Feb. 17, 1841, Verplanck Papers, NYHS.

Charles Cromwell Ingham: MS letter, Charles Ingham to Verplanck, New York, June 22, 1832, Verplanck Papers, NYHS.

Henry Inman: MS letters, Henry Inman to Verplanck, Philadelphia, May 29, 1831, U.S. Hotel, Phila[delphia]., no month given, 1834, 57 White St., Feb. 13, 1835, New York, Oct. 14, 1837, and May 18, 1838, 18 Watkins [?] St., n.d., Verplanck Papers, NYHS.

John Wesley Jarvis: Verplanck once declared that the "faithful and vigorous" portraiture of his friend John Wesley Jarvis "had eminently that same power, so justly ascribed to Reynolds of delineating 'the mind's expression speaking in the face'" (MS address, "Thackeray and the Virginians—John Randolph and the Republican Tory of 1776," Verplanck

Papers, NYHS). Also see Dickson, pp. 161, 298; July, pp. 244-45. Daniel Huntington claimed to have suggested that Verplanck call Jarvis "a Reynolds *unrefined*" instead of "a Reynolds *vulgarised.*" See MS letter, Huntington to Charles Henry Hart, 49 E. 20th, New York, Feb. 11, 1897, Charles Henry Hart Collection of MS letters, Archives of American Art.

John F. Kensett: MS letter, A. B. Durand, William Cullen Bryant, and J. F. Kensett to Verplanck, New York, Dec. 28, 1854, Bryant-Verplanck Correspondence, Berg Collection, NYPL.

Samuel F. B. Morse: MS letters, Samuel Morse to Verplanck, New York, Dec. 21, 1826, Paris, Jan. 2, 1832, New York, April 20, 1837, Verplanck Papers, NYHS.

NATHANIEL PARKER WILLIS

William Bartlett: Willis worked with Bartlett on three landscape gift books: *American Scenery, Canadian Scenery,* and *The Scenery and Antiquities of Ireland.*

John Cranch: Willis, *Pencillings,* pp. 47-52.

Alexander J. Davis: Willis, *Hurry-Graphs,* pp. 143, 176.

Andrew Jackson Downing: Willis, "The Highland Terrace, above West Point," in *Home Book of the Picturesque,* p. 110; Willis, *Rural Letters,* pp. 175, 354, *Hurry-Graphs,* p. 140, *Out-Doors at Idlewild,* pp. 58, 115, 167, 213, *Rag-Bag,* pp. 121-24.

Asher B. Durand: Willis, *Hurry-Graphs,* p. 139, *Out-Doors at Idlewild,* p. 267, "The Highland Terrace, above West Point," in *The Home Book of the Picturesque,* p. 110.

George Flagg: MS letter, N. P. Willis to Albt[.] Mathews, 19 Ludlow Place, Saturday Morning, HM 15591, HHL; Willis, *Hurry-Graphs,* p. 257, *Prose Works,* p. 615, *Rag-Bag,* pp. 294, 337-38. Willis used Flagg, George P. Morris, and himself as a humorous trio in some of his writings. See Daughrity, p. 44.

Thomas Hicks: Beers, p. 332.

John F. Kensett: Beers, p. 332; Willis, *Out-Doors at Idlewild,* pp. 154, 163.

Samuel F. B. Morse: Willis, *Pencillings,* pp. 7, 12, 22, *Rural Letters,* p. 336; Beers, pp. 110-11; MS letters, W[ashington]. Allston to Samuel F. B. Morse, Boston, March 30, 1829, Willis to Morse, Hotel Rivoli [Paris], n.d. [1832 interpolated in pencil], Morse Papers, Vols. X, XI respectively, LC.

Rembrandt Peale: Peale sent Willis a painting, probably one of his portraits of Washington. Willis thanked him for it and mentioned Peale's having visited him at Idlewild in MS letter, N. P. Willis to Rembrandt Peale, Idlewild, Aug. 7, 1859, Society Collection, Historical Society of Pennsylvania, on microfilm at Archives of American Art.

John Rand: Willis sat to John Rand, who furnished him with material for a story. See Beers, p. 227; Willis, "Pencillings by the Way," *NYM*, XII (April 4, 1835), 317. Rand wrote of him from London: "Mr. Willis is . . . very popular here and moves in a high class, his character is not injured for London, tho he moves in a very different circle from myself" (MS letter, Rand to Bryant, London, Aug. 21, 1835, Bryant-Godwin, NYPL).

William Allen Wall: Mary Turlay Robinson, "William Allen Wall of New Bedford," *Magazine of Art*, XXX (Feb., 1937), 108-110, 128.

Robert W. Weir: Willis, *Hurry-Graphs*, pp. 115, 137, *Out-Doors at Idlewild*, pp. 254, 419, 445; Irene Weir, pp. 82-83. In his "Recollections," *NYHSQ*, XLI (April, 1957), 119, John Ferguson Weir, one of Weir's artist-sons, remembered a holiday spent at Idlewild as one of the most pleasant experiences of his youth.

EXHIBITIONS OF THE NATIONAL

ACADEMY:

A CHECK LIST OF REVIEWS IN

KNICKERBOCKER MAGAZINES

(1826-1855)

From 1826 to 1855, the closing date of this study, every annual exhibition of the National Academy of Design was reviewed by at least one literary magazine published in New York. Art historians have made use of these reviews, finding in them not only invaluable aids to identifying sculpture and paintings but also helpful clues to nineteenth-century critical attitudes. But locating these reviews usually proves a difficult and irksome task. To simplify it this appendix lists chronologically all reviews of the National Academy's exhibitions published from 1826 through 1855 in the following journals (abbreviations, if any, are given in parentheses): *The (New York) American Monthly Magazine (AMM); The Broadway Journal; The Corsair; Harper's New Monthly Magazine; The Home Journal*

(HJ); The Knickerbocker (K); The Literary World (LW); Morris's National Press; The New Mirror; The New-York Mirror (NYM); The New-York Weekly Mirror; Putnam's Monthly Magazine; The United States Review and Literary Gazette (USRLG).

1826   *NYM*, III (June 10), 366-67; III (June 17), 375; III (July 1), 391.

1827   *NYM*, IV (June 2), 354.

        USRLG, II (July), 241-63.

1828   *NYM*, V (May 24), 366-67.

1829   *NYM*, VI (May 16), 354-55.

1830   *NYM*, VII (May 15), 359.

1831   *NYM*, VIII (May 7), 350; VIII (May 14), 358.

1832   *NYM*, IX (June 2), 382-83; IX (June 9), 391; IX (June 16), 394-95.

1833   *AMM*, I (July), 331-34; I (Aug.), 401-404. The reviewer was probably Henry William Herbert.

        NYM, X (May 18), 366; X (May 25), 371; X (June 1), 378-79; X (June 8), 387; X (June 15), 398; X (June 22), 406; X (June 29), 410; XI (July 6), 6. The notices for May 18 and June 22 are signed D. Although the other reviews are unsigned, it is assumed that as part of the series they were also written by D., who was William Dunlap. See his *Diary*, III, 679, 683.

1834   *AMM*, III (May), 207-212; III (June), 281-86. The reviewer was probably Henry William Herbert.

        K, III (May), 399-400.

        NYM, XI (May 10), 355; XI (May 17), 367.

1835   *K*, V (June), 550-56.

        AMM, V (June), 312-18; V (July), 391-98. Charles Fenno Hoffman may have been the reviewer.

        NYM, XII (May 16), 366; XII (May 23), 371; XII (May 30), 379; XII (June 6), 390; XII (June 13), 395; XII (June 20), 406; XII (June 27), 413-14; XIII (July 11), 15. The notice for May 16 appeared over the initials C. F. Internal evidence indicates that the remaining seven reviews were written by the same author, who was probably Charles Fenno Hoffman, an editor of the *Mirror*.

1836   *NYM*, XIII (May 7), 358; XIII (May 14), 366; XIII (May 21), 375; XIII (June 4), 390; XIII (June 11), 398; XIII (June 18), 406; XIII (June 25), 414.

        K, VIII (July), 112-15.

1837   *NYM*, XIV (April 29), 351; XIV (May 6), 359; XIV (May 13),
       367; XIV (May 20), 375; XIV (May 27), 383; XIV (June 3), 391;
       XIV (June 10), 399; XIV (June 17), 407.
       K, IX (June), 617-22.

1838   *NYM*, XV (May 26), 382; XV (June 2), 390-91; XV (June 9), 398;
       XV (June 16), 406; XV (June 23), 414; XVI (June 30), 6; XVI
       (July 7), 15.
       AMM, XI (May), 469-72.

1839   *The Corsair*, I (May 4), 121-22; I (May 18), 152-53. Although
       unsigned, both of these reviews were undoubtedly written by Na-
       thaniel Parker Willis.
       NYM, XVI (May 11), 367; XVI (May 18), 375.
       K, XIII (June), 545-49. Signed J. K. F., this review was written
       by John Kenrick Fisher.

1840   *K*, XVI (July), 81-83.

1841   *NYM*, XIX (May 15), 159; XIX (May 22), 167; XIX (May 29),
       175.
       K, XVIII (July), 86-88.

1842   *K*, XIX (June), 588-93.

1843   *The New Mirror*, I (May 6), 76; I (May 13), 94; I (May 20), 108;
       I (May 27), 127.

1844   *K*, XXIII (June), 595-98; XXIV (July), 75-77.

1845   *The New-York Weekly Mirror*, II (April 26), 43; II (May 3), 54,
       56.
       The Broadway Journal, I (April 26), 257-58; I (May 3), 275-76; I
       (May 10), 289-91; I (May 17, erroneously dated May 10), 305-307.

1846   *NYM*, [n.s.] IV (April 25), 46; IV (May 2), 58-59; IV (May 9),
       74-75; IV (May 16), 92; IV (June 6), 139, 140.
       Morris's National Press, I (April 25), [2]; I (May 2), [2]; I (May
       9), [2]; I (May 16), [2]; I (May 23), [4]; I (May 30), [2]; I
       (June 6), [4]; I (June 13), [2]; I (June 20), [4]. The review for
       June 20 was signed T. H. M. (probably Tompkins H. Matteson),
       who in his concluding remarks (*idem*) called himself the author of
       "these notices." He thus admitted to writing all nine reviews. How-
       ever, his own pictures being in the exhibition, he had, he claimed,
       persuaded someone else to comment on them.
       K, XXVII (May), 463-66; XXVII (June), 556-57.

1847   *LW*, (April 17), 256.

      NYM, [n. s. V] (April 17), 24, 26; [n. s. V] (May 1), 59; [n. s. V] (May 15), 90.

      K, XXIX (June), 570-72.

      LW, I (April 24), 279-80; I (May 1), 304; I (May 8), 322-23; I (May 15), 347-48; I (May 22), 370-71; I (May 29), 396-97; I (June 5), 418-20; I (June 12), 447-48; I (June 19), 467-68.

      HJ (May 8), [3].

1848   *LW*, III (April 22), 227-28; III (April 29), 248-49; III (May 6), 266-67; III (May 13), 287-88; III (May 20), 310; III (May 27), 328-29.

      HJ (April 15), 2.

1849   *K*, XXXIII (May), 468-70. Attributed to a correspondent.

      HJ (April 21), 2.

1850   *LW*, VI (April 27), 423-25; VI (May 4), 447-49; VI (May 18), 497-98.

      K, XXXV (June), 558; XXXVI (July), 99.

1851   *LW*, VIII (April 19), 320-21.

      HJ (April 12), [3]; (April 19), [3]; (April 26), [3]; (May 3), [3]; (May 10), [3]. The review for May 3 was "By an Artist."

1852   *K*, XXXIX (June), 563-68. Attributed by Clark to a friend.

      LW, X (April 24), 301-302; X (May 1), 314-16; X (May 8), 331-33. The first two reviews are signed *.

      HJ (April 24), 2; (May 8), 2; (May 15), 2-3; (May 22), 2-3.

1853   *Putnam's Monthly Magazine*, I (June), 700-703.

      K, XLII (July), 93-96.

      LW, XII (April 30), 358-59.

      HJ (April 23), [2]; (April 30), [2]; (May 7), [2].

1854   *Harper's New Monthly Magazine*, VIII (May), 846-47.

      HJ (April 1), [2].

      K, XLIII (May), 539-40.

      Putnam's Monthly Magazine, III (May), 566-68.

1855   *HJ* (March 24), [2]; (March 31), [2]; (April 14), 2.

      Putnam's Monthly Magazine, V (May), 505-510.

      K, XLV (May), 529-33. Attributed by the editor to an unknown friend.

EVALUATIONS OF AMERICAN

LANDSCAPE PAINTERS:

A CHECK LIST OF COMMENTS

IN KNICKERBOCKER BOOKS

AND MAGAZINES

Most of the references in this appendix, which is offered to supplement the closing section of Chapter IV, are made to the following periodicals published in New York and abbreviated as indicated in parentheses: *The Knickerbocker, or New-York Monthly Magazine (K); The New-York Mirror (NYM);* The (New York) *American Monthly Magazine (AMM);* and *The Literary World (LW).* Unless otherwise noted, the articles cited are reviews of the National Academy of Design's annual exhibitions.

Several of the artists listed below were foreigners. Because they worked in America and painted in the characteristic manner of the Hudson River School, they are included in this check list.

William J. Bennett: Favorable notices are in *NYM*, XI (July 27, 1833), 30; *NYM*, XIV (May 6, 1837), 359; *K*, IX (June, 1837), 618.

Thomas Birch: Praise may be found in *NYM*, IX (June 9, 1832), 391; *AMM*, I (July, 1833), 333-34. Less generous estimates are in "American Academy of the Fine Arts," *AMM*, I (July, 1833), 330-31; *AMM*, I (Aug., 1833), 401.

George Loring Brown: Favorable notices include *NYM*, XIV (May 13, 1837), 367; *K*, IX (June, 1837), 619, 620, 622. Brown's faults are noted in *K*, XXIII (June, 1844), 595.

John W. Casilear: Praise may be found in *NYM*, XIII (June 25, 1836), 414; *NYM*, XIV (June 3, 1837), 391.

John G. Chapman: A favorable notice is in *AMM*, V (July, 1835), 392, 397. Censure mixed with praise is in *K*, VIII (July, 1836), 113.

Frederick Edwin Church: Appreciative reviews are in *K*, XLIII (May, 1854), 540; "The Athenaeum Exhibition at Boston," *Putnam's Monthly Magazine*, VI (Sept., 1855), 332. Moderate criticism was expressed in *LW*, III (May 13, 1848), 288; *LW*, VI (April 27, 1850), 424-25; *LW*, VIII (April 19, 1851), 320; *LW*, X (May 8, 1852), 332; *Putnam's Monthly Magazine*, V (May, 1855), 507-508.

Thomas Cole: Many passages on Cole's works are cited and quoted above in Ch. IV. Further praise of Cole's American landscapes is in [William Dunlap], "A Review of the Gallery of the American Academy of Fine Arts, as Now Opened for the Exhibition of Dunlap's Painting of 'Death on the Pale Horse,'" *NYRAM*, II (Dec., 1825), 77, *idem*, II (Jan., 1826), 152-53, and in *K*, III (May, 1834), 400; *K*, XXIX (June, 1847), 572. Cf. the opinion of a reviewer who claimed that Cole was not inherently American in his works: *Putnam's Monthly Magazine*, V (May, 1855), 506. In regard to Cole's fanciful and allegorical paintings, "The Departure" and "The Return" were unfavorably received in *NYM*, XV (June 9, 1838), 398; "Morning" and "Evening," "The Titan's Goblet," and "Dead Abel" were praised in *NYM*, XI (May 17, 1834), 367, and in "Mr. Cole's Last Pictures," *NYM*, XV (Dec. 23, 1837), 203; "The Voyage of Life" and the unfinished "Cross of the World" series were commended and censured in T. S. C., "Cole's Pictures of the Voyage of Life," *NYM*, XIX (Jan. 2, 1841), 3, and in "The Cole Exhibition," *LW*, III (April 15, 1848), 207-208. Other reviews containing disparagement of Cole's fanciful paintings are discussed in LaBudde, pp. 4-6.

Christopher P. Cranch: An unfavorable review is "The Art-Union Pic-

tures," *LW*, II (Oct. 23, 1847), 278. Dislike and approval are mixed in
LW, VI (April 27, 1850), 424.

Jaspar F. Cropsey: Unfavorable notices are in *K*, XXIII (June, 1844),
596; *K*, XXVII (May, 1846), 463-64; *K*, XXXV (June, 1850), 558; *K*,
XXXIX (June, 1852), 567. For balanced appraisals, see *LW*, VI (May 4,
1850), 448; *LW*, X (May 8, 1852), 331-32; *Putnam's Monthly Magazine*,
V (May, 1855), 508.

Thomas Doughty: For representative evaluations of Doughty, see the
articles and books cited in Ch. IV and *NYM*, IV (June 2, 1827), 354;
"The Apollo Gallery," *NYM*, XVII (Nov. 23, 1839), 174; *The New
Mirror*, I (May 6, 1843), 76; *K*, XXXVI (July, 1850), 99; "Editor's
Table," *K*, XLIII (Jan., 1854), 101-102.

Asher B. Durand: Comments in addition to those cited in Ch. IV appear in various places. Durand's tree trunk scenes are condemned, but his
"fine drawing" is praised in *LW*, III (May 13, 1848), 287. Fault is found
with his "Sunday Morning," "Saturday Afternoon," "Morning," and "Evening," in "Our Landscape Painters," *NYM*, XVIII (July 18, 1840), 30.
Several reviews are mixed in their sentiments: *USRLG*, II (July, 1827),
250-51; *K*, XIX (June, 1842), 589; *NYM*, XV (June 9, 1838), 398; *LW*,
VI (April 27, 1850), 424. N. P. Willis wrote a particularly handsome
notice of Durand, mentioning, however, that for the best effect only one or
two of Durand's pictures should be seen at a time. See Willis, *Prose
Works*, pp. 667-68. Other favorable reviews include *K*, XXI (June, 1843),
580; *K*, XXIII (June, 1844), 596-97; *K*, XXIX (June, 1847), 570; *K*,
XXXIII (May, 1849), 469, 470; *K*, XXXV (June, 1850), 558; *K*, XXXIX
(June, 1852), 563, 566-67; *K*, XLIII (May, 1854), 539; *NYM*, XV (June
2, 1838), 391; *AMM*, I (July, 1833), 333; *The New Mirror*, I (May 6,
1843), 76; *LW*, VIII (April 9, 1851), 320; *LW*, X (May 8, 1852), 331 (an
extensive notice); *LW*, XII (April 30, 1853), 358; *Putnam's Monthly
Magazine*, V (May, 1855), 506-507.

Alvan Fisher: Enthusiasm was expressed in *NYM*, IV (June 2, 1827),
354; *NYM*, X (May 25, 1833), 371.

Sanford Robinson Gifford: Merits and defects were weighed in *K*,
XXXIX (June, 1852), 567; *LW*, X (May 8, 1852), 332.

Régis F. Gignoux: Bryant's admiration appeared in *The Home Book
of the Picturesque*, p. 156. Similar feelings are found in *The New Mirror*,
I (May 6, 1843), 77; *idem*, I (May 27, 1843), 127; *K*, XXI (June, 1843),

581; *K*, XXVII (May, 1846), 465. A less generous appraisal was the review in *K*, XIX (June, 1842), 591.

William Hart: A favorable notice is in *K*, XLIII (May, 1854), 540. A more critical attitude was taken by a reviewer in *LW*, III (May 13, 1848), 287.

George Harvey: Merits were discussed in Willis, *Prose Works*, pp. 656, 663; *NYM*, XII (May 30, 1835), 379; *NYM*, XIV (May 20, 1837), 375; *K*, IX (June, 1837), 618. Censure of his paintings is in *K*, V (June, 1835), 554.

John William Hill: Approval characterizes the estimate in *K*, VIII (July, 1836), 113.

Daniel Huntington: Favorable reviews are in *NYM*, XIV (May 20, 1837), 375; *K*, IX (June, 1837), 620; "The Apollo Gallery," *NYM*, XVII (Nov. 23, 1839), 174; *LW*, VI (May 4, 1850), 448; *K*, XXXV (June, 1850), 558. Praise mixed with censure appeared in *NYM*, XV (June 23, 1838), 414; "Our Landscape Painters," *NYM*, XVIII (July 18, 1840), 30.

Henry Inman: "View of Rydal Water" was praised by Bryant in *Orations*, p. 16.

George Inness: In 1849 Inness was criticized for "excessive mannerism" and "sad and heavy tone" (*K*, XXXIII [May, 1849], 468); in 1853 for sacrificing "effect to . . . great love of mere tone" (*K*, XLII [July, 1853], 96). Further criticism is in *LW*, I (May 1, 1847), 304; *LW*, I (May 15, 1847), 347; *LW*, X (May 8, 1852), 332. See also the references cited and quoted above in Ch. IV.

John F. Kensett: Moderate disapproval was expressed in *NYM*, XV (May 26, 1838), 382; *K*, XXXIX (June, 1852), 567; *LW*, X (May 8, 1852), 332; *Putnam's Monthly Magazine*, V (May, 1855), 507. Kensett was praised in *LW*, VI (April 27, 1850), 424; *LW*, VIII (April 19, 1851), 320; "The Athenaeum Exhibition at Boston," *Putnam's Monthly Magazine*, VI (Sept., 1855), 332.

Joshua Shaw: A favorable notice is in *K*, VIII (July, 1836), 112.

Jesse Talbot: Praise may be found in *NYM*, XIX (May 15, 1841), 159; *K*, XXVII (June, 1846), 557; *K*, XXIX (June, 1847), 571. Censure was expressed in *K*, XVIII (July, 1841), 86; *K*, XIX (June, 1842), 589.

William G. Wall: A generous estimate is in *NYM*, V (May 24, 1828), 367. Other favorable notices are given in *K*, VIII (July, 1836), 114; *NYM*, XIV (May 13, 1837), 367; *K*, IX (June, 1837), 619. Wall's faults are enumerated in *NYM*, XIX (May 15, 1841), 159. Merits and defects are weighed in *USRLG*, II (July, 1827), 251, 255-56.

Jacob C. Ward: Ward was praised without reserve in "American Academy of the Fine Arts," *AMM*, I (July, 1833), 330; *AMM*, I (Aug., 1833), 401, 402, 403; "Fine Arts," *AMM*, V (July, 1835), 407. Not so impressed was the reviewer in "American Academy of the Fine Arts," *NYM*, X (June 15, 1833), 398.

Robert W. Weir: Favorable notices of Weir's landscape work appeared in *NYM*, VIII (May 7, 1831), 350; *NYM*, IX (June 9, 1832), 391; *NYM*, IX (June 16, 1832), 395; *AMM*, I (July, 1833), 333; *NYM*, XI (May 10, 1834), 355; *K*, III (May, 1834), 400; *AMM*, V (July, 1835), 396; "Fine Arts," *AMM*, V (July, 1835), 407; *NYM*, XIII (May 14, 1836), 366; *NYM*, XIII (June 11, 1836), 398; "Our Landscape Painters," *NYM*, XVIII (July 25, 1840), 38. More critical appraisals are in "American Academy of Fine Arts," *AMM*, I (July, 1833), 331; *AMM*, V (July, 1835), 393-94, 396.

T. Worthington Whittredge: A favorable review is in *K*, XXVII (May, 1846), 557.

BIBLIOGRAPHY

AND

INDEX

BIBLIOGRAPHY

Manuscripts Arranged by Location

COLLECTION OF MRS. PHILINDA RAND ANGLEMYER:

Franklin, Mary Elizabeth. "John Goffe Rand." (Typewritten monograph.)

ARCHIVES OF AMERICAN ART:

Charles Henry Hart Collection of MS Letters.

COLLECTION OF THE AUTHOR:

Letter from Mrs. Philinda Rand Anglemyer, Washington, D.C., August 19, 1958.

Letter from William P. Campbell, Washington, D.C., July 2, 1963.

Letter from Vernon C. Porter, Director, National Academy of Design, New York, March 27, 1959.

Letter from Mrs. Grinnell Willis (Katherine Tappert Willis), Greenwich, Connecticut, May 29, 1955.

CENTURY ASSOCIATION:

"Minutes of the Sketch Club 1829."

Contains "Constitution and Bye-Laws" (2 pp.); "Report of the

Committee Appointed by the Club to Frame Its Constitution and Bye Laws" (3 pp.); the minutes from Feb. 6, 1829 to April 8, 1830 (69 pp.); a list entitled "Residences of the Members" (2 pp.).

"Minutes of the Sketch Club 27 Dec. 1830 to 4 April 1833."
Contains "S. C.," a poem signed "Mason" (3 pp.); the minutes themselves (104 pp.); a list of officers for 1831 (1 p.); a list of members for 1830 (3 pp.).

["Minutes of XXI: Sketch Club: January 12, 1844 to April 9, 1869."] Title apparently supplied by Theodore Bolton, former librarian of the Century Association.
Contains the minutes themselves (251 pp.); lists of members (5 pp.) and of meetings (4 pp.); a list of the dates of four members' deaths (1 p.).

DETROIT INSTITUTE OF ARTS:
Thomas Cole Papers.

FRICK ART REFERENCE LIBRARY:
[Campbell, Ellen.] "A Forgotten New England Artist and Inventor." (Typewritten monograph.)

HISTORICAL SOCIETY OF PENNSYLVANIA:
Letter from N[athaniel]. P[arker]. Willis to Rembrandt Peale, Idlewild, August 7, 1859. Society Collection.

HENRY E. HUNTINGTON LIBRARY AND ART GALLERY:
Letter from W[illiam]. C[ullen]. Bryant to John Rand, New York, August 13, 1838. BR Box 270.
Letter from N[athaniel]. P[arker]. Willis to Albt[.] Mathews, 19 Ludlow Place, Saturday Morning. HM 15591.

LIBRARY OF CONGRESS:
Samuel F. B. Morse Papers.

MASSACHUSETTS HISTORICAL SOCIETY:
Letter from William Cullen Bryant to Richard H. Dana, New York, August 4, 1843. Dana Papers.

NEW-YORK HISTORICAL SOCIETY:
Gulian C. Verplanck Papers.
Miscellaneous Letters.

NEW YORK PUBLIC LIBRARY:

Bryant Family Papers.

Bryant-Godwin Collection.

Bryant-Verplanck Correspondence. Berg Collection.

Marked copy of *The New-York Review, and Atheneum Magazine* (2 vols.). Berg Collection. The authors of many anonymous articles are revealed through attributions pencilled in the margins by William Cullen Bryant.

A. B. Durand Papers.

Duyckinck Papers.

Goddard-Roslyn Collection of Bryant MSS. (Microfilm of Mr. Conrad Goddard's collection.)

Charles Robert Leslie Folder (Miscellaneous Papers).

Miscellaneous Papers.

Sully, Thomas. "Journal." (Typewritten copy.)

William Henry Powell Miscellaneous Papers.

Wharton, Thomas Kelah. "Journal: 1830-1834."

NEW YORK STATE LIBRARY:

Thomas Cole Papers.

SUFFOLK MUSEUM:

Mount Papers.

YALE UNIVERSITY LIBRARY:

Letter from William C. Bryant to Mr. [John Goffe] Rand, Paris, July 20, 1834.

Letter from John G. Chapman to James F. Cooper, Rome, May 3, 1830.

Letter from John G. Chapman to James F. Cooper, New York, March 21, 1837.

Letter from A. B. Durand to James F. Cooper, New York, September 4, 1837.

Letter from Nathaniel Parker Willis to Francis Alexander, n.p., n.d.

Willis, Nathaniel Parker. "To a Picture of 'Genevieve' by Alexander." (Sonnet.)

Complete or Extended Files of Magazines

The American Monthly Magazine. 12 vols. 1833-1838.
Arcturus. 3 vols. 1840-1842.

The Atlantic Magazine. 2 vols. 1824-1825.

The Columbian Lady's and Gentleman's Magazine. 10 vols. 1844-1849.

The Corsair. 1 vol. 1839-1840.

The Crayon. Vols. I-III. 1855-1856.

The Critic. 2 vols. 1828-1829.

Harper's New Monthly Magazine. Vols. I-XI. 1850-1855.

The Home Journal. Vols. [I]-[IX]. 1846-1855. Variant title: *Morris's National Press.*

The Knickerbocker. Vols. I-XLVI. 1833-1855.

The Literary World. 13 vols. 1847-1853.

The New Mirror. 3 vols. 1843-1844.

The New-York Mirror. 20 vols. 1823-1842.

The New-York Review, and Atheneum Magazine. 2 vols. 1825-1826.

The New-York Weekly Mirror. 6 vols. 1844-1847. Title varies: (a) *The American Literary Gazette and New-York Weekly Mirror,* (b) *Weekly Mirror,* (c) *New-York Mirror.*

Putnam's Monthly Magazine. Vols. I-VI. 1853-1855.

The Union Magazine of Literature and Art. 2 vols. 1847-1848.

The United States Review and Literary Gazette. 3 vols. 1826-1827.

Yankee Doodle. 2 vols. 1846-1847.

Books, Articles, Theses, and Dissertations

Adams, Richard P. "Architecture and the Romantic Tradition: Coleridge to Wright," *American Quarterly,* IX (Spring, 1957), 46-62.

Addison, Agnes. "Early American Gothic," in *Romanticism in America: Papers Contributed to a Symposium Held at the Baltimore Museum of Art: May 13, 14, 15, 1940* (ed. George Boas; Baltimore: Johns Hopkins Press, 1940), pp. 118-37.

Adkins, Nelson Frederick. *Fitz-Greene Halleck: An Early Knickerbocker Wit and Poet.* New Haven: Yale University Press, 1930.

Alison, Archibald. *Essay on the Nature and Principles of Taste.* New York: Harper & Bros., 1846.

Allen, Gay Wilson. *American Prosody.* ("American Literature Series.") New York: American Book Co., 1935.

Allston, Washington. *Lectures on Art and Poems,* ed. Richard Henry Dana, Jr. New York: Baker & Scribner, 1850.

American Art-Union. *Transactions of the American Art Union for the Year 1845.* New York: [American Art-Union, 1846].

——. *Transactions of the American Art-Union, for the Year 1846.* New York: [American Art-Union], 1847.

"American Statuaries." *The North American Magazine,* V (Jan., 1835), 204-7.

Andrews, Wayne. *Architecture, Ambition and Americans: A Social History of American Architecture.* New York: Free Press of Glencoe, 1964.

Arms, George. *The Fields Were Green: A New View of Bryant, Whittier, Holmes, Lowell, and Longfellow, with a Selection of Their Poems.* Stanford: Stanford University Press, 1953.

The Atlantic Club Book: Being Sketches in Prose and Verse, by Various Authors. [Edited by Charles Fenno Hoffman.] 2 vols. New York: Harper & Bros., 1834.

Auser, Cortland P. "The Contribution of George Pope Morris to American Journalism." Unpublished Ph.D. dissertation, New York University, 1960.

Babbitt, Irving. *Rousseau and Romanticism.* Boston: Houghton Mifflin Co., 1919.

Baker, Paul R. *The Fortunate Pilgrims: Americans in Italy, 1800-1860.* Cambridge, Mass.: Harvard University Press, 1964.

Barker, Virgil. *American Painting: History and Interpretation.* New York: Macmillan Co., 1951.

Baur, John I. H. *John Quidor: 1801-1881.* New York: Brooklyn Museum, 1942.

Beard, James F., Jr. "Cooper and His Artistic Contemporaries," in *James Fenimore Cooper: a Re-Appraisal* (ed. Mary E. Cunningham; Cooperstown: New York State Historical Association, 1954), pp. 112-27.

Beers, Henry A. *Nathaniel Parker Willis.* ("American Men of Letters.") Boston: Houghton, Mifflin & Co., 1885.

Benjamin, Park. *Poems of Park Benjamin,* ed. Merle M. Hoover. New York: Columbia University Press, 1948.

Blair, Hugh. *Lectures on Rhetoric and Belles Lettres.* New York: E. Duyckinck, Collins & Hannay, Collins & Co., E. Bliss & E. White, & Valentine Seaman, 1824.

Bloch, E. Maurice. "The American Art-Union's Downfall," *New-York Historical Society Quarterly,* XXXVII (Oct., 1953), 331-59.

Bolton, Theodore. "The Book Illustrations of Felix Octavius Carr Darley," *Proceedings of the American Antiquarian Society,* LXI, Part I (April, 1951), 136-82.

Borgese, G. A. "Romanticism," in *Encyclopaedia of the Social Sciences* (15 vols.; New York: The Macmillan Co., 1934), XIII, 426-33.

Born, Wolfgang. *American Landscape Painting: An Interpretation.* New Haven: Yale University Press, 1948.

Brown, Glenn. *History of the United States Capitol.* 2 vols. Washington: U.S. Government Printing Office, 1900.

Bryant, William Cullen. *Letters of a Traveller; or, Notes of Things Seen in Europe and America.* New York: George P. Putnam, 1850.

———. *Letters of a Traveller: Second Series.* New York: D. Appleton & Co., 1860.

———. *Orations and Addresses.* New York: G. P. Putnam's Sons, 1878.

——— (ed.). *Picturesque America; or, The Land We Live In.* 2 vols. New York: D. Appleton & Co., 1872.

———. *Poems by William Cullen Bryant: with Illustrations by E. Leutze, Engraved by American Artists.* 3d ed. Philadelphia: Carey & Hart, 1847.

———. *The Poetical Works of William Cullen Bryant,* ed. Parke Godwin. 2 vols. New York: D. Appleton & Co., 1883.

———. *Prose Writings of William Cullen Bryant,* ed. Parke Godwin. 2 vols. New York: D. Appleton & Co., 1884.

———. "Reminiscences of Miss Sedgwick," in *Life and Letters of Catharine M. Sedgwick* (ed. Mary E. Dewey; New York: Harper & Bros., 1871), pp. 437-46.

———. Review of *Redwood,* by Catharine M. Sedgwick, *North American Review,* XX (April, 1825), 245-72.

———, and Asher Brown Durand. *The American Landscape, No. I, Containing the Following Views: Weehawken, Catskill Mountains, Fort Putnam, Delaware Water-Gap, Falls of the Sawkill, Winnipiseogee Lake. Engraved from Original and Accurate Drawings; Executed from Nature Expressly for This Work, and from Well Authenticated Pictures; with Historical and Topographical Illustrations.* New York: Elam Bliss, 1830.

[Bryant, William Cullen, Gulian Verplanck, and Robert Sands.] *The Talisman* for 1828. New York: Elam Bliss, 1827.

——— *et al. The Talisman* for 1829. New York: Elam Bliss, 1828.

——— *et al. The Talisman* for 1830. New York: Elam Bliss, 1829.

Bryant II, William Cullen. "Bryant: The Middle Years: A Study in

Cultural Fellowship." Unpublished Ph.D. dissertation, Columbia University, 1954.

Burke, Edmund. *A Philosophical Enquiry into the Origin of Our Ideas of the Sublime and Beautiful*, ed. J. T. Boulton. London: Routledge & Kegan Paul, 1958.

Cahill, Holger, and Alfred H. Barr, Jr. (eds.) *Art in America: A Complete Survey*. New York: Reynal & Hitchcock, 1934.

Caldwell, Henry B. "John Frazee, American Sculptor." Unpublished Master's thesis, New York University, 1951.

Callow, James Thomas. "William Cullen Bryant: Literary Critic." Unpublished Master's thesis, University of Toledo, 1952.

Charvat, William. "Cooper as Professional Author," in *James Fenimore Cooper: a Re-Appraisal* (ed. Mary E. Cunningham; Cooperstown: New York State Historical Association, 1954), pp. 128-43.

———. *Literary Publishing in America: 1790-1850*. Philadelphia: University of Pennsylvania Press, 1959.

———. *The Origins of American Critical Thought, 1810-1835*. Philadelphia: University of Pennsylvania Press, 1936.

Clark, Eliot. *History of the National Academy of Design*. New York: Columbia University Press, 1954.

Clark, Harry H. "Literary Criticism in the *North American Review, 1815-1835,*" *Transactions of the Wisconsin Academy of Science, Arts, and Letters*, XXXII (1940), 299-350.

Clark, L. Gaylord. "Charles Loring Elliott," *Lippincott's Magazine*, II (Dec., 1868), 652-57.

———. *Knick-Knacks from an Editor's Table*. New York: D. Appleton & Co., 1852.

[Clarke, McDonald.] *The Elixir of Moonshine; Being a Collection of Prose and Poetry, by the Mad Poet, a Great Proportion of Which Has Never Before Been Published*. [New York: David Longworth, 1822.]

Clarke, M'Donald. *Poems of M'Donald Clarke*. New York: J. W. Bell, 1836.

Cooper, James Fenimore. *Cooper's Novels*. 65 vols. in 33. New Ed. New York: Stringer & Townsend [1849], 1852-1854. With the exception of *Wyandotte* and *The Deerslayer*, all of Cooper's novels cited in the preceding chapters have been taken from this edition.

———. *Correspondence of James Fenimore Cooper*, ed. James Fenimore Cooper. 2 vols. New Haven: Yale University Press, 1922.

———. *The Deerslayer, or The First War-Path.* Mohawk Ed. New York: G. P. Putnam's Sons, n.d.

———. *Excursions in Switzerland.* Paris: Baudry's European Library, 1836.

———. *Gleanings in Europe: France,* ed. Robert E. Spiller. New York: Oxford University Press, 1928.

[Cooper, James Fenimore.] *Gleanings in Europe: Italy.* 2 vols. Philadelphia: Carey, Lea, & Blanchard, 1838.

Cooper, James Fenimore. *Gleanings in Europe: Volume Two: England,* ed. Robert E. Spiller. New York: Oxford University Press, 1930.

———. *James Fenimore Cooper: Representative Selections, with Introduction, Bibliography, and Notes by Robert E. Spiller,* ed. Robert E. Spiller. ("American Writers Series.") New York: American Book Co., 1936.

———. *The Letters and Journals of James Fenimore Cooper,* ed. James Franklin Beard. Vols. I-IV. Cambridge, Mass.: Harvard University Press, 1960, 1964.

———. *Notions of the Americans Picked up by a Travelling Bachelor.* 2 vols. New York: Stringer & Townsend, 1850.

[Cooper, James Fenimore.] *Wyandotte, or The Hutted Knoll.* 2 vols. Philadelphia: Lea & Blanchard, 1843.

Cowdrey, Mary Bartlett (comp.). *American Academy of Fine Arts and American Art-Union: Exhibition Record: 1816-1852.* New York: New-York Historical Society, 1953.

——— *et al. American Academy of Fine Arts and American Art-Union: Introduction: 1816-1852.* New York: New-York Historical Society, 1953.

——— (comp.). *National Academy of Design Exhibition Record: 1826-1860.* 2 vols. New York: New-York Historical Society, 1943.

———. "William Henry Bartlett and the American Scene," *New York History,* XXII (Oct., 1941), 388-400.

———, and Hermann Warner Williams, Jr. *William Sidney Mount: 1807-1868.* New York: Columbia University Press, 1944.

Cowie, Alexander. *The Rise of the American Novel.* New York: American Book Co., 1948.

Cummings, Tho[ma]s. S. *Historic Annals of the National Academy of Design, New-York Drawing Association, Etc., with Occasional Dottings by the Way-Side, from 1825 to the Present Time.* Philadelphia: George W. Childs, 1865.

Darley, Felix O. C. *The Cooper Vignettes from Drawings by F. O. C. Darley*. New York: James G. Gregory, 1862.

Daughrity, Kenneth Leroy. "The Life and Work of Nathaniel Parker Willis: 1806-1836." Unpublished Ph.D. dissertation, University of Virginia, 1935.

"Death of John Gough Rand," *Evening Post* (New York), Jan. 23, 1873.

Denon. "The Two Academies," *New-York Evening Post*, May 17, 1828.

Dickason, David Howard. *The Daring Young Men: The Story of the American Pre-Raphaelites*. Bloomington: Indiana University Press, 1953.

Dickson, Harold E. *John Wesley Jarvis: American Painter: with a Check-list of His Works*. New York: New-York Historical Society, 1949.

Dorra, Henri. "Parallel Trends in Literature and Art," *Art in America*, XLVII (Summer, 1959), 21-47.

Downing, A[ndrew]. J. *A Treatise on the Theory and Practice of Land-scape Gardening, Adapted to North America; with a View to the Improvement of Country Residences . . . with Remarks on Rural Architecture*. 5th ed. New York: Riker, Thorne, & Co., 1854.

Drake, Joseph Rodman. *The Culprit Fay and Other Poems*. New York: Van Norden & King, 1847.

Dunlap, William. *Diary of William Dunlap: The Memoirs of a Dramatist, Theatrical Manager, Painter, Critic, Novelist and Historian*, ed. Dorothy C. Barck. 3 vols. New York: New-York Historical Society, 1930.

———. *A History of the Rise and Progress of the Arts of Design in the United States*, ed. Frank W. Bayley and Charles E. Goodspeed. 3 vols. New Ed. Boston: C. E. Goodspeed & Co., 1918.

———. *A Trip to Niagara; or Travellers in America. A Farce, in Three Acts*. New York: E. B. Clayton, 1830.

Dunn, N. P. "An Artist of the Past: William Edward West and His Friends at Home and Abroad," *Putnam's Monthly*, II (Sept., 1907), 58-69.

Durand, John. *The Life and Times of A. B. Durand*. New York: Charles Scribner's Sons, 1894.

———. *Prehistoric Notes of the Century Club*. [New York: The Century Club], 1882.

Eaton, Ernest Risley. *William Cullen Bryant, First Advocate of Central Park, New York*. N.p.: Privately printed [1936].

Ekirch, Arthur Alphonse, Jr. *The Idea of Progress in America, 1815-1860.* New York: Peter Smith, 1951.

Fairman, Charles E. *Art and Artists of the Capitol.* Washington: U.S. Government Printing Office, 1927.

Fay, Theodore. *Views in New-York and Its Environs from Accurate, Characteristic, & Picturesque Drawings, Taken on the Spot, Expressly for This Work, by Dakin, the Architect; with Historical, Topographical, & Critical Illustrations, by Theodore Fay ... Assisted by Several Distinguished Literary Gentlemen.* New York: Peabody & Co.; London: O. Rich, 1831.

Fitch, James M. *American Building.* Cambridge: Houghton Mifflin, 1948.

Flagg, Jared Bradley. *The Life and Letters of Washington Allston.* New York: C. Scribner's Sons, 1892.

Flexner, James Thomas. *American Painting: First Flowers of Our Wilderness.* Boston: Houghton Mifflin Co., 1947.

———. *The Light of Distant Skies.* New York: Harcourt, Brace, 1954.

Frazee, John. "The Autobiography of Frazee, the Sculptor," *The North American Quarterly Magazine,* VI (April, 1835), 395-403 (July, 1835), 1-22.

Gardner, Albert TenEyck. *Yankee Stonecutters: The First American School of Sculpture: 1800-1850.* New York: Columbia University Press, 1945.

Gates, W. B. "Cooper's *The Crater* and Two Explorers," *American Literature,* XXIII (May, 1951), 243-46.

Gerdts, William H. "Inman and Irving: Derivations from Sleepy Hollow," *Antiques,* LXXIV (Nov., 1958), 420-23.

Gilchrist, Agnes Addison. *William Strickland: Architect and Engineer: 1788-1854.* Philadelphia: University of Pennsylvania Press, 1950.

Godwin, Parke. *A Biography of William Cullen Bryant, with Extracts from His Private Correspondence.* 2 vols. New York: D. Appleton & Co., 1883.

Goodrich, Lloyd. *American Genre: The Social Scene in Painting & Prints (1800-1935).* New York: Whitney Museum of American Art, 1935.

Greenough, Horatio. *Form and Function: Remarks on Art,* ed. Harold Small. Berkeley and Los Angeles: University of California Press, 1947.

———. *Letters of Horatio Greenough to His Brother, Henry Greenough,* ed. Frances Boott Greenough. Boston: Ticknor & Co., 1887.

Groce, George C., and David H. Wallace. *The New-York Historical*

Society's Dictionary of Artists in America: 1564-1860. New Haven: Yale University Press, 1957.

Grosser, Maurice. *The Painter's Eye.* New York: New American Library of World Literature, 1956.

Hale, Edward Everett, Jr. "American Scenery in Cooper's Novels," *Sewanee Review,* XVIII (July, 1910), 317-32.

Halleck, Fitz-Greene. *The Poetical Writings of Fitz-Greene Halleck, with Extracts from Those of Joseph Rodman Drake,* ed. James Grant Wilson. New York: D. Appleton & Co., 1869.

Hamilton, Sinclair. *Early American Book Illustrators and Wood Engravers.* Princeton: Princeton University Library, 1958.

Hamlin, Talbot. *Greek Revival Architecture in America: Being an Account of Important Trends in American Architecture prior to the War between the States.* . . . London and New York: Oxford University Press, 1944.

Harding, Chester. *A Sketch of Chester Harding, Drawn by His Own Hand,* ed. Margaret White. Boston and New York: Houghton, Mifflin & Co., 1890.

Hazelrigg, Charles Tabb. *American Literary Pioneer: A Biographical Study of James A. Hillhouse.* New York: Bookman Associates [*ca.* 1953].

Herold, Amos. *James Kirke Paulding, Versatile American.* New York: Columbia University Press, 1926.

Herrick, Francis Hobart. *Audubon the Naturalist: A History of His Life and Time.* 2 vols. New York: D. Appleton, 1917.

Hoffman, Charles Fenno. *The Poems of Charles Fenno Hoffman,* ed. Edward Fenno Hoffman. Philadelphia: Porter & Coates, 1873.

Home Authors and Home Artists, or American Scenery, Art, and Literature. New York: Leavitt & Allen, n.d.

The Home Book of the Picturesque: or American Scenery, Art, and Literature. New York: G. P. Putnam, 1852.

Howe, Winifred E. *A History of the Metropolitan Museum of Art, with a Chapter on the Early Institutions of Art in New York.* New York: Metropolitan Museum of Art, 1913.

Huth, Hans. *Nature and the American: Three Centuries of Changing Attitudes.* Berkeley: University of California Press, 1957.

Huxtable, Ada Louise. *Classic New York: Georgian Gentility to Greek*

Elegance. (*The Architecture of New York,* Vol. I.) Garden City, New York: Doubleday & Co., 1964.

"An Illustrated Washington Irving Miscellany," *American Heritage,* XIII (Dec., 1961), 41-55.

Irving, Pierre M. *The Life and Letters of Washington Irving.* 3 vols. Hudson Ed. New York: G. P. Putnam's Sons, 1880.

Irving, Washington. *The Alhambra.* Hudson Ed. New York: G. P. Putnam's Sons [1880].

——. *Biographies and Miscellanies,* ed. Pierre M. Irving. Knickerbocker Ed. Philadelphia: J. B. Lippincott & Co., 1873.

——. *Bracebridge Hall.* Hudson Ed. New York: G. P. Putnam's Sons, 1892.

——. *The Crayon Miscellany.* Knickerbocker Ed. New York: G. P. Putnam's Sons, n.d.

[Irving, Washington] Knickerbocker, Diedrich. *A History of New York, from the Beginning of the World to the End of the Dutch Dynasty.* 2 vols. New York: Inskeep & Bradford, 1809.

Irving, Washington. *The Journals of Washington Irving (Hitherto Unpublished),* ed. William P. Trent and George S. Hellman. 3 vols. Boston: The Bibliophile Society, 1919.

——. "A Letter from Irving to His Architect," *The American Collector,* XVI (Oct., 1947), 47-48.

——. *Letters of Washington Irving to Henry Brevoort,* ed. George S. Hellman. Library Ed. New York: G. P. Putnam's Sons, 1918.

——. *The Sketch-Book.* Hudson Ed. New York: G. P. Putnam's Sons, 1880.

——. *Wolfert's Roost and Other Papers.* Knickerbocker Ed. New York: G. P. Putnam's Sons, n.d.

Irving, William, James Kirke Paulding, and Washington Irving. *Salmagundi; or, The Whimwhams and Opinions of Launcelot Langstaff, Esq., and Others.* Knickerbocker Ed. Philadelphia: J. B. Lippincott & Co., 1873.

Isham, Samuel, and Royal Cortissoz. *A History of American Painting.* New Ed. New York: Macmillan Co., 1927.

Jones, Charles W. "Knickerbocker Santa Claus," *The New-York Historical Society Quarterly,* XXXVIII (Oct., 1954), 357-83.

Jones, Howard Mumford. "James Fenimore Cooper and the Hudson River School," *Magazine of Art,* XLV (Oct., 1952), 243-51.

Judd, David W. (ed.). *Life and Writings of Frank Forester (Henry William Herbert).* 2 vols. New York: Orange Judd Co., 1882.

July, Robert W. *The Essential New Yorker: Gulian Crommelin Verplanck.* Durham, N.C.: Duke University Press, 1951.

Kaser, David. *Messrs. Carey & Lea of Philadelphia: A Study in the History of the Booktrade.* Philadelphia: University of Pennsylvania Press, 1957.

The Knickerbocker Gallery: A Testimonial to the Editor of the Knickerbocker Magazine from Its Contributors, ed. John W. Francis *et al.* New York: Samuel Hueston, 1855.

Knight, Sarah Kemble. *The Journal of Madame Knight, with an Introductory Note by George Parker Winship.* Facsimile Reprint of the 1920 Ed. New York: Peter Smith, 1935.

LaBudde, Kenneth J. "The Mind of Thomas Cole." Unpublished Ph.D. dissertation, University of Minnesota, 1954.

———. "The Rural Earth: Sylvan Bliss," *American Quarterly,* X (Summer, 1958), 142-53.

Larkin, Oliver W. *Art and Life in America.* New York: Rinehart & Co., 1949.

———. *Samuel F. B. Morse and American Democratic Art.* Boston: Little, Brown, 1954.

Lay, Charles Downing, and Theodore Bolton. *Works of Art, Silver and Furniture Belonging to the Century Association.* New York: Century Association, 1943.

Lehmann-Haupt, Hellmut, Lawrence C. Wroth, and Rollo G. Silver. *The Book in America: A History of the Making and Selling of Books in the United States.* 2d ed. New York: R. R. Bowker Co., 1952.

Leslie, Charles Robert. *Autobiographical Recollections,* ed. Tom Taylor. Boston: Ticknor & Fields, 1860.

Lewis, E. Anna. "Art and Artists of America: Asher Brown Durand," *Graham's American Monthly Magazine,* XLV (Oct., 1854), 318-22.

Lounsbury, Thomas R. *James Fenimore Cooper.* ("American Men of Letters.") Boston: Houghton, Mifflin & Co., 1882.

Mabee, Carleton. *The American Leonardo: A Life of Samuel F. B. Morse.* New York: Alfred A. Knopf, 1943.

McCausland, Elizabeth. *George Inness: An American Landscape Painter: 1825-1894.* New York: American Artists Group, 1946.

McKay, George L. "Artists Who Have Illustrated Irving's Works," *American Collector*, XVI (Oct., 1947), 38-40.

Manchester Historic Association. "Arts and Artists in Manchester: By a Staff Contributor," *Manchester Historic Association Collections* (12 vols.; Manchester, N.H.: Manchester Historic Association, 1897-1912), IV (1908), 110-11.

Marckwardt, Albert H. "The Chronology and Personnel of the Bread and Cheese Club," *American Literature*, VI (Jan., 1935), 389-99.

[Mathews, Cornelius] Smith, Ben. *The Motley Book.* New Ed. New York: J. & H. Langley, 1838.

Mathews, Cornelius. *A Pen-and-Ink Panorama of New York City.* New York: John S. Taylor, 1853.

Miller, Perry. *The Raven and the Whale: The War of Words and Wits in the Era of Poe and Melville.* New York: Harcourt, Brace & World, 1956.

Miller, Ralph N. "Thomas Cole and Alison's Essays on Taste," *New York History*, XXXVII (July, 1956), 281-99.

"Mr. Bryant and the National Academy," *Evening Post* (New York), June 14, 1878.

Mize, George E. "The Contributions of Evert A. Duyckinck to the Cultural Development of Nineteenth Century America." Unpublished Ph.D. dissertation, New York University, 1954.

Moore, C. E. *Backgrounds of English Literature, 1700-1760.* Minneapolis: University of Minnesota Press, 1953.

Morris, George Pope (ed.). *American Melodies.* New York: Linen & Fennell, 1840.

———. *The Deserted Bride and Other Poems.* New York: D. Appleton & Co., 1843.

———. *The Deserted Bride, and Other Productions.* New York: Charles Scribner, 1853.

———. *The Little Frenchman and His Water Lots, with Other Sketches of the Times.* Philadelphia: Lea & Blanchard, 1839.

Morrison, Hugh. *Early American Architecture from the First Colonial Settlements to the National Period.* New York: Oxford University Press, 1952.

Morse, Samuel F. B. *Samuel F. B. Morse: His Letters and Journals,* ed. Edward Lind Morse. 2 vols. Boston: Houghton, Mifflin Co., 1914.

Mott, Frank Luther. *A History of American Magazines: 1741-1850.* New York: D. Appleton & Co., 1930.

"The National Academy," *New York Mirror* [n. s. V] (May 1, 1847), 59.

Nevins, Allan. *The Evening Post: A Century of Journalism.* New York: Boni & Liveright [*ca.* 1922].

The New-York Book of Poetry. [Ed. Charles Fenno Hoffman.] New York: G. Dearborn, 1837.

New York Metropolitan Museum of Art. *Annual Report.* New York: Metropolitan Museum of Art, 1877-1878.

Newton, Annabel. *Wordsworth in Early American Criticism.* Chicago: University of Chicago Press, 1928.

"19th Century American Genre Painting," *Panorama,* IV (Nov., 1948), 27-33.

Noble, Louis L. *The Course of Empire, Voyage of Life, and Other Pictures of Thomas Cole, N. A., with Selections from His Letters and Miscellaneous Writings: Illustrative of His Life, Character, and Genius.* New York: Cornish, Lamport & Co., 1853.

"Notes on New Books: *The Architect . . . by William H. Ranlett, Architect . . . ," The New York Mirror,* [n. s. V] (Oct. 17, 1846), 26-27.

Odell, George C. D. *Annals of the New York Stage.* Vol. III: *1821-1834.* New York: Columbia University Press, 1928.

Olmsted, Frederick Law, Jr., and Theodora Kimball. *Frederick Law Olmsted: Landscape Architect: 1822-1903.* 2 vols. New York: G. P. Putnam's Sons, 1928.

Orians, G. Harrison. "The Cult of the Vanishing American," *Bulletin of the University of Toledo,* XIII (Nov., 1935), 3-15.

————. "The Rise of Romanticism: 1805-1855," in *Transitions in American Literary History* (ed. Harry Hayden Clark; Durham, N.C.: Duke University Press, 1953), pp. 163-244.

————. *A Short History of American Literature Analyzed by Decades.* New York: F. S. Crofts & Co., 1940.

Overmyer, Grace. *America's First Hamlet.* New York: New York University Press, 1957.

Patterson, Samuel White. *The Poet of Christmas Eve: A Life of Clement Clarke Moore, 1779-1863.* New York: Morehouse-Gorham, 1956.

Paulding, James Kirke. *The Backwoodsman.* Philadelphia: M. Thomas, 1818.

———. *A Christmas Gift from Fairy Land.* New York: D. Appleton & Co. [*ca.* 1838].

———. *The Letters of James Kirke Paulding,* ed. Ralph M. Aderman. Madison: University of Wisconsin Press, 1962.

[Paulding, James Kirke.] *Salmagundi, Second Series, by Launcelot Langstaff.* 2 vols. New York: Harper & Bros., 1835.

———. "Sketch of the Life of Mr. Joseph Wood," *Port Folio,* New (Third) Ser., V (Jan., 1811), 64-68.

Paulding, William I. *Literary Life of James K. Paulding.* New York: Charles Scribner & Co., 1867.

Philbrick, Thomas. *James Fenimore Cooper and the Development of American Sea Fiction.* Cambridge, Mass.: Harvard University Press, 1961.

Pochmann, Henry A. (ed.). *Washington Irving: Representative Selections, with Introduction, Bibliography, and Notes.* ("American Writers Series.") New York: American Book Co., 1934.

Price, Uvedale. *Sir Uvedale Price on the Picturesque: with an Essay on the Origin of Taste, and Much Original Matter, by Sir Thomas Dick Lauder, Bart. and Sixty Illustrations, Designed and Drawn on the Wood, by Montagu Stanley, R. S. A.* Edinburgh: Caldwell, Lloyd, & Co., 1842.

Prown, Jules David. "Washington Irving's Interest in Art and His Influence upon American Painting." Unpublished Master's thesis, University of Delaware, 1956.

Putnam, George Haven. *George Palmer Putnam: A Memoir.* . . . New York: G. P. Putnam's Sons, 1912.

Rathbone, Perry T. (ed.), *Mississippi Panorama.* New ed. rev. St. Louis: City Art Museum of St. Louis, 1950.

Richards, T. Addison. "Idlewild," *Harper's New Monthly Magazine,* XVI (Jan., 1858), 145-66.

Richardson, E. P. *Painting in America: The Story of 450 Years.* New York: Thomas Y. Crowell, 1956.

Ringe, Donald A. "Chiaroscuro as an Artistic Device in Cooper's Fiction," *PMLA,* LXXVIII (Sept., 1963), 349-57.

———. "James Fenimore Cooper and Thomas Cole: An Analogous Technique," *American Literature,* XXX (March, 1958), 26-36.

———. "Kindred Spirits: Bryant and Cole," *American Quarterly,* VI (Fall, 1954), 233-44.

Robinson, Mary Turlay. "William Allen Wall of New Bedford," *Magazine of Art*, XXX (Feb., 1937), 108-10, 128.

Rutledge, Anna Wells (comp.). *Cumulative Record of Exhibition Catalogues: The Pennsylvania Academy of the Fine Arts, 1807-1870: The Society of Artists, 1800-1814: The Artists' Fund Society, 1835-1845.* Philadelphia: American Philosophical Society, 1955.

Sanford, Charles L. "The Concept of the Sublime in the Works of Thomas Cole and William Cullen Bryant," *American Literature*, XXVIII (Jan., 1957), 434-48.

Schmitt, Evelyn L. "Two American Romantics—Thomas Cole and William Cullen Bryant," *Art in America*, XLI (Spring, 1953), 61-68.

Scott, Leonora Cranch. *The Life and Letters of Christopher Pearse Cranch, by His Daughter Leonora Cranch Scott.* Boston: Houghton Mifflin, 1917.

Scott, Walter. "On Ornamental Plantations and Landscape Gardening," *Quarterly Review*, XXXVII (March, 1828), 302-44.

Scudder, Harold H. "Cooper's *The Crater,*" *American Literature*, XIX (March, 1947), 109-26.

Scully, Vincent J., Jr. "Romantic Rationalism and the Expression of Structure in Wood: Downing, Wheeler, Gardner, and the 'Stick Style,' 1840-1876," *The Art Bulletin*, XXXV (June, 1953), 121-42.

Sears, Clara Endicott. *Highlights among the Hudson River Artists.* Boston: Houghton Mifflin Co., 1947.

Shelley, Donald A. "American Painting in Irving's Day," *American Collector*, XVI (Oct., 1947), 19-21, 50.

———. "William Guy Wall and His Watercolors," *The New-York Historical Society Quarterly*, XXXI (Jan., 1947), 25-45.

Shepard, Paul H., Jr. "American Attitudes toward the Landscape in New England and the West, 1830-1870." Unpublished Ph.D. dissertation, Yale University, 1954.

Sotheran, Charles. "The Theaters of New-York," in *The Memorial History of New-York: from Its First Settlement to the Year 1892* (ed. James Grant Wilson; 4 vols.; New York: New-York History Co., 1893), IV, 456-97.

Spivey, Herman E. "*The Knickerbocker Magazine*, 1833-1865: A Study of Its History, Contents, and Significance." Unpublished Ph.D. dissertation, University of North Carolina, 1936.

Stearns, Bertha Monica. "Nineteenth-Century Writers in the World of Art," *Art in America*, XL (Winter, 1952), 29-41.

Still, Bayrd. "The Personality of New York City," *New York Folklore Quarterly*, XIV (Summer, 1958), 83-92.

Street, Alfred B. *The Poems of Alfred B. Street.* Complete Ed. New York: Clark & Austin, 1845.

Sweet, Frederick A. *The Hudson River School and the Early American Landscape Tradition.* New York: Whitney Museum of American Art & The Art Institute of Chicago, 1945.

Sweet, William Warren. *Religion in the Development of American Culture: 1765-1840.* New York: Charles Scribner's Sons, 1952.

Taft, Kendall (ed.). *Minor Knickerbockers: Representative Selections, with Introduction, Bibliography, and Notes.* ("American Writers Series.") New York: American Book Co., 1947.

——. "Samuel Woodworth." Unpublished Ph.D. dissertation, University of Chicago, 1936.

Taft, Lorado. *The History of American Sculpture.* New Ed. New York: Macmillan Co., 1930.

Taylor, Joshua. *William Page: The American Titian.* Chicago: University of Chicago Press, 1957.

Thompson, Ralph. *American Literary Annuals & Gift Books.* New York: H. W. Wilson Co., 1936.

Thorpe, T[homas]. B[angs]. "Lewis Gaylord Clark," *Harper's New Monthly Magazine*, XLVIII (March, 1874), 587-92.

——. "New-York Artists Fifty Years Ago," *Appleton's Journal*, VII (May 25, 1872), 572-75.

——. "Painters of the Century, No. II; Birth of the National Academy of Design," *Baldwin's Monthly*, XI (Dec., 1875), 5.

——. "Painters of the Century, No. IX; Characteristic Incidents—Cole and Elliott," *Baldwin's Monthly*, XIII (Sept., 1876), 1.

Thrall, William Flint, and Addison Hibbard. *A Handbook to Literature: With an Outline of Literary History, English and American.* New York: Odyssey Press, 1936.

Tuckerman, Henry T. *A Memorial of Horatio Greenough.* New York: G. P. Putnam, 1853.

Vail, R. W. G. "An Encore for Santa Claus," *New-York Historical Society Quarterly*, XXXVII (Oct., 1953), 327-30.

———. "Santa Claus Visits the Hudson," *New-York Historical Society Quarterly*, XXXV (Oct., 1951), 337-43.

Van Winkle, William Mitchell, and David A. Randall (compilers). *Henry William Herbert [Frank Forester]: A Bibliography of His Writings: 1832-1858.* Portland, Maine: Southworth-Anthoensen Press, 1936.

Vaux, Calvert. *Villas and Cottages.* New York: Harper & Bros., 1857.

Verplanck, Gulian Crommelin. *Discourses and Addresses on Subjects of American History, Arts, and Literature.* New York: J. & J. Harper, 1833.

Wallace, C. W. "John Rand," *Granite Monthly*, X (Jan., 1887), 1-5.

Weir, Irene. *Robert W. Weir, Artist.* New York: House of Field-Doubleday, 1947.

Weir, John Ferguson. "The Recollections of John Ferguson Weir: I. Memories of West Point," *New-York Historical Society Quarterly*, XLI (April, 1957), 109-41.

Weitenkampf, Frank. "Early American Landscape Prints," *Art Quarterly*, VIII (Winter, 1945), 40-68.

Wetmore, Prosper Montgomery. *Lexington, with Other Fugitive Poems.* New York: Carvill, 1830.

Williams, Stanley T. *The Life of Washington Irving.* 2 vols. New York: Oxford University Press, 1935.

Willis, Nathaniel Parker. *A l'Abri, or The Tent Pitch'd.* New York: Samuel Colman, 1839.

———. *American Scenery; or, Land, Lake, and River: Illustrations of Transatlantic Nature.* 2 vols. London: George Virtue, 1840.

———. *Canadian Scenery . . . Illustrated in a Series of Views by W. H. Bartlett.* 2 vols. London: George Virtue, 1840.

———. *The Convalescent.* New York: Charles Scribner, 1859.

[Willis, Nathaniel Parker.] "The Editor's Table," *The* (Boston) *American Monthly Magazine*, II (May, 1830), 147-48.

Willis, Nathaniel Parker. *Famous Persons and Places.* New York: Charles Scribner, 1854.

———. *Fun-Jottings.* New York: Charles Scribner, 1853.

———. *Hurry-Graphs, or Sketches of Scenery, Celebrities and Society, Taken from Life.* Detroit: Kerr, Doughty, & Lapham, 1853.

———. *Inklings of Adventure.* 2 vols. New York: Saunders & Otley, 1836.

———— (ed.). *The Ladies' Souvenir.* New York: Leavitt & Allen, n.d.

————. *Out-Doors at Idlewild; or, The Shaping of a Home on the Banks of the Hudson.* New York: Charles Scribner, 1855.

————. *Paul Fane; or, Parts of a Life Else Untold.* New York: C. Scribner, 1857.

————. *Pencillings by the Way: Written during Some Years of Residence and Travel in France, Italy, Greece, Asia Minor, Turkey, and England.* "The First Complete Edition." New York: Morris & Willis, 1844.

————. *People I Have Met.* New York: Baker & Scribner, 1850.

————. *Picturesque American Scenery: A Series of Twenty-Five Beautiful Steel Engravings.* Boston: Estes & Lauriat, 1883.

————. *Poems of Early and After Years.* Philadelphia: Carey & Hart, 1848.

————. *Poems of Nathaniel Parker Willis . . . with a Memoir of the Author, by H. L. Williams.* New York: Hurst & Co., 1882.

————. *The Prose Works of N. P. Willis.* New Ed. Philadelphia: Henry C. Baird, 1852.

————. *The Rag-Bag, a Collection of Ephemera.* New York: Charles Scribner, 1855.

————. *Rural Letters.* New York: Baker & Scribner, 1849.

———— (ed.). *Trenton Falls, Picturesque and Descriptive: . . . Embracing the Original Essay of John Sherman. . . .* New York: George P. Putnam, 1851.

————, and J. Sterling Coyne. *The Scenery and Antiquities of Ireland. Illustrated by Drawings from W. H. Bartlett. The Literary Portion of the Work by N. P. Willis and J. Sterling Coyne, Esqs.* London: George Virtue, 1842.

Wilson, James Grant. *Bryant and His Friends.* New York: Fords, Howard, & Hulbert, 1886.

Wish, Harvey. *Society and Thought in America.* 2 vols. New York: Longmans, Green & Co., 1950.

Wittke, Carl. *We Who Built America: The Saga of the Immigrant.* New York: Prentice-Hall, 1939.

Woodworth, Samuel. *The Poetical Works of Samuel Woodworth. Edited by His Son* [Frederick A. Woodworth]. 2 vols. New York: Charles Scribner, 1861.

Wright, Nathalia. "The Chanting Cherubs: Horatio Greenough's Marble

Group for James Fenimore Cooper," *New York History*, XXXVIII (April, 1957), 177-97.

———. *Horatio Greenough: The First American Sculptor*. Philadelphia: University of Pennsylvania Press, 1963.

INDEX

National Academy, 31-32; lectures on mythology, 31; and Durand, 32, 66n, 68-69, 141-42, 164-67; and Morse, 32, 46, 63n, 64, 234; and American Art-Union, 33, 34-36; and T. W. Whitley, 36; recommends Allston, Morse, and Sully for Rotunda jobs, 46; acquainted with largest number of artists, 62-63; and Sketch Club members, 63-69; and Weir, 63-64; and Rand, 69-79; miscellaneous artist-friends of, 79-81, 232-35; and sculptor-friends, 80; honored by Century Club, 80-81; analyzes reasons for fraternizing with artists, 81; and Metropolitan Museum, 81; edits *New-York Review*, 93; edits *United States Review*, 94n; chief Knickerbocker druid, 119, 120; celebrates nature's therapeutic and educative powers, 122; "To a Waterfowl" and Doughty's "In Nature's Wonderland," 122-23; praises native mountains, 128; values untamed scenery, 130; supplies American landscape with legend, 131; and Mound Builders, 135; creates panoramas of the mind, 147; and imbalance of "Monument Mountain," 151; creates Gothic landscapes, 156-57; and *American Landscape*, 164-67 *passim*; edits *Picturesque America*, 170-71; provides critical theory for native genre, 175-76; bases writings on pictures by friends, 181-82; works of illustrated, 183, 184n; provides scenes for Beard, Audubon, Mozier, 190; extends pantheism to city, 194; on architecture, 195n, 204n, 206n; prefers informal gardening, 215-16; and city planning, 218; promotes Central Park, 219; indirect influence on other parks, 219-20; mentioned, vii, viii, 3-4, 5, 8, 12, 25, 28, 29, 45n, 60n, 86n, 87, 116, 118, 124n, 129n, 132n, 135, 137, 143, 144, 150n, 155, 163n, 170, 221-22, 224, 225, 226, 227, 236, 239, 240, 248, 249

Bulwer-Lytton, E. G., 177
Burke, Edmund, 125n, 126, 147
Burns, Robert, 128, 150, 183
Buss, H. R., 101
Byron, George Gordon, 18, 42, 177, 183

C

Calhoun, John C., 88
Canadian Scenery, 168-69
Canova, Antonio, 87
Capitol (Washington, D.C.), architecture of, 202-4; columns of, 214
Carlyle, Thomas, 214
Carpets, 211
Casilear, John W., 89, 100, 156n, 235, 247
Catherwood, Frederick, 213n
Catlin, George, 156, 238
Central Park, 219-20, 234
Century Association, 15, 62, 80-81, 221-22
Cervantes Saavedra, Miguel de, 183
Chapman, John G., in Sketch Club, 14, 19n; and Paulding, 88; and Bryant, 232; mentioned, 7, 19, 48, 49, 56, 60-61, 63, 100, 107, 110, 117, 183n, 225, 236, 247
Character sketches, and genre, 173
Charleston, 204, 228
Checks and balances, 174
Chiaroscuro, 145n
Chicago, 228
Christ's Church (New York), 199
Church, Frederick E., 81, 117, 152, 169, 247
Church of the Holy Innocents (West Point), 204n
Cincinnati, 228
City Hall (New York), 196-97
City Planning, 218-20
Clark, Lewis Gaylord, as Sketch Club guest, 16; as editor of *Knickerbocker*, 102-7 *passim*; and Cole, 103-4, 105-6; and Elliott, 106, 235; work of illustrated, 184n; mentioned, 5, 6, 65n, 90, 218, 224, 235
Clark, Willis Gaylord, 120
Clarke, McDonald, and Durand's studio, 89; and Page, 89-90; and genre, 176; artist-friends of, 235-36; mentioned, 4, 8, 120n, 135, 221
Classical architecture, revival of criticized by Cooper, Willis, and anonymous author, 207-8, 213; mentioned, 199, 200, 223
Clay, E. W., 237
Closed scenes, 152
Clover, Lewis P., 89, 235